Shaw, Glen Byam.

Macbeth onstage

26.00

MACBETH ONSTAGE

Act III, Scene ii. Sir Laurence Olivier and Vivien Leigh.

MACBETH ONSTAGE

An Annotated Facsimile of Glen Byam Shaw's 1955 Promptbook

Edited by Michael Mullin

University of Missouri Press

Columbia & London, 1976

TO MARY CATHERINE MULLIN

sine qua non

University of Missouri, Columbia, Missouri 65201
Printed and bound in the United States of America

Library of Congress Cataloging in Publication Data

Shaw, Glen Byam.
Macbeth onstage.

1. Shakespeare, William, 1564–1616. Macbeth.
2. Shakespeare, William, 1564–1616—Stage history—
1950– I. Shakespeare, William, 1564–1616. Macbeth. 1976. II. Mullin, Michael, 1944
III. Title.
PR2823.S48 822.3'3 76-15589
ISBN 0-8262-0212-8

Facsimile of promptbook and typescript comments from various notebooks reproduced by permission of Glen Byam Shaw.

Photographs of the 1955 Stratford-upon-Avon production *Macbeth* by Angus McBean, in the Harvard Theatre Collection, Harvard University, Cambridge, Mass.

Facsimile of text of *Macbeth*, New Temple Shakespeare, edited by M. R. Ridley (1935), reproduced by permission of J. M. Dent & Sons Ltd. Publishers, London.

PREFACE

In 1955 Glen Byam Shaw directed a production of *Macbeth* at Stratford-upon-Avon—a production that has come to be regarded not only splendid in its kind, but one of the most thoroughly satisfying *Macbeths* of the twentieth century. Well in advance of that production Shaw worked up a carefully planned promptbook (or director's script) and also a notebook in which he wrote out a vast number of comments on every scene and character. He has now graciously permitted his promptbook and notes to be made public in this volume. His notes appear next to the page of the facsimile promptbook to which they pertain. Thus any reader, and any practitioner of theatre arts can, as it were, sit in at rehearsals, look over Glen Byam Shaw's shoulder as he guides a famous *Macbeth* to realization.

Theatre historians, and especially historians of staged Shakespeare, have long attempted through close study of stage documents, eye-witness accounts, and other primary sources to recover the facts of the actors' and directors' essential art—the produced play. At the same time, many modern directors are careful to record their art in all its subtlety and complexity, as Glen Byam Shaw has in this promptbook. Young directors and actors turn to the promptbooks of past productions for guidance and inspiration, especially at the Shakespeare Festival Theatre, Stratford, Ontario, at the Royal Shakespeare Theatre, Stratford-upon-Avon, and at the National Theatre, London, where promptbooks are kept for reference. Classroom teachers of Shakespeare are coming to recognize that focus on stage production (not literal staging, but consideration of staging) is one of the most fruitful of pedagogical techniques. A class studying Shakespeare that spends its *Macbeth* sessions analyzing and realizing the Shaw promptbook will know the play far more vividly than they ever could know it from the text alone.

I have added to Shaw's promptbook certain aids to the reader. In the Introduction I have described the design of the costumes, the sets, and the Shakespeare theatre at Stratford, so one can visualize both from the front and backstage exactly what is happening. I have also described rehearsal practices. At the head of each of the three parts into which Shaw divided the play, I have described what is next to be seen in the performance. The glossary is a guide to Shaw's abbreviations and to technical terms. At the end of the book, I have presented the critics' response to the acting, some reminiscences of actors who participated, and an essay on Shaw's style as a producer-director.

This book has enjoyed the advice and criticism of many friends and colleagues. Most especially I wish to thank Glen Byam Shaw for permitting me to publish his notebooks and promptbook and for answering my questions about them. From Maynard Mack at Yale University I received the inspiration and guidance that led me to study Shakespeare in performance and thence to Shaw's *Macbeth*. Charles H. Shattuck at the University of

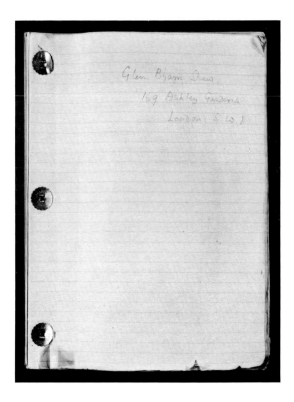

Illinois has given me untold help: his expertise helped me solve many of the riddles the promptbook poses, his keen eye has often saved me from error, and his friendship has encouraged me. Desmond Hall and Roger Howells of the Royal Shakespeare Company stage management have scrutinized my account of the performance for factual accuracy. Through careful reading and long discussions, James Hurt at the University of Illinois has helped me clarify my ideas; Maurice Charney at Rutgers University has advised me on organization of my own parts of the book. Maxine Audley, Trader Faulkner, Emrys James, Keith Michell, and Lee Montague, actors in the production and members of the company in 1955, have given me first-hand accounts of the rehearsals and the performance. Dr. Levi Fox, Director of the Shakespeare Birthplace Trust, Stratford-upon-Avon, and the Board of Governors of the Royal Shakespeare Theatre granted me access to the theatre records at the Shakespeare Centre Library; Marguerite Darvill, Marian Horn, Roger Pringle, and Eileen Robinson all helped in my research there. Dr. Jeanne Newlin, Curator of the Harvard Theatre Collection, located the production photographs and has arranged permission for their reproduction here. The National Endowment for the Humanities and the University of Illinois have sustained this research at various phases.

Most of all, for their love and understanding during the long odyssey this work has taken us on, I thank my wife Cate and my daughters Catie and Bridie.

M. M.
Urbana, Illinois
23 April 1976

CONTENTS

INTRODUCTION

Although *Macbeth* looks easy to stage, it is not. True, it is short, and its plot is simple. Yet the changes in stage conventions and common beliefs that make all Renaissance plays difficult for modern audiences make *Macbeth* especially difficult. The play is set in a barbaric past that was remote even in Shakespeare's time, and his audience's preoccupation with witchcraft and Scotland has long since faded. When Davenant updated the play for the late seventeenth-century theatre, popular belief already found the Witches implausible. Disbelief has grown since then, and to compensate for it, contemporary directors like Komisarjevsky (Stratford-upon-Avon, 1933) and Polanski (film, 1969) have tried to rationalize the Witches as old crones looting corpses on the battlefield. Inevitably, the supernatural dimension shrinks.

In order to restore the play's atmosphere of medieval superstition, it has long been performed in period costumes and scenery. The resultant need for set changes has often slowed the rapid pace the play should have, and elaborate feudal ceremonies with crowds of supers in shaggy fur and feathers have often smothered in spectacle the subtle poetry and nuances of feeling experienced by the play's readers.

Besides these difficulties, casting and directing present extraordinary problems. The director must strike the right balance between Macbeth and Lady Macbeth, and between the title roles and the rest of the cast. The leading man must strive to be at once poet and soldier, hero and criminal—he must trace the symptoms of violent ecstacy (without seeming ludicrous) and, having succeeded at these physically taxing feats, he must end the performance with a vigorous sword fight. Lady Macbeth's part also tends to extremes. If she is strong—a Sarah Siddons—Macbeth's responsibility is diminished; if weak, or underplayed—as in Polanski's film—his need for her love and respect seems merely trivial. In contrast to the title roles, the supporting roles are small, even "bitty," and are hard to cast because they often go unnoticed in reviews.

With difficulties of acting go difficulties of staging: the play is foreshortened. The "big" scenes—the Witches, the murder of Duncan and its discovery, the Banquet Scene, and the Cauldron Scene—fill the first two-thirds of the play. Then the pace slows and the narrative focus widens with the Lady Macduff Scene, the long scene in England, and the Sleepwalking. The last act is cluttered with little scenes—the gathering of English and Scots forces, the picking up and casting off of branches, Macbeth's reception of the reports, and the great soliloquies they draw from him. Instead of rising to a climax by the resolution of subplots (as does *Hamlet*, for example, with the elimination of Polonius, Ophelia, Rosenkrantz, and Guildenstern well before the end), at the end of *Macbeth*, the narrative branches out, and sympathy begins to shift away from Macbeth to those around him, with the danger that the performance will shrink into a melodramatic hunting down of the tyrant. As a result, just as *Hamlet* is know proverbially as a play that never utterly fails, *Macbeth* is famous as one that almost never fully succeeds.

Glen Byam Shaw's *Macbeth* at Stratford-upon-Avon in 1955 was a notable exception to the play's tradition of theatrical failure. The newspaper critics recognized it at once as a classic. It was "Nonpareil," as Harold Hobson proclaimed, concurring with the other critics, among them Alan Dent, who called it "the crown of the season at Stratford-upon-Avon," and Kenneth Tynan who

Glen Byam Shaw in 1955.

praised "all the speed and clarity we associate with Glen Byam Shaw." Theatre historians have since judged it one of the best *Macbeths*, if not the best, in our time. Richard David wrote in *Shakespeare Survey*, "Byam Shaw gave us Shakespeare's tragedy in all its balanced perfection." In *Macbeth and the Players*, Dennis Bartholomeusz judged it "the most successful interpretation of *Macbeth* in this century." And Gareth Lloyd Evans, writing in *Theatre Quarterly*, placed it "at the peak of interpretations of this century." [1]

1. Richard David, "The Tragic Curve," *Shakespeare Survey* 9 (1956): 127; David Bartholomeusz, *Macbeth and the Players* (Cambridge, 1969), p. 254; Gareth Lloyd Evans, "*Macbeth* in the Twentieth Century," *Theatre Quarterly* 1 (1971): 39.

How did this performance succeed where so many others did not? From reviews we can find out a good deal about how Sir Laurence Olivier and Vivien Leigh interpreted the main roles. Yet our knowledge of the production as a whole is fragmentary; its overall design is lost in the conflicting impressions of different reviewers. That there was a design is certain, however, for the director made a detailed record of his work, a promptbook and two notebooks. The promptbook shows with detailed stage directions and maps how Shaw staged the play. The notebooks analyze each scene and each character. Taken together, promptbook and notebooks not only document one of the best professional productions of the play in this century, but also give us a blueprint of the play's nonverbal dimension: the actions, sights, and sounds implicit in the text, which come to life only in performance.

DOCUMENTS

Among the documents I consulted to create a complete view of Shaw's production of *Macbeth* were not only the director's own plans and descriptions but also photographs, the Stratford promptbook, and published resources.

1. *Glen Byam Shaw's Promptbook and Notebooks.* In 1953 Glen Byam Shaw went to Stratford's Shakespeare Memorial Theatre to be codirector there with Anthony Quayle.[2] Unlike later directors, such as Peter Hall and Peter Brook, whose rehearsal methods favored improvisation by the actors, Shaw mapped his staging beforehand; then, during rehearsals, he instructed his actors to follow it. His promptbook and notebooks record this staging. In the first notebook, entitled "The Play," he analyzed each scene, naming the place and time of day, and describing the scene's major events and its purpose in the progress of the play. In the second notebook, entitled "The Characters," he analyzed each role, naming age, appearance, and the actor who would play it. For the major roles, Shaw laid down a line of characterization for the actor to follow. In rehearsal Shaw read these notes to the actors, telling them how he wished them to act as he told them where to go onstage.

Before rehearsals began Shaw had carefully choreographed the play in his promptbook. With a model of the set, he worked out the blocking—the movement of the actors onstage—and the sound and light effects. All this he set down in the promptbook. Physically, the promptbook consists of one hundred and six sheets of ruled notepaper, with pages from the New Temple edition of *Macbeth* pasted on the recto of each sheet, and the whole bound together with brad fasteners. The rectos are marked with stage directions, notes on time and place, and cues for light and sound effects. On the verso, the blank left-hand page, Shaw often added further directions and stage maps. The date on the title page of the promptbook, 17 March 1955, shows that Shaw was planning his production of *Macbeth*, his first production of the season, more than two months before it opened on 7 June 1955, and more than a month before it went into rehearsal at the end of April. The frequent erasures and the re-markings by the same hand with different pencils attest to great care in the promptbook's making, and the wear on the heavily thumbed pages shows how much it was used.

2. Glen Byam Shaw was born in 1904. He made his first appearance as an actor at the Pavilion Theatre in Torquay, England, in 1923. Two years later he played Yasha in *The Cherry Tree* in London. He acted in productions in the United States and London until the outbreak of World War II. After the war he became director of the Old Vic Dramatic School, where he produced several plays before his appointment to the Shakespeare Memorial Theatre, Stratford-upon-Avon. The 1955 production of *Macbeth* was the first time Shaw directed the play. He became sole director at Stratford after Quayle left in 1956.

In 1960, Shaw left Stratford to become Director of Productions at the Sadler's Wells Opera (now the English National Opera), a post he holds today. Peter succeeded him at Stratford.

For more details of his career, see *Who's Who in the Theatre*, 15th ed. (London, 1972), pp. 1400–1401; *l'Enciclopedia dello spettacolo* (Rome, 1961), vol. 8, p. 1933; and Phyllis Hartnoll, ed., *Oxford Companion to the Theatre* (New York, 1967), pp. 879–80.

2. *The Stratford Promptbook.* In format, this promptbook is not unlike Shaw's. Bound in a black spring binder are sheets of ruled notepaper with pages from the New Temple *Macbeth* pasted on the rectos. Cues for lights, sound effects, and set changes are entered in colored pencil alongside the words of the text, and directions for actors, referred to by name rather than role, are penciled on the facing pages. These directions, some of them erased, are in several hands (presumably those of stage manager Jean Roberts and her assistants Hal Rogers and Margaret Hilder). With these very full stage directions are stage maps (mimeographed floor plans for each setting, with actors' positions penciled in), a typed fight routine for the Macbeth-Macduff fight, and understudy lists. The Stratford promptbook is kept at the Shakespeare Centre Library, Stratford-upon-Avon (call number O.S. 71.21/1955 M).

Although the Stratford promptbook is a very accurate record of the production onstage, it is ultimately less useful to scholars and teachers than Shaw's promptbook. Where Shaw made his promptbook to plan the production, the Stratford stage management made theirs to run it. Consequently, the Stratford promptbook is a set of practical instructions to actors and stagehands. Although Shaw never forgets the practicalities (he sets down, one by one, the order each actor in a group is to exit, for example, and which exit to use), his concerns are much wider than those of the stage management, and his promptbook shows it. Shaw's arrows, maps, and written directions tell us exactly what is happening every moment onstage and his notes often tell us why.

3. *Production Records.* These are the loose working papers made by the stage management. Besides cast and understudy lists, they include "plots" or instruction sheets for the various offstage activities: "Flys plot," and "Hanging plot" (for the crew who moved cloths and drops from the fly-space above the stage); "Understage plot" (for the trap from which Banquo's Ghost and the apparitions came); "Running plot" (for moving stage settings); lighting chart and plot; music plot, music cues, and musicians' rehearsal sheets; the "Working division" (a list of the actors required for each scene); a "Wardrobe plot"; and even an inventory of armor. Architects' drawings give the ground plan for each setting. Although not especially useful in themselves, the various "plots" were indispensable in performance, being the instructions to which the cues in the Stratford promptbook refer. Often I have used them to make my description of the staging more specific. The production records are kept in the Shakespeare Centre Library.

4. *Photographs.* Sixty photographs taken by the Company photographer Angus McBean record the production in detail. Many of them are reproduced in this book.

5. *Theatre Records.* Press cuttings from every British publication were collected by the Theatre's publicity department, and are now kept in a scrapbook at the Shakespeare Centre Library. These record the production as it was seen by reviewers in the audience.[3]

6. *Interviews.* I interviewed a number of the actors who played in the 1955 *Macbeth*, and I also spoke with the Stratford theatre management. The actors interviewed were: Maxine Audley (Lady Macduff), Trader Faulkner (Malcolm), Emrys James (Sewer, Thane), Keith Michell (Macduff), and Lee Montague (Seyton). Excerpts from the interviews with Audley, Faulkner, and Montague appear near the end of the book. Desmond Hall (who was production manager in 1955) and Roger Howells (who succeeded him) have both checked my account of the staging for factual accuracy.

3. The publications in which these reviews appeared are:
Birmingham Evening Despatch, 8 June 1955, Norman Holbrook.
Birmingham Gazette, 8 June 1955.
Birmingham Mail, 8 June, 9 June 1955.
Birmingham Post, 9 June, 15 June 1955, J. C. Trewin.
Birmingham Weekly Post, 10 June 1955.
Coventry Evening Telegraph, 8 June 1955.
Coventry Standard, 10 June 1955.
Daily Herald, 11 June 1955.
Daily Mail, 8 June 1955.
Daily Mirror, 8 June 1955.
Daily Sketch, 8 June 1955, Harold Conway.
Daily Telegraph, 8 June 1955, Patrick Gibbs.
Daily Worker, 9 June 1955.
Drama, August 1955, Ivor Brown.
Evening News, 8 June 1955, Stephen Williams.
Evening Standard, 8 June 1955, Milton Shulman.
Evesham Journal, 11 June 1955, 18 June 1955.
Financial Times, 8 June 1955, Peter Foster.
Gloucester Echo, 8 June, 9 June 1955.
Illustrated London News, 25 June 1955, J. C. Trewin.
Lady, 23 June 1955, J. C. Trewin.
Leamington Spa Courier, 10 June 1955.
Manchester Guardian, 9 June 1955, Philip Hope-Wallace.
Manchester Guardian Weekly, 16 June 1955.
Morning Advertiser, 15 June 1955.
New Statesman, 18 June 1955.
News Chronicle, 8 June 1955, Alan Dent.
Nottingham Guardian Journal, 8 June 1955.
Observer, 12 June 1955, Kenneth Tynan.
Punch, 15 June 1955.
Scotsman, 15 June 1955.
Sketch, 13 June, 13 July 1955.
Solihull and Warwick County News, 11 June 1955.
South Wales Argus, 8 June 1955, Marion Rathbone.
Spectator, 24 June 1955.
Stage, 9 June 1955.
Stratford-upon-Avon Herald, 10 June 1955, James Courtenay.
Sunday Times, 12 June 1955, Harold Hobson.
Theatre World, July 1955.
Times, 8 June, 16 June 1955.
Time and Tide, 18 June 1955.
Tribune, 8 July 1955.
Truth, 17 June 1955.
Warwickshire Advertiser, 10 June 1955.
Western Daily Press, 9 June 1955, Peter Rodford.
Western Independent, 19 June 1955.
Wolverhampton Express and Star, 8 June, 10 June 1955.
Yorkshire Post, 8 June 1955, Desmond Pratt.

7. *Published References.* The importance of recording the actual performance of plays, especially Shakespeare's plays, has not gone unnoticed in the past. In the last part of the nineteenth century, the theatre critic William Winter recorded Edwin Booth's Shakespearean acting through "promptbook editions" and descriptions of Booth's "dramatic characters," and, at the end of his life, Winter completed *Shakespeare on the Stage* (issued first in 1911 and reissued with additions in 1915 and 1916), accounts of the stage history of individual plays. G. C. D. Odell's *Shakespeare from Betterton to Irving* (2 vols., 1920) provides a detailed chronological account of Shakespeare's plays on the English and American stages. In *Shakespeare and the Actors* (1945) and in subsequent books and articles Arthur Colby Sprague has described the theatrical traditions of the acting and staging of the plays. G. Blakemore Evans has analyzed and published facsimiles of seventeenth-century Shakespeare promptbooks. G. Winchester Stone and Kalman Burnim, experts in eighteenth-century theatre, have applied close scrutiny to the promptbooks of David Garrick. Charles H. Shattuck, whose catalogue *The Shakespeare Promptbooks* has made possible far-ranging investigations of Shakespeare's plays onstage, has analyzed and published promptbooks of the nineteenth-century actor William Charles Macready and has used promptbook records to reconstruct Edwin Booth's *Hamlet*. Other scholars have also based their work upon promptbook research: among the more important recent books are biographies of William Charles Macready by Alan S. Downer, Charlotte Cushman by Joseph Leach, and Samuel Phelps by Shirely S. Allen. Joseph Price's *The Unfortunate Comedy* examines stage history as a guide to understanding *All's Well That Ends Well.*

In my description of the performance I have also drawn on Richard David's vivid account in *Shakespeare Survey* (9 [1956]: 123–31) and on Dennis Bartholomeusz's account in *Macbeth and the Players* (Cambridge, 1969), pp. 254–66.

TEXT

As his basic text, Shaw used the New Temple edition (edited by M. R. Ridley, London: J. P. Dent & Co., 1935, reprinted 1949), an edition long favored by actors and directors because the book is small, the print is large with modern spelling, and the text is not cluttered by scholarly notes. From the start, Shaw treated the text as an acting script, shaping it as he worked with it. He cut up two copies of the book and then pasted one page of text onto the recto of each sheet in his promptbook. While keeping the text nearly intact, Shaw cut the Hecate scene (III, v) and the scene following between Lennox and Another Lord (III, vi), not even pasting these into the promptbook. He united various messengers' and servants' lines under the single character Seyton. Here and there he penciled out a line or two that would be obscure to his audience, and from time to time he changed a word for better sense (*chair* for *cheer* in V, iii, 21), or to avoid a distracting double entendre (*orbs* for *balls* in IV, i, 121). The actual cuts are:

> I, ii, 25–28a, 46–47a, 59–63; iii, 93b–97a; II, iii, 80b; III, i, 22, 80b–82a, 132b–133a; iv, 14; v and vi in toto; IV, i, 37–43, 78, 125–132; ii, 38b–43; iii, 27, 53b–55a, 63b–65a, 70b–72, 82b–85a, 108b–111a, 125b–131a, 136b–137a, 140–159a, 166b–170a, 174b–177a, 191–192a; V, ii, 27–30; iv, 14b–16a, 19–20; vi, 6b–8; vii, 12–29; viii, 50b–53.

In all, these come to 204 lines out of the 2,091 lines printed in the New Temple *Macbeth.* Although Shaw has told me that he was "not generally in favour of carving up Shakespeare," he did in fact pare away about 10 per cent of *Macbeth,* which may seem to be a good deal of paring to readers unfamiliar with common stage practice. At the turn of the century it was not uncommon to remove as much as one-third of the text through cutting—as in Sir Herbert Beerbohm Tree's 1911 *Macbeth.* By midcentury, respect for the text had restrained such flagrant excisions, especially at

Stratford-upon-Avon, where Anthony Quayle in 1949 trimmed only 156 lines (7 per cent) from his *Macbeth*, and John Gielgud in 1952, 88 lines (about 5 per cent). In the *Macbeth* that followed Shaw's, Peter Hall's 1967 production, only 40 lines were cut. In short, although Shaw cut somewhat more than average, he was exercising a director's established prerogative. For sanction he could look both to stage practice and to textual scholarship, which has long questioned the integrity of the Folio text of *Macbeth*.

STAGE

Although there have been modifications since 1955, Shakespeare Memorial Theatre was essentially the same as the present Royal Shakespeare Theatre (as it was renamed in 1961). The house then seated 1,301, with room for 76 standing, and then, as now, every seat was usually taken. By 1955 the stage and seating of the theatre, which had been built in 1932 with a small forestage and a picture-frame proscenium arch, had been changed to bring the audience and actors closer together. The upper and lower balconies (called the Balcony and the Dress Circle) had been extended toward the stage, and so had the stalls. The orchestra pit was covered to create a forestage in front of the proscenium arch, and the arch itself was camouflaged behind false walls. The layout and dimensions of the theatre are shown in the theatre plans on p. 14. Although complicated in practice, the mechanics of the stage were simple in principle. Above the stage in the fly-space were cloths and drops that could be raised and lowered. Under the stage was a machine to work the trap and a smoke-generating device (used in *Macbeth* for the Cauldron Scene). Shaw's promptbook refers to eight entrances, each entrance being the space between two "wings," or scene flats at the side of the stage. On stage right (referred to as "Opposite Prompt" or simply "OP"), in front of the proscenium arch was the assembly entrance (Assey), and behind it, the proscenium entrance (Pros), the middle entrance (Mid), and the back entrance (Back). Stage left ("Promptside," "PS," or "P") repeated the same sequence of entrances. On the stage itself were two permanent lifts, which, as the plan shows, were used to raise and lower sets (or, in the first scene, to lower the Witches). In front of the lifts, a small trap was installed for Banquo's Ghost and for the Cauldron's apparitions.

Just behind the proscenium arch was the prompter's box, a control center manned by the assistant stage manager, who sat with the promptbook and ran the cue board. Although he was rarely called upon to actually prompt a forgetful actor, his main task was to run the production by signaling actors, stagehands, musicians, and electricians. The Stratford promptbook told him when to warn and cue the actors and the others. For each "stand by" and "cue" in the promptbook, he threw a switch on the cue board, and a "warn" or "cue" light went on to signal the actor or stagehand. For the knocking at the gate, for example, when Lady Macbeth said, "Why did you bring the daggers from the place?" the prompter turned on the "stand by" light in the promptside assembly entrance ("P Assey"), and, at her exit, he turned on the cue light. Then a stagehand knocked, repeating the knock every time the cue light flashed. As the play went forward, the assistant stage manager kept it running smoothly and checked the actors' "moves" against the notes made in the promptbook, so that from one night to the next the performances were as uniform as possible. It was with this system in mind that Shaw prepared his promptbook.

DESIGN

Working with designer Roger Furse, Shaw had established the design of costumes and settings early in the planning, before he began work on the promptbook. Roger Furse (1903–1973) had

THE SHAKESPEARE
MEMORIAL THEATRE, 1955.

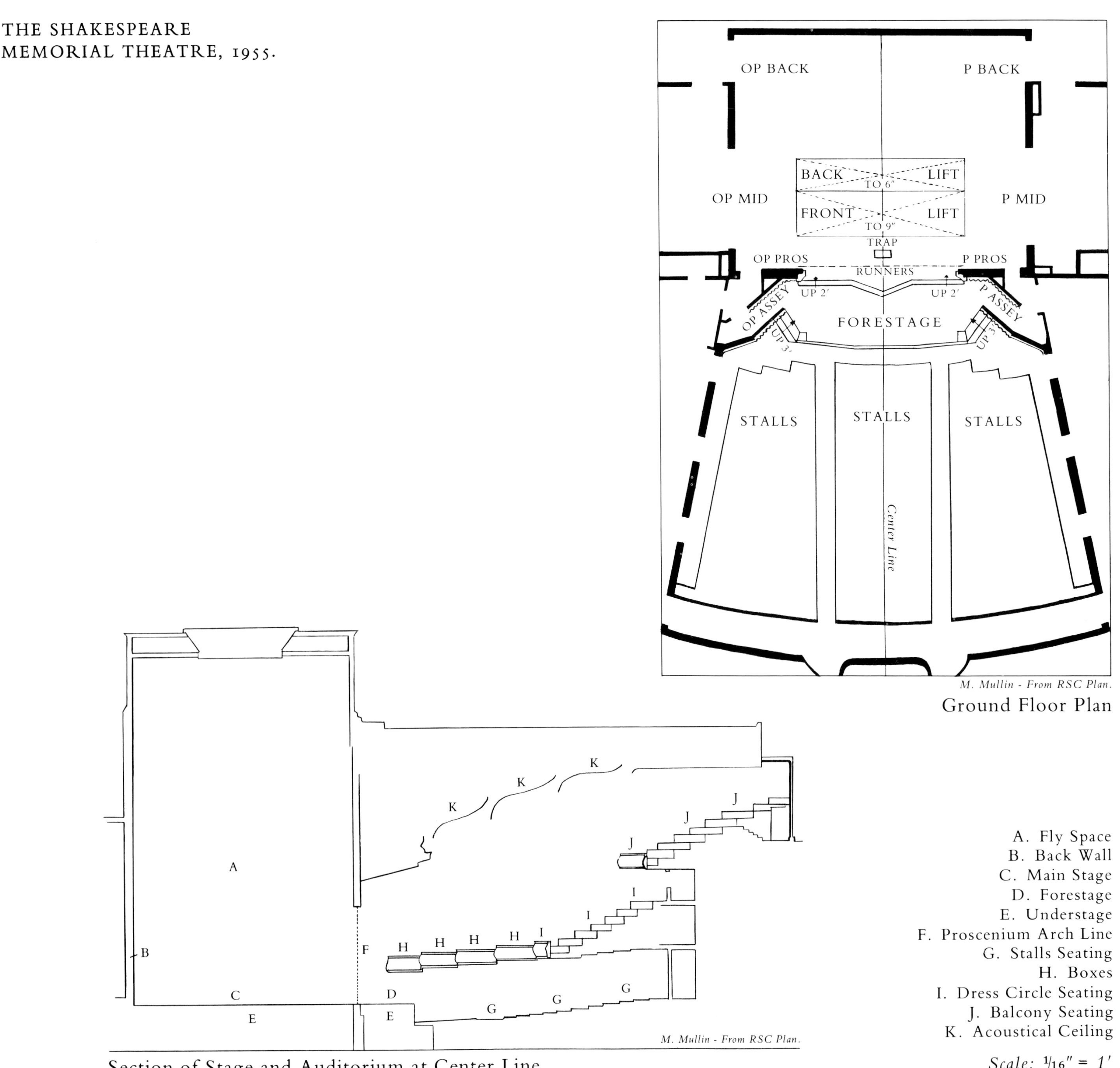

Ground Floor Plan

Section of Stage and Auditorium at Center Line

A. Fly Space
B. Back Wall
C. Main Stage
D. Forestage
E. Understage
F. Proscenium Arch Line
G. Stalls Seating
H. Boxes
I. Dress Circle Seating
J. Balcony Seating
K. Acoustical Ceiling

Scale: 1/16" = 1'

wide experience with Shakespeare's plays, having done the designs for a dozen productions at the Old Vic from 1937 to 1955, as well as designs for Olivier's films of *Henry V* (1944) and *Hamlet* (1948). For the 1955 *Macbeth*, Furse designed eight sets: The Heath, Macbeth's Courtyard, The Banquet Hall, The Cavern, Macduff's Castle, England, Dunsinane, and The Battlements. Multiple acting areas in each set permitted the action to move swiftly around the stage, and in Macbeth's Courtyard, the setting approximated the Elizabethan Globe playhouse, with an upper level, an inner stage, several openings backstage, and a large downstage area. Furse solved the problem of disruptive set changes by drawing the "runners," curtains just upstage of the proscenium line, at the end of one scene, so that the action continued on the forestage while stagehands changed the set behind the runners. For example, the setting for the first three scenes of the play was a mountain-filled backdrop with a prop tree and three "crags" placed further downstage. Then, for the next scene (set in "Forres" says the promptbook), the runners closed off the stage behind the proscenium arch and they opened at the end of the Forres Scene to reveal the courtyard of Macbeth's Inverness, where the next scenes (I, v to II, iv) were acted without a break (see illustrations).

The settings blended traditional medieval architecture with modern expressionism. Rough stone steps in wide halls under arches and vaulting dated the scene, and distortions of these familiar shapes gave an emotional tone to the settings, so that, said the *Birmingham Mail* (8 June), they "were in thorough keeping with the mood and spirit of the play, offering as they did the impression of rude and massive halls and storm-racked wastes in which the gloomy and lurid story unfolded itself with perfect propriety." Russets, browns, shades of gray on rough stone-textured surfaces created a harsh, foreboding atmosphere. For the interior scenes, the angular arches, tumbled askew as if wrenched by earthquake, created a world of caverns, deep misshapen recesses from which the human figures came forward into the light. In the Sleepwalking Scene, for example, Lady Macbeth stepped slowly forward, her candle shining at the end of a long, cavernous tunnel, made longer by the series of bent arches that receded into the gloom. The shape of the twisted archway, an irregular pentagon, appeared not only in the architecture, but also as a decorative motif on Lady Macduff's tapestry and on the battlements, and in the shape of the thrones in the Banquet Hall. Even in the England Scene (IV, iii), which is usually thought of as a point of brightness and sunlight, the sunlit backdrop was overhung with the dark shapes of huge trees that met overhead to form another twisted archway.

The costumes combined splendor and sensuality. The men, all armed, were dressed in breeches and tunics, with leather armor, boots, and gloves. Speaking about all the men, *Punch* reported that Macbeth "goes to a good barber and is not hung about with old rugs." The women wore long, graceful gowns with tight-fitting bodices of clinging jersey on which shadows and highlights had been painted to accentuate their figures. The colors of their garments identified each group of characters. The Scots wore dark plaids. Except for a spot of bright color like Malcolm's cream-colored tunic, Duncan's yellow gloves, or Macbeth's crimson cape, the dominant colors were dark: tan, rust, browns, blacks, greens, and grays. Macbeth and Lacy Macbeth's color was green—hers a vivid emerald accentuated by touches of red in her wig; his, more muted, and set off by red cape and trim. The English and their Scots allies wore blue cloaks and tunics and breeches in shades of cream, silver, and white. Banquo appeared in a blue tunic after the show of Kings (IV, i), and Lady Macduff and her family were dressed in shades of blue and gray. Although muted in color, the costumes were by no means drab. In color transparencies, the group scenes glow with a rich variety of color. One can almost feel the soft dresses of the women, the cold steel and leather armor of the men. "Always we are conscious of the sword and dagger, the thrust of steel," said J. C. Trewin in the *Birmingham Post* (9 June). Light glints from the swords and daggers at every man's side, and gold shines from the King's crown, from his red, gold-embossed belt, from Lady

Design for Macbeth's costume, by Roger Furse, 1955.

Design for Lady Macbeth's costume, by Roger Furse, 1955.

Design for the Porter's costume, by Roger Furse, 1955.

Macbeth's golden bracelets, from her gold and topaz earrings, and from the gold trim that adorns Macbeth's royal robes.

Although Furse's settings depicted a dark, barren world, his costumes decked that world with bright pageantry. This grandeur, visually exciting simply as theatre, was important to the play. It made kingship a thing of beauty as well as of power, and suggested that it appealed to Macbeth's vivid imagination (as it does to ours), as well as to his ambition. Against this beauty stood the loathsome Witches, made more hideous by tricks of make-up and by gray, ragged clothes that suggested in color and roughness the wasteland from which they come. The Banquet Scene showed at once how much Macbeth longs for the dignity and beauty that attended Duncan, and how little of it his crimes have won. Macbeth and Lady Macbeth, resplendent in their royal habillements, were stripped of pomp, ceremony, and dignity by the coming of Banquo's Ghost, the hideous embodiment of Macbeth's evil.

REHEARSAL

At the first rehearsal, reading from his notebook, Shaw spoke to the assembled actors, setting forth his ideas on the meaning of the play and what he hoped the production would attain.

> The theme of *Macbeth* is, of course, ambition, but it seems to me that the terrifying atmosphere that pervades the play is due to the fact that the two central characters in the tragedy consciously & deliberately give their souls to the Devil to achieve their end. Lady Macbeth evokes the powers of darkness to take possession of her & give her the strength to resist any feelings of remorse or pity that may interfere with the fulfillment of her purpose.
>
> Macbeth knows that to murder the King would be the most appalling & monstrous crime, & yet he allows himself to be goaded into committing the murder. He is not a victim of the Fates & he could have said "Get thee behind me, Satan," but he doesn't. I think that it is for this reason that this play is the most awe-inspiring & terrifying of all the tragedies.
>
> These two human beings are not monsters; if they were, the play would be infinitely less terrible and tragic. Lady Macbeth is not by nature a "fiend-like Queen" for if she were there would be no necessity for her to call on evil spirits to help her; & having achieved her object she would be able to enjoy it, monstrously. That is, certainly, not the case.
>
> Macbeth is a great soldier & a great man & has the imagination of an artist, which is not so unusual as people sometimes think with men of action. At the start of the play he has nobility as well as a dynamic personality & it is only after he has given way to temptation that he becomes morose, suspicious, savage, & cruel, though to the very end he remains human & magnificent: "I'll fight, till from my bones my flesh be hack'd." He gets absolutely no enjoyment from his crimes, each one of which sinks him deeper into hell.
>
> In the other great tragedies there are expressions of pity & respect when the central character or characters die. We feel that they will, at least, be at peace in "the life to come." At the end of *Hamlet* Horatio says "Good-night sweet Prince & flights of Angels sing thee to thy rest." There is enormous pity & heart-felt sorrow for Lear when he dies, & also for Othello, & we feel sure that Antony & Cleopatra are going to meet again "where souls do couch on flowers"; & the same could be said about Romeo and Juliet.
>
> But in *Macbeth* it is utterly different. Not a word of sympathy or sorrow is said about Lady Macbeth when she commits suicide, except by her husband. Her body will be thrown into an unhallowed grave & her soul will be in torment forever. All the other great tragic heroes are happy to die but Macbeth fights for life to the end because he knows that he is going to eternal hell. His head is cut from his body & stuck on the battlements of his own castle. He is mourned by no one. Certainly this is the most moral play, & is the strongest possible warning against

evil & sin. The play should have a compelling & horrifying effect on the audience. There is tremendous action in it from beginning to end. There is not a single scene in the play that should not hold the audience spell-bound. I don't tell stories well but when my step-daughter Jane was a little girl I told her the story of *Macbeth* & my wife Angela was very angry with me because Jane woke up screaming every night for a week.

We should set out to tell this marvellous & horrifying story of Shakespeare's with all the imagination, strength, & reality that we can muster. We can't expect to enjoy rehearsing this play any more than one can enjoy the thought of hell, but we can live through the next four weeks in a ferment of imagination, excitement & endeavour. Let us, from the very start imagine to ourselves, that this play has never been seen before. Let us come at it absolutely freshly. Let us base our presentation on a determination to tell the story clearly & to the full. That can only be done by means of imaginative acting of the highest grade.

It has been said that Shakespeare poured all his creative genius into the characters of Macbeth & Lady Macbeth & left very little over for the other characters. To me that is a wrong way to put it.

I believe that he did exactly what he set out to do, which was to show us these two exceptional human beings with the flames of hell burning them up & the horror of those flames reflected on the faces of the normal human beings who look on. It is like people looking into a volcano. One sees in the expression of their faces the awe & fear which they feel at what they see.

Macbeth & Lady Macbeth can only achieve their right significance in the story if everyone around them re-acts to them in the right way.

The discovery of the King's murder can only have its true impact on the audience if *every* individual on the stage is imagining the terrible situation to the full.

The sleep-walking scene depends on the acting of three people, not just one; & so forth.

It is not a matter of inventing details of character that the genius of the author has told him are not only unnecessary but wrong. The difference between such characters as Angus, Menteith, Caithness, etc. is negligible, but it is through the re-actions of these men that we see the reflections of the fire that burns at the centre of the play.

An actor who has no imagination cannot even walk on in this play without doing harm. And one can't act in an imaginative way unless one does everything one can to stimulate one's imagination to the full, & use every bit of personal experience that one has had to help. You can't imagine out of nothing.

I remember being in this very room when I was told that King George VI had died. An extraordinary atmosphere was immediately created, but what would have been the effect of us if we had been told that he had been murdered? And how should we have felt if we had been present at Windsor Castle at the time? From start to finish of this play we are very near to death, so near in fact that the tragic hero sees shadows from the other world.

Everyone in the play must feel this nearness of death just as we all did during the War.

The rhythm of the play is extraordinary. There is a feeling of tremendous speed. As though one were running down a great dark flight of steps in a night-mare. This is something which must be conveyed to the audience if the story is to have its full effect.

The acting needs urgency, vitality, & power. By that I don't mean shouting. One can't imagine this story taking place anywhere except in the highlands of Scotland. Scottish people are by nature strongly passionate but they are also dour. They don't go about shouting at each other. Their feelings are deep & hidden but when they do break out they can be appalling in their fierceness & strength. If ever a play needed a feeling of suppressed tension, interspersed with great waves of emotional outbreak, it is this one. If it is under-acted, it cannot have the right impact on the audience, in fact I would say that so long as it is truly acted it cannot be over-acted. I am not for any of the characters using Scottish accents because I don't think it was the author's intention & if one or two characters speak with an accent, then why not all? This I'm quite sure would be wrong.

I feel that it is a great experience in my life to try to produce this play; I feel that what Roger Furse has given us for the sets & costumes is of exactly the right nature, but, I'm sure he will agree with me when I say that the only thing that really matters is the acting.

I would like to stun the audience with our performance, but we will never do that if we are indefinite, half-hearted, timid, or over-detailed. Think of the play as a whole. Act each scene to the full, but don't anticipate what is to come. This is great tragedy & must never be allowed to sink below that level. Let us be "bloody, bold & resolute" from the start.

As Shaw's remarks implied, the cast included a diversity of talents and interests. At their head was Sir Laurence Olivier as Macbeth, with his wife Vivien Leigh as Lady Macbeth. And following were a company of actors less well known. Many of them were actors in the making like Maxine Audley (Lady Macduff), Emrys James (Sewer, Thane), Keith Michell (Macduff), and Ralph Michael (Banquo); some, like Lee Montague (Seyton), had followed Shaw from the Old Vic Dramatic School; others, like Patrick Wymark (the Porter), were old hands in supporting roles at Stratford. As a director, Shaw exercised much greater control over the actors than most directors do today—and his power was leagued with Olivier's great prestige.

To understand the effect Olivier had on the cast, we need to remember that he was then at midcareer. He was known as an actor who had done great things on the stage, but who had not done them recently. His work in films and his involvement with his wife's stage career had led to world tours and light comedy but had kept him from Shakespearean tragedy since his famous Richard III at the Old Vic in 1949.[4] Vivien Leigh was a successful film star, but was somewhat distrusted by the theatre crowd, actors and audiences being divided about her "real" talents. Olivier wanted to put Vivien Leigh on equal footing with himself as a stage actor. He was making opportunities for her and giving her all the benefit of his own influence and experience. One would expect that this would make difficulties with the rest of the actors. Yet so great was the fame of Olivier and Shaw that they inspired admiration and acquiescence, not jealousy, and the strength of director and star helped pull the varied company together.[5] Indeed, the actors remembered taking a personal interest in the leading man and lady as people, in some ways remarkably akin to the interest other characters in the play have in Macbeth and his wife.

It would be wrong to suppose that Shaw lavished all his attention on Olivier, at the expense of the others. Unlike today, when Peter Hall's ideal of an "actors' company" (with each actor more or less equal) has taken root, in Shaw's time the actors took the star system of talent and credit for granted.[6] The play itself favors such an arrangement. The towering stature of the two Macbeths and the consequent flattening out of the other parts has long made it a vehicle for great actors. Simply because the Macbeths are so often onstage alone or at the center of attention in a group, the other parts blur together into group reactions with a few individual "cameo" appearances. Even when we recall the small parts distinctly—the Porter, Banquo's murder, Lady Macduff's murder, or Macduff grieving for his loss—we think of separate scenes, "bits," rather than fully developed characterizations. For this reason, and because he must have been well aware of an actor's tendency to feel slighted with a small part, Shaw emphasized the need for each actor to fill out his role with an awareness of its importance to the entire staging, and his notes show that he had given careful thought to every character, in every scene, even to such minor characters as Seyton. Lee Montague, who had that part, told me that, unlike some directors, Shaw did not simply tell an actor where to stand, but would always give his actors reasons for standing and moving.

It wasn't just a question of "Go there." He would provide a reason, a motivation, a very *good* motivation. . . . He wouldn't give you the deepest motivation. He'd give you a motivation that was sufficient for you to go *there*. . . . When in fact you started to drop the book and started to talk about it and really rehearse it, then he would provide you with even more, and deeper motivations.

4. "A year ago it looked as if Olivier might do nothing more of importance in the theatre. His play appearances had been uninteresting for some time, and his film activities, while often worthwhile in their sphere, seemed to absorb his attention to the detriment of his acting. . . . The news of Olivier's departure for Stratford gave one a little thrill of hope," said *The Stage* (1 September 1955), summing up Olivier's success during the 1955 Stratford season.

5. "They worked devotedly with their team and their director. There was no exhibitionism, and much hard, well shared labour," reported Ivor Brown in *Drama* (August 1955): 34.

6. During an experimental season without stars in 1954, the Shakespeare Memorial Theatre suffered a decline in attendance. The success of the 1955 season with Olivier and Leigh confirmed management's belief in the star system. *Birmingham Post*, 14 July 1955.

The key to these motivations lies in the analyses Shaw made in his notebooks.

In practical terms, of course, Shaw spent more time with Olivier and Leigh than with the others, simply because as Macbeth and Lady Macbeth they had more acting to do. The scenes were prepared individually, actors coming to the theatre to rehearse only "their" scenes. This isolated preparation created a feeling of excitement among the actors because, as several actors have told me, until the first full-scale rehearsals, they were aware only of their own scenes, and could only guess at what Olivier had in store. As it reached the final stages of rehearsal, the play lived up to its reputation as a dangerous undertaking. Keith Michell (Macduff) and Trader Faulkner (Malcolm) remembered that during the rehearsal of the fight between Macbeth and Macduff, Olivier's sword went into Michell's eye, cutting the cornea, and almost blinding him, and that, another time, the stairs they fought on began to give way. "We all thought, 'This is it!' We were always expecting something dreadful to happen in this play," said Trader Faulkner. Despite these near misses, there were no serious mishaps. Although quiet about his own work, Olivier helped the younger actors. When Trader Faulkner, for instance, wanted to resist Shaw's notion that Malcolm is young and inexperienced, Olivier (who had played the part in 1928) supported Faulkner, and urged him to try a more virile Malcolm. Urging others on, but holding himself back, Olivier built up suspense among his fellow actors about his own plans. "He'd been very quiet, and had not *done* a great deal, just walking through quite quietly," remembered Lee Montague. "And then we were going to do a read-through, one of the final read-throughs onstage, and he decided to give a performance. Suddenly one realized what a tremendous performance it was going to be."

CAST LIST

THE WITCHES Dilys Hamlett, Nancye Stewart, Mary Law
DUNCAN Geoffrey Bayldon
MALCOLM Trader Faulkner
DONALBAIN Ian Holm
A SERGEANT David King
ROSS William Devlin
LENNOX James Grout
ANGUS John Springett
MENTEITH Robert Hunter
CAITHNESS Gabriel Woolf
MACBETH Sir Laurence Olivier
BANQUO Ralph Michael
FLEANCE Paul Vieyra
LADY MACBETH Vivien Leigh
SEYTON Lee Montague
A PORTER Patrick Wymark
AN OLD MAN John MacGregor
TWO MURDERERS Ron Haddrick, Hugh Cross
MACDUFF Keith Michell
LADY MACDUFF Maxine Audley
MACDUFF'S SON John Rogers
A SHEPHERD Mervyn Blake
A DOCTOR Geoffrey Bayldon
A GENTLEWOMAN Rosalind Atkinson
A SERVANT Richard Coe
SIWARD Mervyn Blake
SIWARD'S SON Robert Arnold
A SENTRY Rex Robinson
LORDS, SOLDIERS, ATTENDANTS Jill Dixon, Ann Firbank, Leon Eagles, Peter Van Greenaway, Alan Haywood, Emrys James, George Little, Kevin Miles, Geoffrey Sassé, John Southworth, Philip Thomas

GLOSSARY

For the terms and abbreviations below, I list the most common form first, then variants. Notes in parentheses indicate the first occurrence of each term in the promptbook. Roman numerals refer to the act and scene; arabic numerals refer to the pages in this book. Thus, for example, *Ang., An.* (I, iii, 47) means that the abbreviation first appears in Act One, Scene Three, page 9 of the promptbook (p. 47 of this book), and *Cham* (I, iv, 52), in Act One, Scene Four, page 52 of this book.

Ang., An. Angus (I, iii, 47).
Ban. Banner or Banner Carrier (I, ii, 33).
Ban. Banquo (I, iii, 42).
C. Center stage (I, ii, 32), that is, the visual center of the stage, a spot downstage from the physical center. The lines of sight from all seats in the house converge at center stage.
C Arch. The center archway in the palace set (I, v, 59).
Caith. Caithness (I, ii, 33).
Cham. Chamberlain (I, iv, 52), one of Duncan's men, later Macbeth's.
Cloth flied in. The backdrop for the Lady Macduff scene (IV, ii, 173) is "flied" (Shaw's idiosyncratic usage for "flown") or lowered from the flies above the stage during the blackout. See notes on *Drape flied*, *England clothes flied*, and *Gauze flied*, and also the illustrations for the Lady Macduff scene.
D., Doc. The Doctor (IV, iv, 204).
D, Dun. Duncan (I, ii, 33).
DS. Downstage (I, ii, 32), nearer the audience and traditionally "below" upstage because the stage sloped downwards. In fact, the stage in 1955 was flat.
Don. Donalbain (I, ii, 33).
Drape flied. The backdrop for the England scene is lowered from the flies above the stage (IV, iii, 185). See notes on *Cloth flied in*, *England clothes flied*, and *Gauze flied*, and also the illustration for the England scene.
Drawer closed. The cover or "slider" over the front lift, on which the rock rests, is shut (I, i, 31), after the Witches exit stage right.
E Sol. English Soldier (V, vi, 230), one of Siward's men.
England clothes flied, Sleepwalking clothes flied in. The backdrop for the England Scene is raised, and the backdrop for the Sleepwalking Scene is lowered (IV, iii, 203). See notes on *Cloth flied in*, *Drape flied*, *Gauze flied*, and also the illustrations for the England and Sleepwalking scenes.
Fade In, Fade Out. A sound cue and/or a light cue (I, ii, 33) for an effect that gradually grows stronger or weaker.
Fle. Fleance (I, v, 66).
Forestage. The area in front of the proscenium arch (I, iii, 43), down two steps from the main stage.
Front lift. A platform in the stage, used for the Witches to descend (I, i, 31). The lifts, front and back, could be raised as part of the set (as they appear to be for I, ii, 32, for example). All were part of the original 1932 stage; the trap for Banquo's Ghost was built for this production.
G., GW. Gentlewoman (IV, iv, 205):
Gauze flied. A gauze or scrim, behind which the Witches appeared, is raised into the flies, the open space above the stage, in preparation for the next scene (I, i, 31). See notes on *Cloth flied*, *Drape flied*, *England clothes flied*, and also the illustration showing the Witches seeming to hover in air behind the scrim.
L. Lord (III, i, 116).
Lady M. Lady Macbeth (I, v, 62).
Lady Mac. Lady Macduff (IV, ii, 174).
Len. Lennox (I, ii, 33).

Lighting preset behind runners. The stage lighting is already set when the runners open (III, iv, 137) as distinguished from a fade-in.

Loon. The Messenger whom Macbeth calls a cream-fac'd loon (V, v, 226).

M. Macbeth (I, iii, 42).

M. S. Macbeth's servant, as distinguished from a "Royal Servant" to Duncan, one of the Sewer's nine assistants in the dumbshow (I, vii, 71).

M. Sols. Macbeth's soldiers (V, v, 226).

Mac. Macduff (II, iii, 94).

Mal. Malcolm (I, ii, 33).

Men. Menteith (I, ii, 33).

Mid. The middle entrance (I, i, 31), the entrance on either side of the stage between the backstage entrance and the proscenium entrance.

Murd, M. Murderer (III, i, 122).

OM. Old Man (II, iv, 110).

OP. Opposite Promptside, or stage right (I, ii, 32). Instead of the stage right and stage left customary in American theatres, the British theatre marks directions by the promptside (stage left at Stratford and most modern theatres), and opposite promptside. See note on *PS.*

OP Ass. The Assembly entrance stage right (I, iii, 39), just in front of the proscenium arch.

Offc. Officer (I, ii, 32).

PS. Promptside, or stage left (I, ii, 32). Here is located the prompter's box with the promptbook and the switches for cue lights. See note on *OP.*

PS Ass. The Assembly entrance stage left (I, ii, 32), just in front of the proscenium arch.

Port., Por. The Porter (II, iii, 92).

Pros. The proscenium entrance (I, ii, 32), the entrance just behind the proscenium arch, on either side of the stage.

R. Ross (I, ii, 36).

RS. Royal Servant (I, iv, 52), one of Duncan's men, later Macbeth's.

R Standard. Royal Standard, Duncan's banner (I, ii, 37).

Runners. The curtains which could be drawn across the stage to separate the forestage from the main stage (I, iv, 53).

SB. Standard Bearer (I, ii, 33).

S. M. T. The Shakespeare Memorial Theatre (title page, 30), now renamed the Royal Shakespeare Theatre.

S. Sol. Scots Soldier (V, ii, 212).

Second cloth. The curtain drawn across the second arch by the Gentlewoman after Lady Macbeth leaves at the end of the Sleepwalking Scene (V, ii, 213).

Shep. The shepherd (IV, ii, 179), who warns Lady Macduff.

Sey. Seyton (I, v, 66).

Siw. Old Siward (V, iv, 224).

Sjt. Sergeant, the bloody captain who reports to Duncan (I, ii, 32).

Sol. Soldier (I, ii, 32).

S, Son. One of Lady Macduff's sons (IV, ii, 174).

Sound effects. Indicated by a vertical line alongside the text, with the effect described at its onset. See for example "Thunder" and "Vibration in the air" (I, i, 31).

Truck off. The truck on which the wall for the England Scene rested is pushed offstage into the wings (IV, iii, 203).

Turret door. The door leading to Lady Macbeth's apartments (I, vi, 67).

US, Up. Upstage (I, iii, 39), away from the audience. See note on *DS.*

W. Witch (title page, 30).

Xs, Xing. Crosses, crossing (I, ii, 33). An actor moves from one side of the stage to the other, usually in front of another actor.

Y. Siward, Y. Siw. Young Siward (V, iv, 222).

PERFORMANCE

In the account of the performance I draw on and quote from all the theatre documents, indicating the particular source only for published records. I divide the play as it was divided in Shaw's production, indicating the standard act and scene divisions in parentheses and Shaw's name for the scene afterwards. There follows the time for each scene in standard notation (2:05 means two minutes and five seconds). Note that the time taken for an entire "Part" is a bit longer than the total for its individual scenes, because some time passed between each scene.

> I remember on the first night, there was a terrible thunderstorm in the afternoon. We went to the theatre, and the thing took off like a rocket.
>
> —Trader Faulkner (Malcolm)

PART I (I, i to II, iv). 52:30

Scene 1 (I, i), Opening Scene. 0:33.

The "house lights fade to blackout." "Thunder, very loud," echoes through the darkened theatre. The curtain springs up, and the stage glows with dim light, so that the audience can just glimpse the Witches descending, as if hovering in fog and filthy air, half-concealed behind a backlit gauze. "A weird high sound like the howling of the wind—but more unearthly—continues throughout the scene." The Witches speak as they come to earth, a cat screeches, a toad croaks, and the Witches vanish into the darkness, no sooner seen and heard than gone. This scene is prologue, like the one that follows, to Macbeth's entry in I, iii, and Shaw moves through it quickly, with minimal stage business.

Scene 2 (I, ii), Bloody Sergeant Scene. 2:57.

As the stage grows light again, the trumpets ring out, drums beat, and shouts presage Duncan's arrival. "Throughout this scene we hear the sounds of battle in the distance." The gauze is gone, and we can now see the heath, its gray expanse broken only by rough-edged boulders. The King marches in, flanked by his nobles and by soldiers with banners. The company halts, grouped around the King at its head, and from across the stage the wounded Sergeant staggers forward, to stand swaying, waiting for the King to give him leave to speak. Malcolm goes to him and, as he delivers his report, Duncan moves forward. The Sergeant proclaims victory, the soldiers cheer, a "big reaction from all." A nobleman (Lennox) helps the wounded man offstage. As they go, another messenger arrives from the battlefield stage right, telling of another victory. Again the King and company move downstage in their eagerness to hear his news, and again the soldiers cheer, raising all the banners at news of fresh victory. His report given, the orders for Cawdor's execution issued, and Macbeth's reward received, the messenger leaves the way he came, toward the battlefield stage right. The King and his retinue stride off stage left, to the sounds of cheering and trumpets. Empty, the stage grows quiet; the light grows dimmer.

Scene 3 (I, iii), Witches Scene. 8:00.

Thunder rolls away in the distance. One by one the Witches enter, each from a different corner of the stage. Dressed in gray rags, the color of the stone itself, they sit on the great boulder downstage center. At the ominous sound of Macbeth's drum, they rise, take hands, and dance in a circle while chanting their incantation in time to the drumbeats. The lights come up a shade brighter when Macbeth enters, resplendent in his cape and armor, and leaps up to bestride the boulder. With the strong light of the setting sun upon him, he surveys the field, then stops "transfixed" at the sight of the Witches crouched downstage, and remains, silently gazing, "like a man *dazed* by a lot of battle and a lot of fighting," while Banquo speaks to them. They come up to Macbeth, who still stands atop the boulder, and they all-hail him, their voices growing softer with each greeting, to whisper the promise of kingship—at which "Macbeth makes slight start." All eyes—in the audience and onstage—are on Macbeth. "He radiates a kind of brooding sinister energy, a dazzling darkness, . . . and one glimpses the black abysses in the general's mind" (*Tribune*). Then Banquo speaks, the Witches regroup to all-hail him. Unable to restrain his own eager ambition, Macbeth leaps from the rock, hurrying after first one Witch and then another as they "vanish" in turn. Richard David describes how this was done:

> As Macbeth fixed on the second Witch the first slid like a lizard from the scene; when attention shifted to the third the second was gone; and as Macbeth and Banquo turned on each other in eager surmise the third too vanished. This was genuine producer's sleight of hand.

Macbeth and Banquo draw off to stage right, half laughing about what they have seen, and the lights "start to fade to night," when Ross and Angus bring their news. At first Macbeth and Banquo stay together, exchanging hurried questions, then, as Banquo goes to join Ross and Angus, Macbeth comes down to the forestage to ponder the supernatural soliciting. Here in small is an important movement onstage that the script invites, and Shaw stressed. Macbeth is physically isolated from others onstage, and, in his isolation, he moves downstage to speak directly to the audience. The others, in turn, draw together behind him, speaking inaudibly of their own affairs, and occasionally remarking loudly on how their partner is rapt, until at last Macbeth recovers himself and they go out together across the now dimly lit stage. Night has fallen.

Scene 4 (I, iv), Forres Scene. 3:10.

The first "movement" has come to an end. Then, as Royal Trumpets blare (to cover the noise of the change) the runners close, the forestage lighting comes up, and servants enter bearing flickering candelabra. Duncan's royal standard is brought on. The trumpets stop, and the King enters with his stately entourage, filling the forestage with pageantry. This is Duncan's court. The men have shed their armor, keeping only swords and daggers, and one, who stands nearest Duncan, bears a coronet on a red cushion. All is ceremony and dignity. Malcolm, touching the coronet, reports Cawdor's execution to Duncan. Macbeth and Banquo enter, still clad in battle gear, and they kneel in obeisance to the King, who raises each of them in turn. His captains greeted, Duncan then proceeds with the main business of the scene, Malcolm's investiture as Prince of Cumberland. "Mal kneels. Standard Bearer moves forward, Duncan takes coronet from cushion & puts it on Mal's head & kisses his forehead." "The old King senses the power & ambitions of Macbeth. Having honored him, he deliberately chooses this moment to name Malcolm as his successor & make him Prince of Cumberland." The crowning is a political gambit, meant to set up the new order, and Duncan follows it up quickly with another ploy by announcing that he will now go to Inverness to solidify his ties with Macbeth. Crowning Malcolm is a calculated risk, and by favoring Macbeth with his presence, Duncan hopes to cancel any resentment Macbeth might feel. Although Macbeth mouths a gracious acceptance, this is belied by his asides, downstage, apart from the others, and by his hasty exit, before the King and court leave to the flourish of trumpets.

Scene 5 (I, v to II, iv), Murder Scene. 37:10.

As the sound of trumpets dies away, the runners open to disclose the setting of Macbeth's courtyard. The twisted central arch dominates the castle. Beneath it stands Lady Macbeth, her serpent-green figure framed by the archway, an image of her that will return when she sits in state at the banquet and when she comes forward from the black depths carrying her candle at the end. Like Macbeth's first appearance, Lady Macbeth's is important. The great arch and massive stone slabs make her seem the one bright spark of life in dead, stone-gray Inverness. After the servant Seyton comes with his news, she returns to center stage, again framed by the arch, and stretches out her arms high overhead to invoke the spirits, writhing as she bids them take control of her body. Just as she has reached full pitch, Macbeth enters, still in battle dress, and stands, waiting, under the central arch. It is an electric moment, as she turns to welcome him in words that echo the Witches' prophetic greeting. "They meet mid C stage and embrace." Even as she tells him to beguile the time, "he turns slightly away from her," and makes a "slight move away," saying only that they will speak further. Even in their first meeting, there is an inkling of the division the crime will work between them.

At the sound of a distant trumpet, Duncan's herald, Lady Macbeth ascends the stairs to make preparations for the King. Macbeth is again alone. The trumpets sound again, recalling him to himself, and he goes off the way he has come. The trumpets grow louder, and then Duncan comes in with his men; on his right hand is Malcolm, and all around him are his nobles and servants. His company fills the grim setting with color and life, just as his words fill the air with beauty, an ironic contradiction between his innocent perceptions and the evil realities that we know exist in the grim castle. Lady Macbeth comes slowly down the stairs she had just rushed up. "The King greets his hostess with great courtesy and charm." Her manner too is formal, like her speech. She curtseys in greeting, and Duncan raises her. As they go into the banquet hall, just offstage right, he takes her hand, and the company files out afterwards. Evening has fallen, and from the banquet hall there comes a "warm light."

Seyton remains. Shaw says he is "the head manservant of the Macbeth household. He is trusted, absolutely, by his employer." Besides giving Seyton the messengers' and the third murderer's lines, the director made him a frequent silent witness onstage. Here his importance in Macbeth's household is established; he makes "a sign offstage," and then "servants carrying torches cross the courtyard with food & wine & the musicians play." Their entrance not only sets the time of day, it also tells us that the banquet is about to begin offstage right, where Duncan and the others have gone, from whence Macbeth now enters, once more isolated from company by his secret thoughts. As he questions the deed, he moves away from Duncan. When Lady Macbeth comes in, she circles around Macbeth, edging him back toward Duncan; she then "attacks him violently, calls him a coward, and refers to their son—who has died as a baby—in the most ghastly way." (Thus Shaw accounts for her reference to children and the strange effect it has on Macbeth.) "He takes her hand without looking at her," and they return to the banquet. A harp cadenza swells from the hall, the banquet draws to an end.

At this point Shaw had at first worked out a dumbshow to balance the one that opened the "banquet" part of the scene. On their way to bed, nobles and torchbearers were to cross the stage, and the Sewer was to come out with a bag of gold to tip the various servants. Both this business and the "harp cadenza," which seems to have replaced it in the Stratford promptbook, are good examples of the way the play invites directors to fill in its occasionally broken narrative, a temptation Shaw resisted, but one to which others have yielded. Beerbohm Tree at His Majesty's in 1911 had Duncan enter, bless the assembled court, and then retire to a hymn and harp cadenza. In their films of *Macbeth*, George Schaeffer (1960) and Roman Polanski (1969) put in some business to get Duncan to bed and elsewhere provided visual continuity. Although Shaw's notes show that he filled in the narrative between scenes for himself and for his actors, in actual performance he only suggested it with such techniques as light changes, for instance the shift to moonlight here at this point, and sometimes sound effects, for example the trumpets signaling "last post" in this scene and the earlier warning of Duncan's approach (I, v).

To see what Shaw has achieved, we need to look not only at what he has *done*, but also at what he has *not* done. Duncan's murder and its discovery (II, i to iii) show his great restraint: he builds from slow, fearful movements at the outset to a dazzling burst of terror at the end of the scene. "Banquo and Fleance come from the Royal Apartments & cross the Courtyard on their way to their own room. Banquo . . . already feels the evil insinuations of the Witches tormenting him at night. He suddenly hears a sound and is frightened for himself and his son." He snatches back the sword he has handed to Fleance and then sees Macbeth, again framed by the center arch, with Seyton standing behind him with a torch. The two men approach each other cautiously. Banquo gives Macbeth the ring, then leaves with Fleance. Seyton follows them halfway up the stairs with the torch, as if to light their way, or to make certain that they have gone. He returns, Macbeth hands him the diamond and "is giving last instructions to the servants," wrote Richard David:

> The man is still beside him when he sees the spectral dagger and checks at it like a pointer. With a terrible effort he withdraws his gaze for a moment and dismisses the servant; then with a swift and horrid compulsion swings round again. The first part of the dagger speech was spoken with a sort of broken quiet, only the sudden shrillness of "Mine eyes are made the fools o' th' other senses" and "There's no such thing" revealing the intolerable tension that strains the speaker. . . . The second part of the speech sunk to a drugged whisper and, speaking, Macbeth moved, as in a dream, towards Duncan's room, but with his face turned away from it. . . . It was the already trodden stones behind him that Macbeth, with deprecating hand, implored to silence. It was this scene above all that brought the audience under the enchantment.

The courtyard is empty. "An owl cries in distance." Then Lady Macbeth enters from stage right, "Duncan's side" of the stage, and stops, poised atop the great slab that lies across the center arch.

Full of suppressed excitement, she comes down the steps as the owl cries again. Halfway down them, she freezes, listens, and hears Macbeth's shout. He enters, the two long daggers glinting in his blood-stained hands. As she nervously questions him, circling around him, he moves slowly, as if dazed or drugged, making only a "slight move" away from her. She seizes the daggers and carries them—awkwardly it seems in the photograph—back to Duncan's room. The knocking sends him deeper into his trance—"to Macbeth it has an unearthly significance, but to his wife, who is still, just, in command, of the situation, it means the danger of detection & she forces her husband to retire," "pushing him towards PS steps," as Macbeth "turns at the OP doorway." "They go slowly upstairs and into the bedroom."

The stage is empty, and it begins to grow light with the dawn. The Porter enters, "putting on his clothes & carrying his boots and keys." He stands under the center arch "with one boot off." He is "not a comic character," Shaw insists, "but a real person. He is gross and bestial (A porter of Hell), full of drink & lust." He is also an actor ("Pray you, remember the porter," he bids us), and the business of putting on his boots gives him a half-serious reason for delay, which he makes the most of, before he begins another routine with Macduff. First, he leads the men onto center stage, then he "stops & turns to Mac," springing the joke about the three things that drink provokes. Although the Porter dominates the scene, Macduff is no less important. "This is the first time that we have seen him & we must recognize at once in him the strength & power & determination of goodness. . . . The inflexible nature of a man of God." Keith Michell was not only young—twenty-six years old—with make-up that stressed his youth, he was also impressive physically. His six feet four inches towered over the others; a fur hat added to his height; and his great cloak made his broad-shouldered frame appear even larger. While the Porter finishes his joke, we may laugh with him, but we also watch to see how the joke is taken by this giant who has come to awaken Duncan. As if bid by Macduff's query, "Macbeth comes from his chamber aloft garbed in a long, black, monkish gown, as if from some unholy rite, furtively inspecting his washed hands, & greets them in subdued tones, tacitly owning the presence of a corpse" (*Theatre World*). The Porter scurries away through the center arch at the sight of his master. Macbeth "has recovered his nerve; from now on until his second hallucination [Banquo's Ghost], he is completely in control of himself." He directs Macduff to the door, and the tension, which has been growing ever tighter since Banquo left the stage, is now stretched to the breaking point: "Macduff goes into the King's apartment, there are a few agonising moments of suspense which should seem like an eternity, & then the appalling crime is discovered." Macduff's great voice cries "Horror, horror, horror!"—and sets off a dazzling theatrical explosion. "The whole castle is in an uproar. The Alarum bell crashes out and half-naked figures stand about in the Courtyard confused and terrified." From every entrance and at every level actors rush out into the courtyard, dishevelled and half-dressed; terror and amazement run through them, darting from the discoverers of the crime to Duncan's sons, who begin to panic. The alarum bell stops and into this sudden silence Macbeth comes back, once more bloody-handed, from the slaying of the grooms. "He almost takes a ghastly delight in describing the horror of the scene in full detail." The terror now seizes Lady Macbeth, who comes forward slowly toward Macbeth and collapses nearly at his feet, downstage center. "Immediately, the focus, if not suspicion, centres on her. Her husband goes to her at once & as she recovers they are face to face with the knowledge of their guilt & surrounded by those strained, white faces peering at them out of the darkness." For a moment, the crowded stage forms a tableau, eloquent in its depiction of the isolation the crime enforces upon Macbeth and Lady Macbeth, and the chaos it has brought to those around them.

As Lady Macbeth is helped up the stairs to her chamber, there begins the gradual winding down of tension. The crowd disperses in every direction. Macbeth goes up to his chambers. Malcolm and Donalbain, standing downstage center, "realise the danger of their position & being young & inexperienced they do the worst possible thing & decide to fly the country." As they speak, the audience sees, but they do not, that a dark figure stands watching them from the top of the stairs. Turning to go, "they get to the arch, they see [Macbeth]," and they run off. He turns to see Banquo enter, and goes down to him. Macbeth "walks to PS, looks back at [Banquo], and walks off OP Assey followed by him." Not only does Macbeth's silent entry emphasize his new role—he has become a "watcher," an overseer and planner of action now—it enables Shaw to give real urgency to the Princes' flight. And Banquo's meeting with Macbeth suggests a silent complicity in his crime, a complicity based "mostly on . . . his own interest in the future of the crown. In which case," Shaw writes, "he is a guilty man & to some extent gets what he deserves."

"A lament starts to be played as though on Bagpipes or Chanter in the distance. It is for the dead King, and continues to the end of the scene." Into the empty Courtyard now come an Old Man and one of the Scots nobles (Ross). The Old Man looks at Duncan's doorway when he speaks of the deed that's done. As they talk over the strange portents, Macduff comes "from the conference," which Shaw thinks of as taking place somewhere just offstage. The three men part, their different states of mind suggested by the different directions they go: Macduff goes stage left, to Fife; Ross, stage right, to Scone; and the Old Man, "slowly US towards C arch as Curtain falls."

Glen Byam Shaw.
169 Ashley Gardens
London. S.W.1

The Production

We will present the play in three parts. Part I ends with the scene between Macduff, Ross & the Old Man, page 42 in the New Temple Edition.

Part II ends with the Banquet Scene, page 61 in the New Temple Edition.

This I think is the best way to divide the play from the story point of view, which I consider the most important, but it does mean that Part III is considerably longer than Part II. That is a danger & we must do everything we can to keep the third part moving along at the right tempo.

We know a certain amount about their [the Witches'] appearance from what Banquo says. That they have hair on their chins & that they are withered & wild in their attire. That their fingers are wrinkled & their lips are skinny. And that they "look like the inhabitants o' the earth."

We know that they can disappear & that they can conjure up Spirits. We know that everything they say is either cruel, insinuating or horrifying.

What are they? They are certainly not the Fates. If we felt that Macbeth was, through them, fated to murder the King it would completely destroy the tragedy of the story.

Are they three cackling, dirty old women? No, because they have supernatural powers. We see them three times in the play. First, in the air descending to the earth. Secondly on the earth; & thirdly in their cavern below the earth, in fact, in hell. And they are, as the Second Witch says, preparing a HELL-broth.

To me they are the instruments of the devil, the powers of darkness. They should be terrible & yet strangely wonderful—because anything evil is, always, fascinating & wonderful in some way.

They never laugh or cackle, they are far too evil & intent on destruction for that. I think of them as condemned souls out of hell. They must have tragic stature.

Macbeth, Act I, Scene i

Glen Byam Shaw.
S.M.T. 17 MAR 55.

1 Witch
Standing
2 W
Sitting
3W sitting

HOUSE LIGHTS FADE to BLACK OUT.

THUNDER very loud.

CURTAIN UP.

THE TRAGEDY OF

MACBETH

PART I

~~Act First~~

FADE IN — SCENE I — Opening.

~~A desert place~~

Thunder and Lightning. ~~*Enter*~~ *three Witches*

Vibration in the air

1. W. When shall we three meet again?
In thunder, lightning, or in rain?
2. W. When the hurlyburly 's done,
When the battle 's lost, and won.
3. W. That will be ere the set of sun.
1. W. Where the place?
2. W. Upon the heath.
3. W. There to meet with Macbeth. — Screech of a cat
1. W. I come, Graymalkin. — Croak of a toad
2 W. ~~All.~~ Paddock calls:—anon! (rises with 3 W.)
All Fair is foul, and foul is fair.
Hover through the fog and filthy air. *Exeunt*

FADE TO BLACK OUT

1

FRONT LIFT DESCENDING

GAUZE FLIED

OR Mid DRAWER CLOSED

Act I, Scene i. The Witches.
Nancye Stewart, Mary Law, and Dilys Hamlett.

No Time. The Witches hover through the fog & filthy air & arrive on the earth with the intention of meeting & tempting Macbeth.

Duncan. 70 [years old]. Geoffrey Bayldon.

He is old but he must be every inch a King. He is gentle & gracious but he is certainly not a silly, senile old man. He should look frail—"Who would have Thought the old man to have had so much blood in him"—with a parchment skin & the beauty & serenity of old age. Whenever he is present there must be no question as to who is the King. We must understand that his word is law. It is the position of supreme power that Lady Macbeth is determined her husband shall have, & we must see that Duncan holds that position.

The Bloody Sergeant. 28 [years old]. David King.

A magnificent Scottish soldier, fierce & tough as nails. He has been badly wounded in the battle & is bleeding, but I don't want him to be soused in blood. The sight of blood in the play is so important that we must not over-use it.

Macbeth, Act I, Scene ii

Enter. Duncan
PS Ass. Royal Standard Bearer (Geoffrey Sassi)
Malcolm
Donalbain
1st Sol with Banner (Hugh Cross)
4th " " " (Kevin Miles)

Enter PS mid Across PS corner of DS lift
Lennox
Menteith
Caithness
3rd Sol with Banner (Emrys James)
2nd " " " (Leon Eagles)
5th " " " (Robert Arnold)

below DS lift
Offr (Ron Haddrick)
6th Sol (John Southworth)
7th Sol (Alan Haywood)

Enter OP Pros
Bloody Sgt & comes towards C. stage

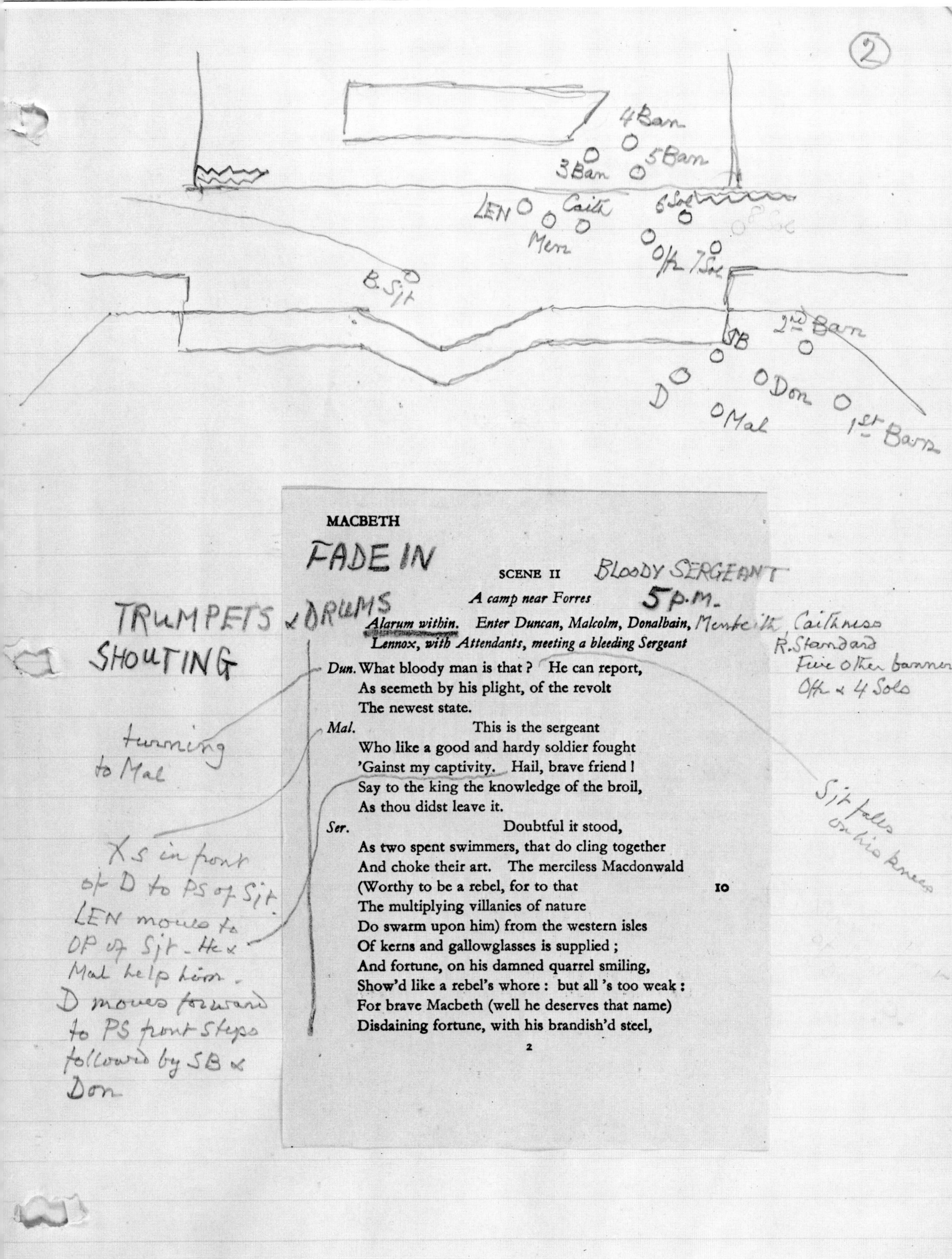

MACBETH

SCENE II

A camp near Forres

Alarum within. Enter Duncan, Malcolm, Donalbain, Lennox, with Attendants, meeting a bleeding Sergeant

Dun. What bloody man is that? He can report,
As seemeth by his plight, of the revolt
The newest state.

Mal. This is the sergeant
Who like a good and hardy soldier fought
'Gainst my captivity. Hail, brave friend!
Say to the king the knowledge of the broil,
As thou didst leave it.

Ser. Doubtful it stood,
As two spent swimmers, that do cling together
And choke their art. The merciless Macdonwald
(Worthy to be a rebel, for to that
The multiplying villanies of nature
Do swarm upon him) from the western isles
Of kerns and gallowglasses is supplied;
And fortune, on his damned quarrel smiling,
Show'd like a rebel's whore: but all 's too weak:
For brave Macbeth (well he deserves that name)
Disdaining fortune, with his brandish'd steel,

2

Bloody Sgt Scene. 5 pm.
Duncan meets a wounded Sergeant who tells him of the magnificent courage & leadership of Macbeth & Banquo. Ross & Angus arrive from the battlefield to tell the King of the victory & the treachery of the Thane of Cawdor. The King orders them to have Cawdor put to death & confer the title on Macbeth.

Malcolm. 18 [years old]. Trader Faulkner.

Donalbain. 17 [years old]. Ian Holm.

Unless the two Royal Princes are young I feel that the story doesn't make sense. Macbeth says "What's the boy Malcolm." And Malcolm says to Macduff, "I am young . . . . and wisdom to offer up a weak, poor innocent lamb to appease an angry God." No man could talk like that unless he was very young.

Also I cannot believe that the Royal Princes would panic, as they most certainly do, after the murder of their father, if they were experienced men of the world.

We know Malcolm has fought against the rebels & been saved from being taken prisoner by the Sergeant, but perhaps that also is an indication that he is not a very experienced soldier. I think of them both as having lived a very sheltered life.

The sons of an old father. We must, of course, at the end feel that Malcolm will make a good young King.

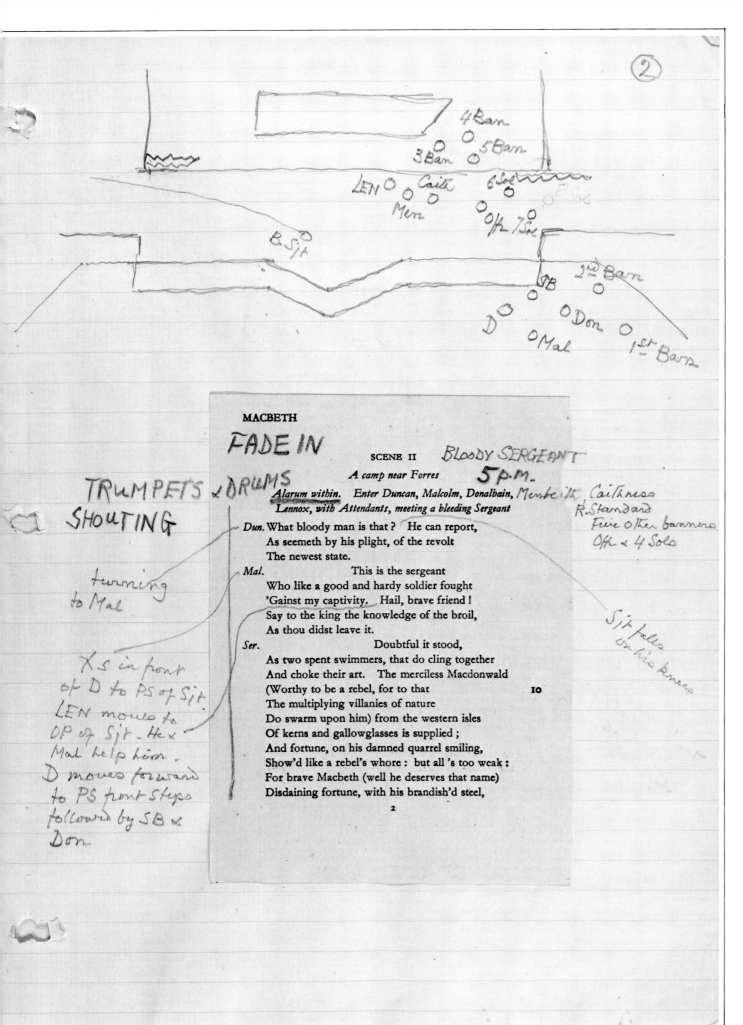

(3)

Act I Sc. ii

Which smok'd with bloody execution,
Like valour's minion, carv'd out his passage,
Till he fac'd the slave;
Which ne'er shook hands, nor bade farewell to him, †
Till he unseam'd him from the nave to the chops,
And fix'd his head upon our battlements.

Dun. O valiant cousin, worthy gentleman!

Ser. ~~As whence the sun 'gins his reflection~~
~~Shipwrecking storms and direful thunders break,~~
~~So from that spring, whence comfort seem'd to come,~~
~~Discomfort swells.~~ Mark, king of Scotland, mark,
No sooner justice had, with valour arm'd,
Compell'd these skipping kerns to trust their heels,
But the Norweyan lord, surveying vantage,
With furbish'd arms, and new supplies of men,
Began a fresh assault.

Dun. Dismay'd not this
Our captains, Macbeth and Banquo?

Ser. Yes,
As sparrows eagles; or the hare the lion.
If I say sooth, I must report they were
As cannons overcharg'd with double cracks;
So they doubly redoubled strokes upon the foe:
Except they meant to bathe in reeking wounds,
Or memorize another Golgotha,

3

Xing in front of Mal to OP of D

Lennox. James Grout.
Menteith. Robert Hunter.
Angus. John Springett.
Caithness. Gabriel Woolf.

I don't find anything in the text which is particularly characteristic for any one of these Noblemen & I certainly don't intend to make up characters for them. Whether Menteith is married or not is simply nothing to do with the play, but that doesn't mean that they are not, either separately or collectively, of considerable importance. Unless they are strongly & truly acted they could be dreary & dull. That they must not be. What they must appear to be are Noblemen of very great authority & importance.

I use them throughout the play.

I see no reason why the actors playing them should not be their own ages.

Act I, Scene ii. "Whence cam'st thou, worthy Thane?" William Devlin (Ross), Trader Faulkner (Malcolm), Geoffrey Bayldon (Duncan), Gabriel Woolf (Caithness), Robert Hunter (Menteith), James Grout (Lennox), Ian Holm (Donalbain) (see opposite page).

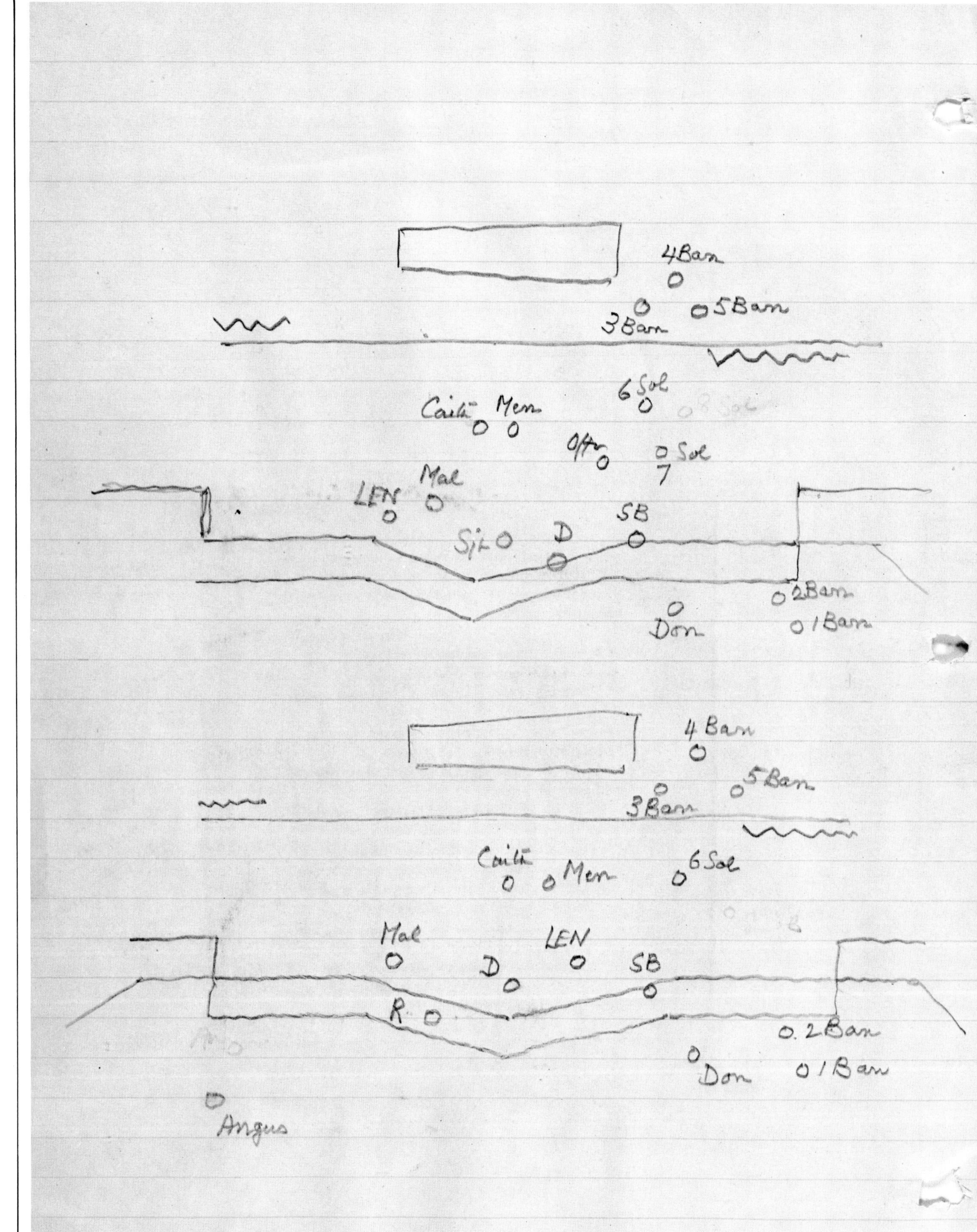

Macbeth, Act I, Scene ii

MACBETH

I cannot tell—
But I am faint, my gashes cry for help.
Dun. So well thy words become thee as thy wounds;
They smack of honour both. Go get him surgeons.
Exit Sergeant, attended
Who comes here?
Enter Ross and Angus
Mal. The worthy thane of Ross.
~~*Len.* What a haste looks through his eyes! So should he look~~
~~That seems to speak things strange.~~
Ross. God save the king!
Dun. Whence cam'st thou, worthy thane?
Ross. From Fife, great king,
Where the Norweyan banners flout the sky
And fan our people cold.
Norway himself with terrible numbers,
Assisted by that most disloyal traitor,
The thane of Cawdor, began a dismal conflict,
Till that Bellona's bridegroom, lapp'd in proof,
Confronted him with self-comparisons,
Point against point, rebellious arm 'gainst arm,
Curbing his lavish spirit: and, to conclude,
The victory fell on us.
Dun. Great happiness!

4

Ross. 40 [years old]. William Devlin.

He is a quiet gentle, & good man & the loyal & true friend.

He is, also, a great Nobleman & a soldier, Macduff's cousin. Notice that when Macduff calls him "my ever gentle cousin." He goes to see Lady Macduff when she is left alone with her children; & he has the agonising duty of going to England to tell Macduff what has happened to his wife and family.

(5)

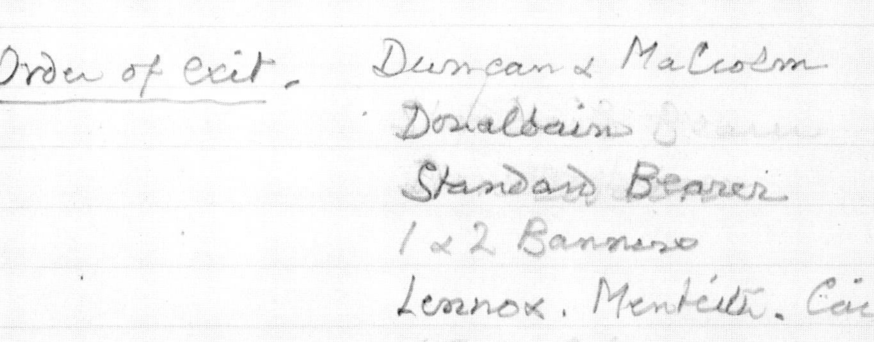

Order of exit. Duncan & Malcolm
Donalbain
Standard Bearer
1 & 2 Banners
Lennox. Menteith. Caithness

3, 4, 5 Banners

Act I Sc. iii

~~*Ross.* That now~~
~~Sweno, the Norways' king, craves composition~~;
~~Nor would we deign him burial of his men,~~
~~Till he disbursed, at Saint Colme's inch~~
~~Ten thousand dollars, to our general use.~~
Dun. No more that thane of Cawdor shall deceive
Our bosom interest: go pronounce his present death,
And with his former title greet Macbeth.
Ross. I 'll see it done.
Dun. What he hath lost, noble Macbeth hath won.

Exeunt

SCENE III

The heath

Thunder. Enter the three Witches

1. *W.* Where hast thou been, sister?
2. *W.* Killing swine.
3. *W.* Sister, where thou?
1. *W.* A sailor's wife had chestnuts in her lap,
And mounch'd, and mounch'd, and mounch'd.
'Give me,' quoth I:
'Aroint thee, witch!' the rump-fed ronyon cries.
Her husband 's to Aleppo gone, master o' the Tiger;
But in a sieve I 'll thither sail,

5

CHEERING
TRUMPETS
LIGHTING CHANGE
WITCHES 6pm
ROLLING away in the distance
bows & exit OP [illegible] followed by Angus
PS [illegible]
2 W enters OP mid & sits on Draw
1 W enters US PS & comes to PS of 2W & sits on DRAW
3 W enters PS Pros & sits PS of 1W

Witches Scene. 6 pm.
The Witches meet on the heath & wait for the arrival of Macbeth.

The Heath.

MACBETH

And, like a rat without a tail,
I 'll do, I 'll do, and I 'll do.
2. *W*. I 'll give thee a wind.
1. *W*. Thou 'rt kind.
3. *W*. And I another.
1. *W*. I myself have all the other,
And the very ports they blow, †
All the quarters that they know
I' the shipman's card.
I 'll drain him dry as hay :
Sleep shall neither night nor day
Hang upon his pent-house lid ;
He shall live a man forbid :
Weary se'nnights, nine times nine,
Shall he dwindle, peak, and pine :
Though his bark cannot be lost,
Yet it shall be tempest-tost.
Look what I have.
2. *W*. Show me, show me.
1. *W*. Here I have a pilot's thumb,
Wreck'd as homeward he did come. *Drum within*
3. *W*. A drum, a drum !
Macbeth doth come.
All. The weird sisters, hand in hand
Posters of the sea and land, †

6

will

fumbling in her dress

takes thumb out of her dress

Regals rise & move DS & take hands

Banquo. 38 [years old].
Ralph Michael.

He is Macbeth's best friend. A soldier & a man of courage. He is the only other person in the world, apart from Lady Macbeth, who knows of Macbeth's meeting with the Witches, & he is personally involved in what they said.

Macbeth. 42 [years old].
Laurence Olivier.

A superb leader & soldier with the courage of a lion & the imagination of a poet.

A man of iron discipline & will-power & an almost hypnotic personality.

There is something marvellously mysterious about him. The sort of man who can make one nervous by just looking at one.

No one would ever dare to slap Macbeth on the back or be jolly with him. Even his friends find him a bit over-powering & his soldiers & servants are terrified of his anger. He is tremendously proud & confident, but never shows off or blusters. When he speaks other people remain silent.

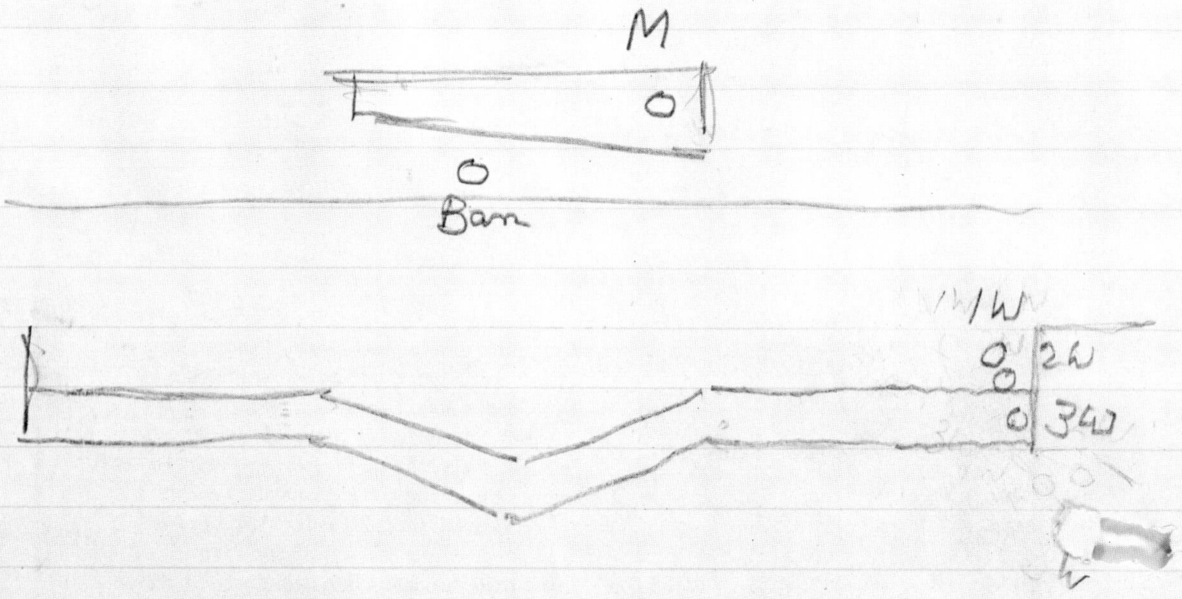

M

Ban

1W

2W

3W

(7)

* Macbeth enters & moves to top of C Rock. Slight pause – Banquo enters & moves to OP of Macbeth – Macbeth Speaks. Then sees the Witches. Banquo asks his question but gets no answer. He looks at Macbeth & sees that he is transfixed – Banquo follows his gaze & sees the Witches himself –

Act I Sc. iii

Thus do go, about, about,
Thrice to thine, and thrice to mine,
And thrice again, to make up nine.
Peace, the charm 's wound up.

* *Enter Macbeth and Banquo*

Mac. So foul and fair a day I have not seen.
Ban. How far is 't call'd to Forres? What are these
So wither'd, and so wild in their attire,
That look not like the inhabitants o' the earth,
And yet are on 't? Live you or are you aught
That man may question? You seem to understand me,
By each at once her choppy finger laying
Upon her skinny lips: you should be women,
And yet your beards forbid me to interpret
That you are so.
Mac. Speak, if you can: what are you?
1. W. All hail, Macbeth, hail to thee thane of Glamis!
2. W. All hail, Macbeth! hail to thee thane of Cawdor!
3. W. All hail, Macbeth, that shalt be king hereafter!
Ban. Good sir, why do you start, and seem to fear
Things that do sound so fair? I' the name of truth,
Are ye fantastical, or that indeed
Which outwardly ye show? My noble partner
You greet with present grace, and great prediction
Of noble having, and of royal hope,

7

DRUM FADES to silence

they bow three times to OP

Putting his sword in scabbard

bow three times US PS

bow three times PS

OP US

They move to forestage extreme PS & crouch down.

looking about

Witches put their fingers to their lips

Witches rise

Witches bow to M – M makes slight start

Soft

Softer

Whispered –

Act I, Scene iii.
Macbeth's first entrance.
Sir Laurence Olivier.

When he and Banquo come, they hail him as Thane of Glamis, Thane of Cawdor, & King that shalt be. From the way he behaves we see at once that the possibility of becoming the King & the idea of murdering Duncan is already in Macbeth's mind, however vaguely.

Act I, Scene iii. Macbeth meets the Witches. Ralph Michael (Banquo), Sir Laurence Oliver (Macbeth), Dilys Hamlett, Nancye Stewart, and Mary Law (Witches).

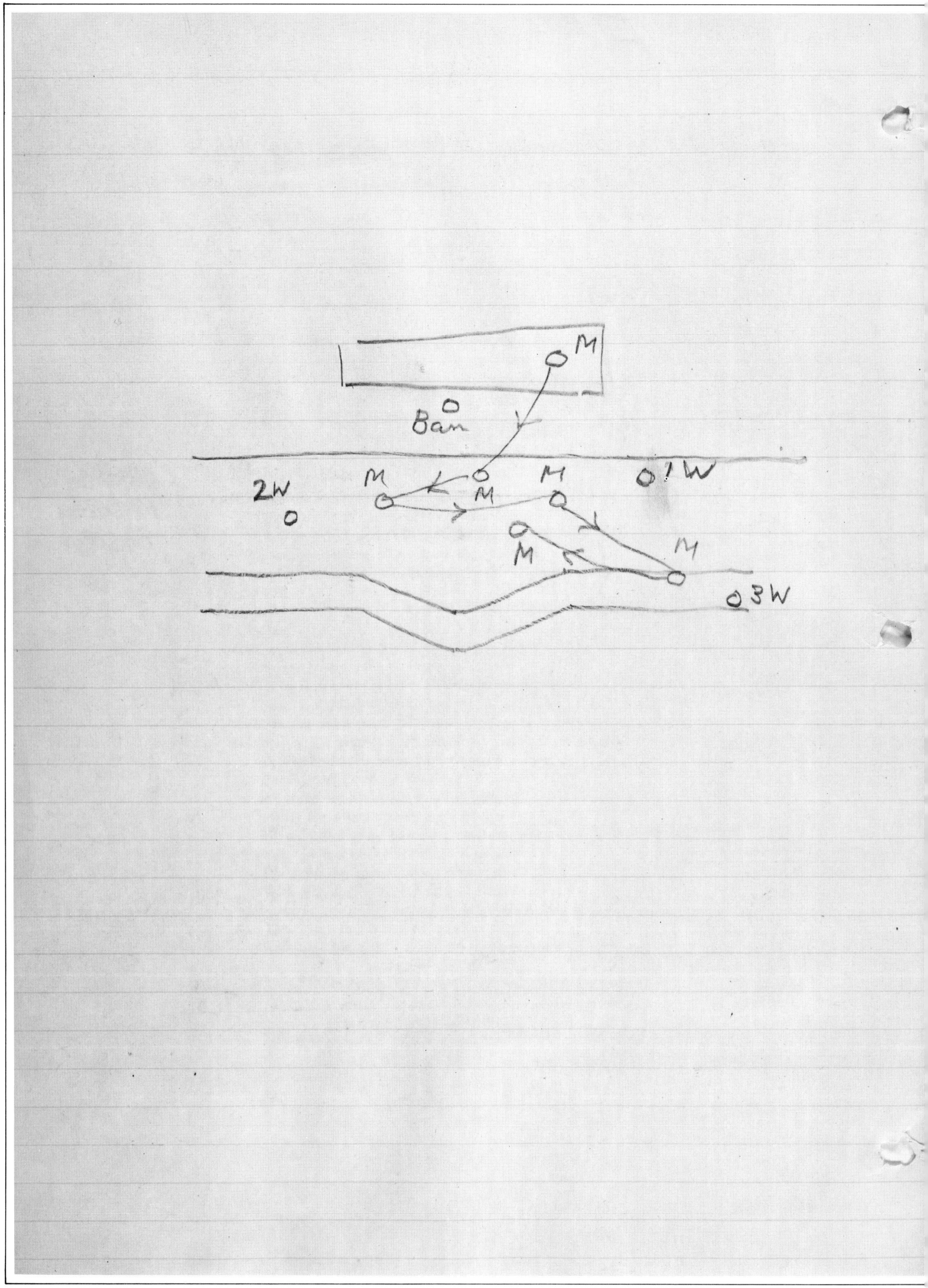

M
Ban
2W
M
M
M
1W
M
M
3W

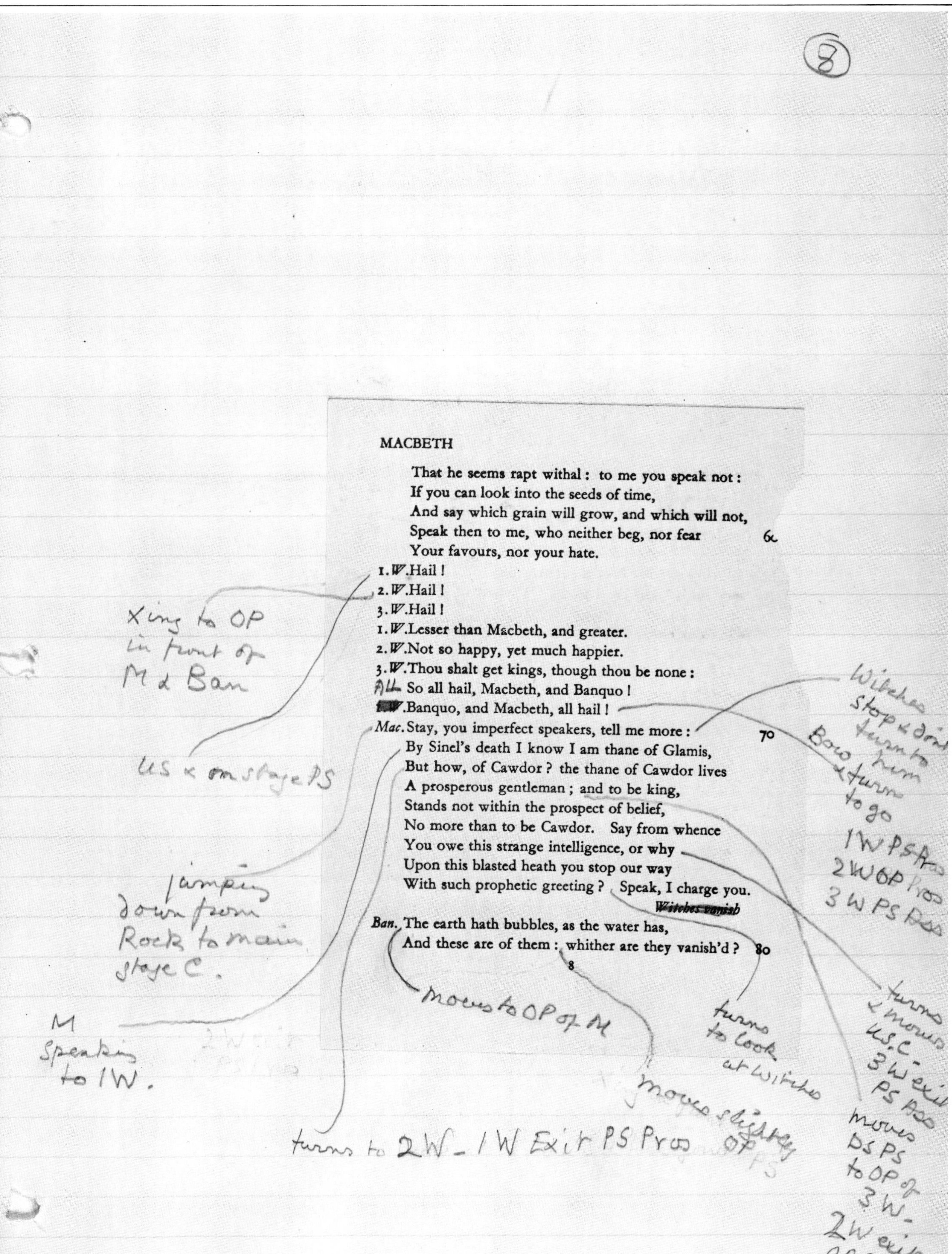

MACBETH

That he seems rapt withal: to me you speak not:
If you can look into the seeds of time,
And say which grain will grow, and which will not,
Speak then to me, who neither beg, nor fear
Your favours, nor your hate.
1. W. Hail!
2. W. Hail!
3. W. Hail!
1. W. Lesser than Macbeth, and greater.
2. W. Not so happy, yet much happier.
3. W. Thou shalt get kings, though thou be none:
All. So all hail, Macbeth, and Banquo!
W. Banquo, and Macbeth, all hail!
Mac. Stay, you imperfect speakers, tell me more:
By Sinel's death I know I am thane of Glamis,
But how, of Cawdor? the thane of Cawdor lives
A prosperous gentleman; and to be king,
Stands not within the prospect of belief,
No more than to be Cawdor. Say from whence
You owe this strange intelligence, or why
Upon this blasted heath you stop our way
With such prophetic greeting? Speak, I charge you.
~~Witches vanish~~
Ban. The earth hath bubbles, as the water has,
And these are of them: whither are they vanish'd?

8

Xing to OP in front of M & Ban

US & on stage PS

Jumping down from Rock to main stage C.

M Speaking to 1W.

turns to 2W – 1W Exit PS Pros

moves to OP of M

moves slightly OP PS

turns to look at witches

Witches stop & don't turn to him

Bao & turns to go

1W PS Pros
2W OP Pros
3W PS Pros

turns & moves U.S.C. – 3W exit PS Pros

moves DS PS to OP of 3W – 2W exit OP Pros

The Witches also hail Banquo as the father of Kings.

The Witches disappear.

Ross & Angus arrive to tell Macbeth that he is now Thane of Cawdor.

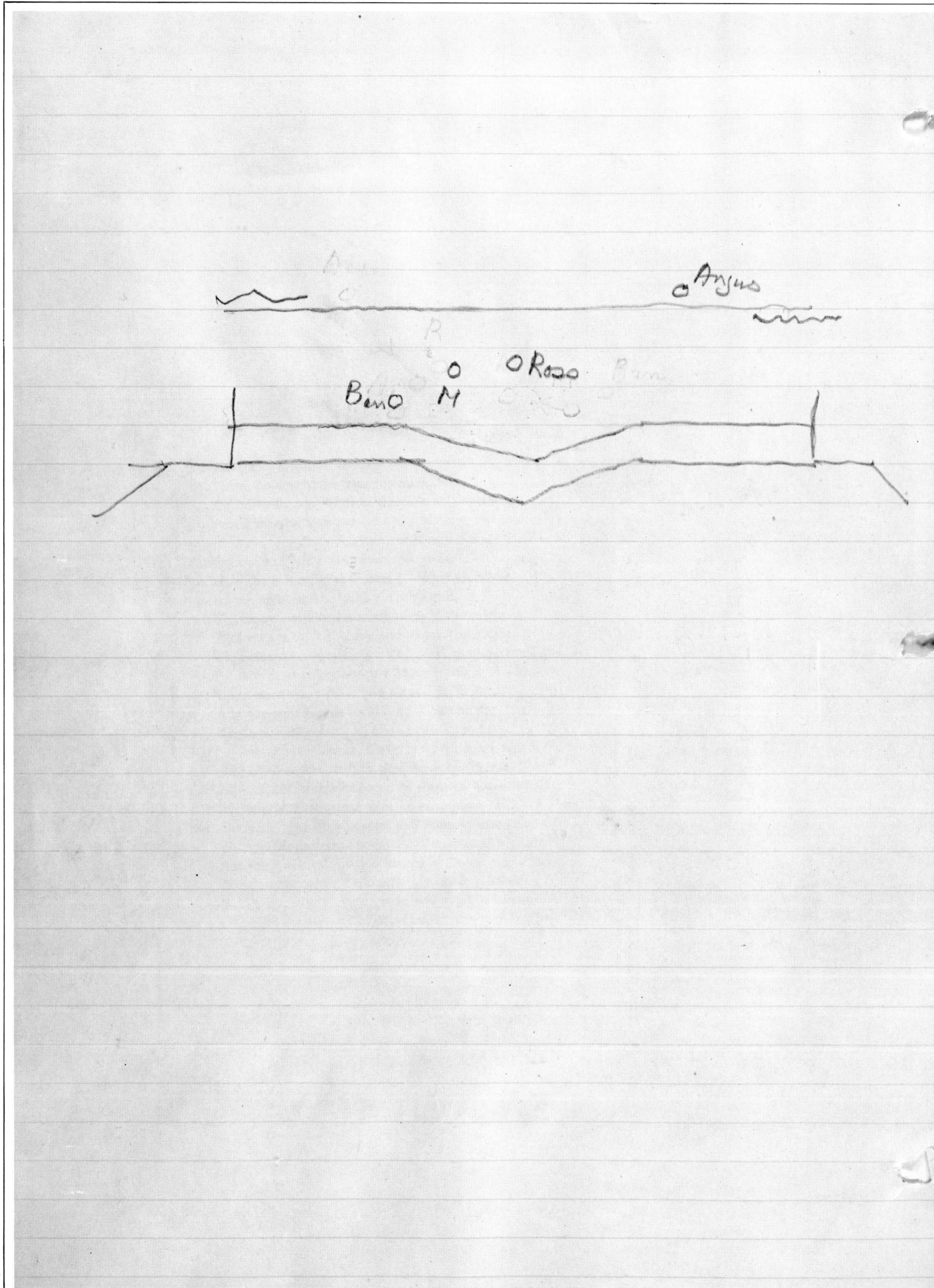

(9)

Act I Sc. iii

Mac. Into the air : and what seem'd corporal melted
As breath into the wind. Would they had stay'd !

Ban. Were such things here, as we do speak about ?
Or have we eaten on the insane root,
That takes the reason prisoner ?

Mac. Your children shall be kings.

Ban. You shall be king.

Mac. And thane of Cawdor too : went it not so ?

Ban. To the selfsame tune, and words. Who 's here ?

Enter Ross and Angus

Ross. The king hath happily receiv'd, Macbeth,
The news of thy success : and when he reads
Thy personal venture in the rebels' fight,
His wonders and his praises do contend,
Which should be thine, or his : ~~silenc'd with that,~~
~~In viewing o'er the rest o' the selfsame day,~~
~~He finds thee in the stout Norweyan ranks,~~
~~Nothing afeard of what thyself didst make,~~
~~Strange images of death.~~ As thick as hail †
Came post with post, and every one did bear
Thy praises in his kingdom's great defence,
And pour'd them down before him.

Ang. We are sent
To give thee from our royal master thanks,
Only to herald thee into his sight,

21 c 9

Slight move to PS of Ban

Start of FADE to Night

Slight move C by M-

PS back Ross moves PS of M Ang in front of lift PS

moving to OPDS of Ross

R
M
A
B
M
B

MACBETH

Not pay thee.
Ross. And for an earnest of a greater honour,
He bade me, from him, call thee thane of Cawdor:
In which addition, hail, most worthy thane,
For it is thine.
Ban. What, can the devil speak true?
Mac. The thane of Cawdor lives: why do you dress me
In borrow'd robes?
Ang. Who was the thane, lives yet,
But under heavy judgement bears that life,
Which he deserves to lose. Whether he was combin'd
With those of Norway, or did line the rebel
With hidden help and vantage, or that with both
He labour'd in his country's wreck, I know not;
But treasons capital, confess'd, and prov'd,
Have overthrown him.
Mac. (*aside*) Glamis, and thane of Cawdor:
The greatest is behind.—Thanks for your pains.—
Do you not hope your children shall be kings,
When those that gave the thane of Cawdor to me
Promis'd no less to them?
Ban. That, trusted home,
Might yet enkindle you unto the crown,
Besides the thane of Cawdor. But 'tis strange:

10

We see the poison beginning to work in him [Macbeth].

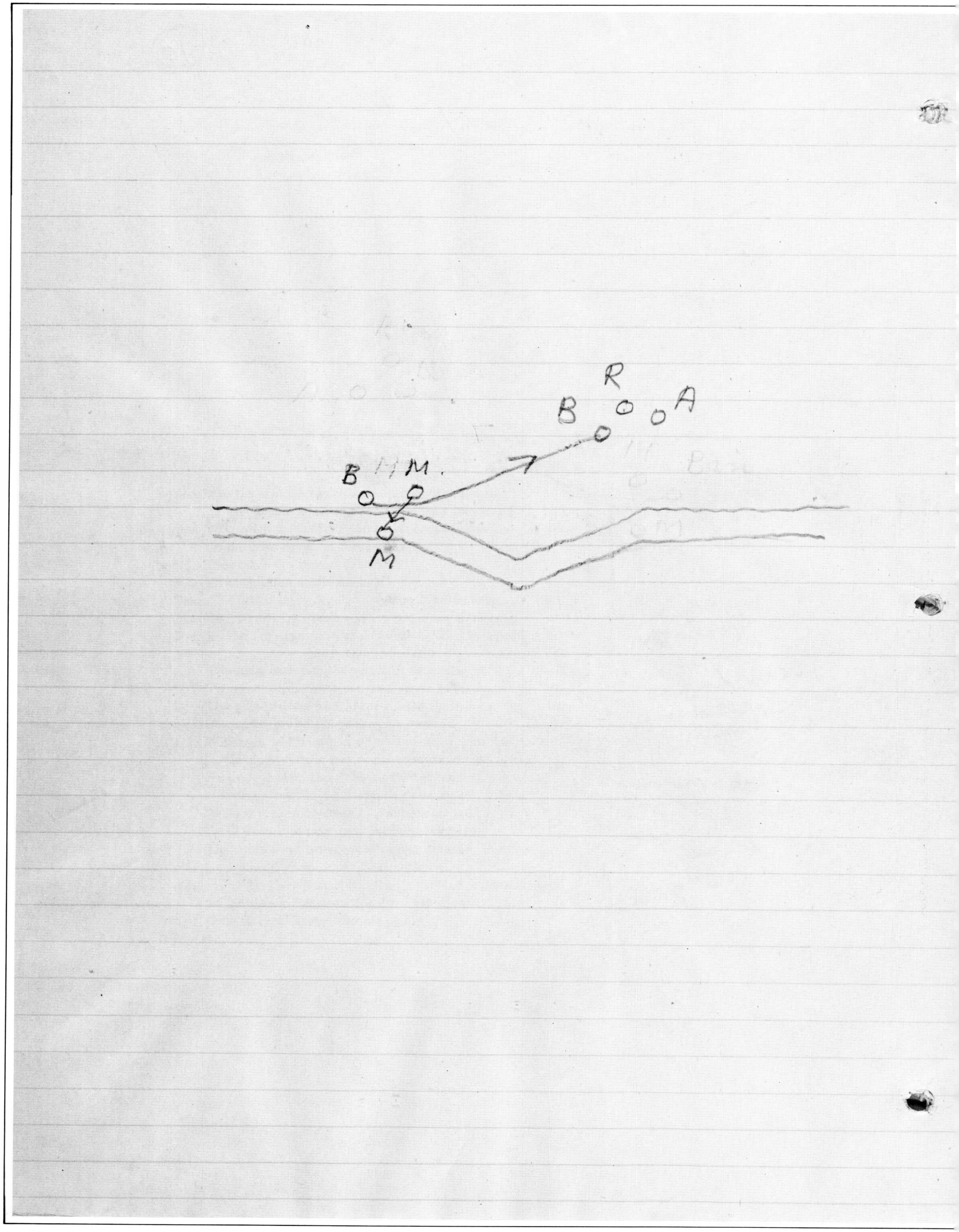

Macbeth, Act I, Scene iii

(11)

And oftentimes, to win us to our harm,
The instruments of darkness tell us truths,
Win us with honest trifles, to betray 's
In deepest consequence.
Cousins, a word, I pray you.

Mac. (*aside*) Two truths are told,
As happy prologues to the swelling act
Of the imperial theme.—I thank you, gentlemen.—
(*aside*) This supernatural soliciting
Cannot be ill ; cannot be good : if ill ? †
Why hath it given me earnest of success,
Commencing in a truth ? I am thane of Cawdor :
If good ? why do I yield to that suggestion, †
Whose horrid image doth unfix my hair,
And make my seated heart knock at my ribs,
Against the use of nature ? Present fears
Are less than horrible imaginings :
My thought, whose murder yet is but fantastical,
Shakes so my single state of man that function
Is smother'd in surmise, and nothing is,
But what is not.

Ban. Look how our partner 's rapt.

Mac. (*aside*) If chance will have me king, why, chance may crown me,
Without my stir.

Ross & Angus make move to go X ing in front of M to OP of R & A

Slight move DS

Ban turns to M

coming down steps on to forestage OP

turns to look at M

Macbeth, Act I, Scene iii

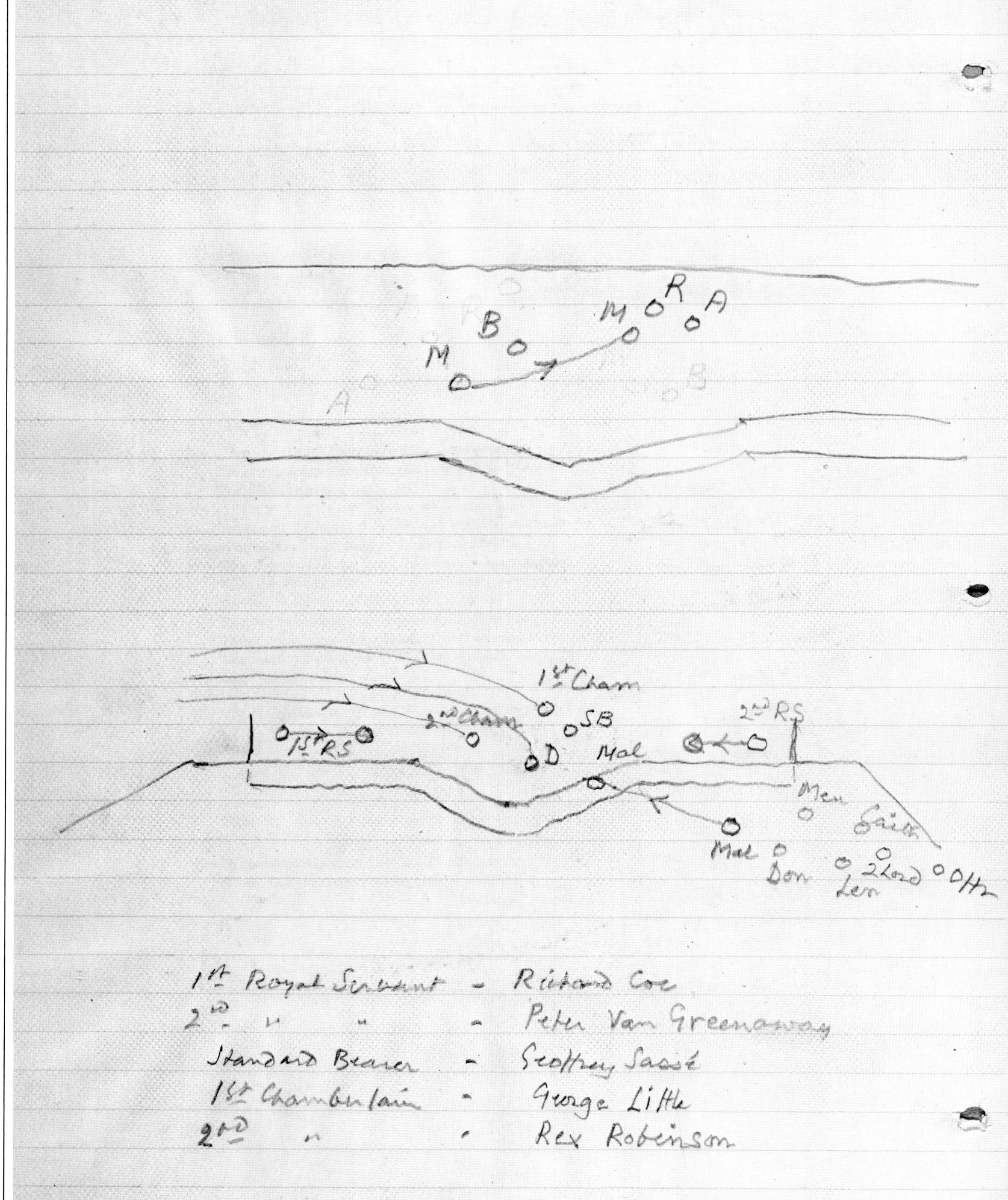

Forres Scene. 9 pm.

We are in the Royal Palace at Forres. Malcolm tells his father that he has heard that Cawdor has been executed.

The Scottish Soldiers

They should look tough & fierce. Scottish troops are always supposed to be exceptionally good at hand-to-hand fighting.

1st Chamberlain. George Little.
2nd Chamberlain. Rex Robinson.

They are the King's personal body-guard. Like two private detectives, but instead of revolvers they carry daggers.

Order of Exit PS back { M (DS) Ross { Banquo (U.S) Angus

MACBETH

Ban. New honours come upon him,
Like our strange garments, cleave not to their mould,
But with the aid of use.
Mac. (*aside*) Come what come may,
Time, and the hour, runs through the roughest day.
Ban. Worthy Macbeth, we stay upon your leisure.
Mac. Give me your favour: my dull brain was wrought
With things forgotten. Kind gentlemen, your pains
Are register'd where every day I turn
The leaf to read them. Let us toward the king;
Think upon what hath chanc'd; and at more time,
The interim having weigh'd it, let us speak
Our free hearts each to other.
Ban. Very gladly.
Mac. Till then, enough. Come, friends. *Exeunt*

going to OP of Ban

moving slightly towards M

turns to Ross & Angus

turning to Ban & moving to PS of him

Xing in front of Ban to R & A

PS back

LIGHTING CHANGE

RUNNERS CLOSED

TRUMPETS

FORRES 9 PM.

SCENE IV

Forres. The palace

Flourish. Enter Duncan, Malcolm, Donalbain, Lennox, and Attendants

Dun. Is execution done on Cawdor? Are not
Those in commission yet return'd?
Mal. My liege,

12

moves to C Stage

Coming to steps PS of D

Dun puts his hand on Coronet

(3) 1st R. Servant enters with Candelabra OP Pros & goes to (extreme) OP Pros Arch.

(1) 2nd R Servant enters with Candelabra & goes to (extreme) PS Pros Arch.

(2) Enter Malcolm, Donalbain, Lennox, Menteith, Caithness PS Ass, 2 Lord. Offr & stand on forestage PS Standard Bearer

(4) Enter Duncan followed by 1st & 2nd Chamberlains OP Pros. 1st Cham US of 2nd carrying Coronet. S. Bearer

Forres, the royal palace.

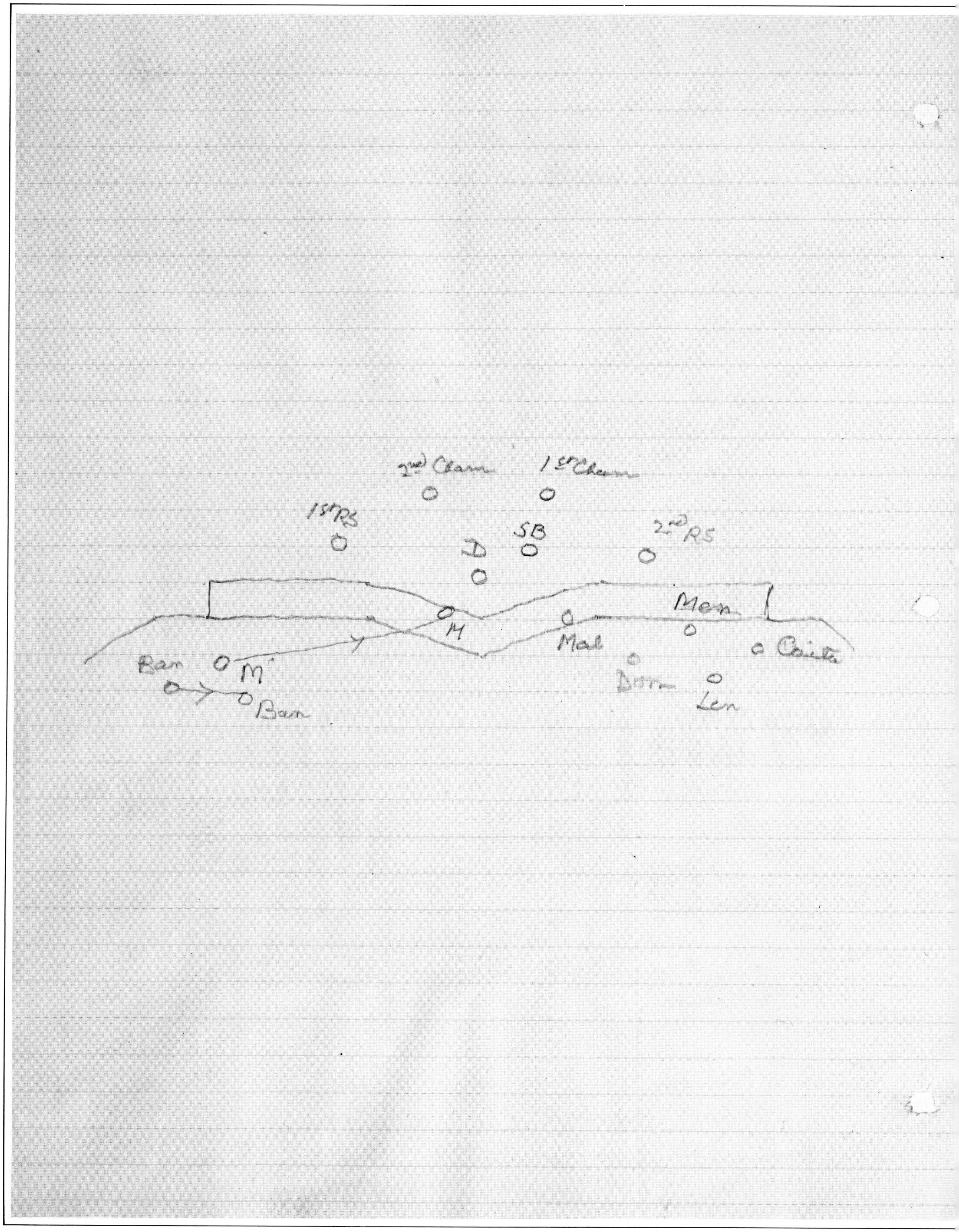

Macbeth and Banquo arrive & are greeted by Duncan.

(13)

Act I Sc. iv

They are not yet come back. But I have spoke
With one that saw him die; who did report
That very frankly he confess'd his treasons,
Implor'd your highness' pardon, and set forth
A deep repentance: nothing in his life
Became him like the leaving it; he died
As one that had been studied in his death,
To throw away the dearest thing he ow'd
As 'twere a careless trifle.

Dun. There 's no art
To find the mind's construction in the face:
He was a gentleman, on whom I built
An absolute trust.

Enter Macbeth, Banquo, ~~Ross, and Angus~~

OP Aoo

O worthiest cousin!
The sin of my ingratitude even now
Was heavy on me: thou art so far before,
That swiftest wing of recompense is slow,
To overtake thee. Would thou hadst less deserv'd,
That the proportion both of thanks, and payment,
Might have been mine! only I have left to say,
More is thy due than more than all can pay.

Mac. The service, and the loyalty I owe,
In doing it, pays itself. Your highness' part
Is to receive our duties: and our duties

13

M Xs to OP of C & kneels on top step Ban moves toward slightly

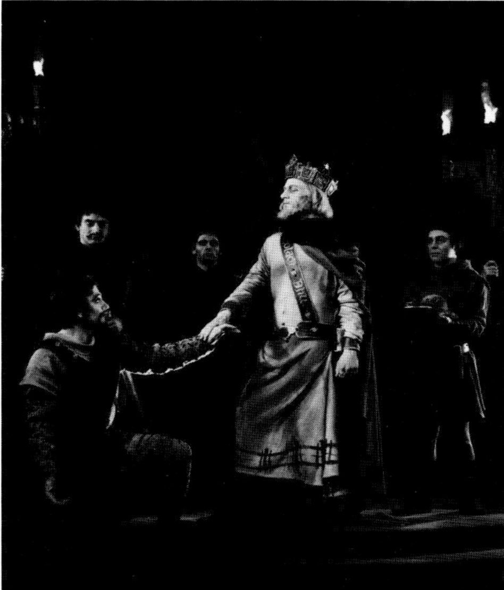

Act I, Scene iv. "The service and the loyalty I owe." Sir Laurence Olivier (Macbeth, kneeling), George Little (Royal Servant, US of Olivier), Rex Robinson (Royal Servant), Geoffrey Bayldon (Duncan), Geoffrey Sassé (Standard Bearer, with coronet), actor holding candelabra is unidentified.

The old King senses the power & ambitions of Macbeth & having honoured him, deliberately chooses this moment to name Malcolm as his successor & make him prince of Cumberland.

I think that he senses a certain danger of ambition in Macbeth & that is why he names Malcolm as his heir when he does. I don't, of course, mean that he imagines for a moment that Macbeth would murder him, but I do think that he may well feel that, should he die in the near future, the election would fall on Macbeth & that is not what he wants to happen.

He again shows his good will to Macbeth by telling him that he will spend the night at his Castle at Inverness.

Macbeth, Act I, Scene iv

(14)

MACBETH

Are to your throne, and state, children, and servants ;
Which do but what they should, by doing every thing
Safe toward your love and honour.

Dun. Welcome hither :
I have begun to plant thee, and will labour
To make thee full of growing. Noble Banquo,
Thou hast no less deserv'd, nor must be known
No less to have done so : let me enfold thee,
And hold thee to my heart.

Ban. There if I grow,
The harvest is your own.

Dun. My plenteous joys,
Wanton in fulness, seek to hide themselves
In drops of sorrow. Sons, kinsmen, thanes,
And you whose places are the nearest, know,
We will establish our estate upon
Our eldest, Malcolm, whom we name hereafter
The Prince of Cumberland : which honour must
Not unaccompanied invest him only,
But signs of nobleness, like stars, shall shine
On all deservers. From hence to Inverness,
And bind us further to you.

Mac. The rest is labour, which is not us'd for you : †
I'll be myself the harbinger, and make joyful
The hearing of my wife with your approach ;

14

Slight move back PS
Ban moves slightly OP
Standing next to M

Mal kneels
S. Bearer moves forward - D takes Coronet from cushion & puts it on Mal's head & kisses his forehead
S.B. - steps back US

D raises M

M moves slightly US. Ban kneels or steps

Ban rises

Mal rises & D turns to M

Order of Exit

1st Royal Servant
Duncan & Malcolm
Banquo & Donalbain
Standard Bearer
1st & 2nd Chamberlains
2nd Royal Servant
Lennox
Menteith
Caithness
2 Lord
Offr

So humbly take my leave.
Dun. My worthy Cawdor!
Mac. (*aside*) The Prince of Cumberland! that is a step,
On which I must fall down, or else o'erleap,
For in my way it lies. Stars, hide your fires,
Let not light see my black and deep desires:
The eye wink at the hand; yet let that be,
Which the eye fears, when it is done, to see. *Exit*
Dun. True, worthy Banquo; he is full so valiant,
And in his commendations I am fed;
It is a banquet to me. Let 's after him,
Whose care is gone before, to bid us welcome:
It is a peerless kinsman. *Flourish. Exeunt*

LIGHTING CHANGE RUNNERS OPEN TRUMPETS

SCENE V

Inverness. Macbeth's castle

Enter Lady Macbeth, reading a letter

L.M. 'They met me in the day of success; and I have learn'd by the perfect'st report, they have more in them than mortal knowledge. When I burn'd in desire to question them further, they made themselves air, into which they vanish'd. Whiles I stood rapt in the wonder of it, came missives from the

15

Murder Scene. 5 pm to next morning.
Lady Macbeth has just received the letter from Macbeth telling her of his meeting with the Witches.

Lady Macbeth. 36 [years old]. Vivien Leigh.
She has an excessively passionate nature & an extraordinary intensity of purpose. She adores her husband. Her ambition for him is beyond everything. Anybody who stands in his way, even the King, must be got rid of.

Act I, Scene v.
The Letter Scene. "Glamis thou art."
Vivien Leigh (Lady Macbeth).

We realise that although she admires him enormously & loves him devotedly she knows that he is far from ruthless or cruel by nature.

She is the only person who has any real power over Macbeth & she knows it. She thinks that she understands him well, & she does, to a very considerable degree, but the strange, imaginative, Celtic side of his nature she doesn't understand.

She mistakes it for lack of determination & firmness of purpose, & is sure that she is justified in driving him on to achieve what she knows, in his heart, he wants, & what she considers is his right.

MACBETH

king, who all-hail'd me Thane of Cawdor, by which title, before, these weird sisters saluted me, and referr'd me to the coming on of time, with "Hail, king that shalt be!" This have I thought good to deliver thee, my dearest partner of greatness, that thou mightst not lose the dues of rejoicing by being ignorant of what greatness is promis'd thee. Lay it to thy heart, and farewell.'

Glamis thou art, and Cawdor, and shalt be
What thou art promis'd : yet do I fear thy nature,
It is too full o' the milk of human kindness
To catch the nearest way. Thou wouldst be great,
Art not without ambition, but without
The illness should attend it. What thou wouldst highly,
That wouldst thou holily ; wouldst not play false,
And yet wouldst wrongly win. Thou 'ldst have, great Glamis,
That which cries 'Thus thou must do, if thou 'ldst have it;'
And that which rather thou dost fear to do,
Than wishest should be undone. Hie thee hither,
That I may pour my spirits in thine ear,
And chastise with the valour of my tongue
All that impedes thee from the golden round,
Which fate and metaphysical aid doth seem

16

moves slightly R of C stage

looking at letter

Inverness, Macbeth's castle.

Everything points to the fact that her will-power & passionate ambition are out of all proportion to her physical strength. It is because of this that she calls on the evil Spirits to help her. It is because of this that she has to fortify herself with drink before she rings the bell that summons her husband to commit the murder. It is this which makes her faint after the discovery of the murder, & which makes her walk in her sleep & finally commit suicide.

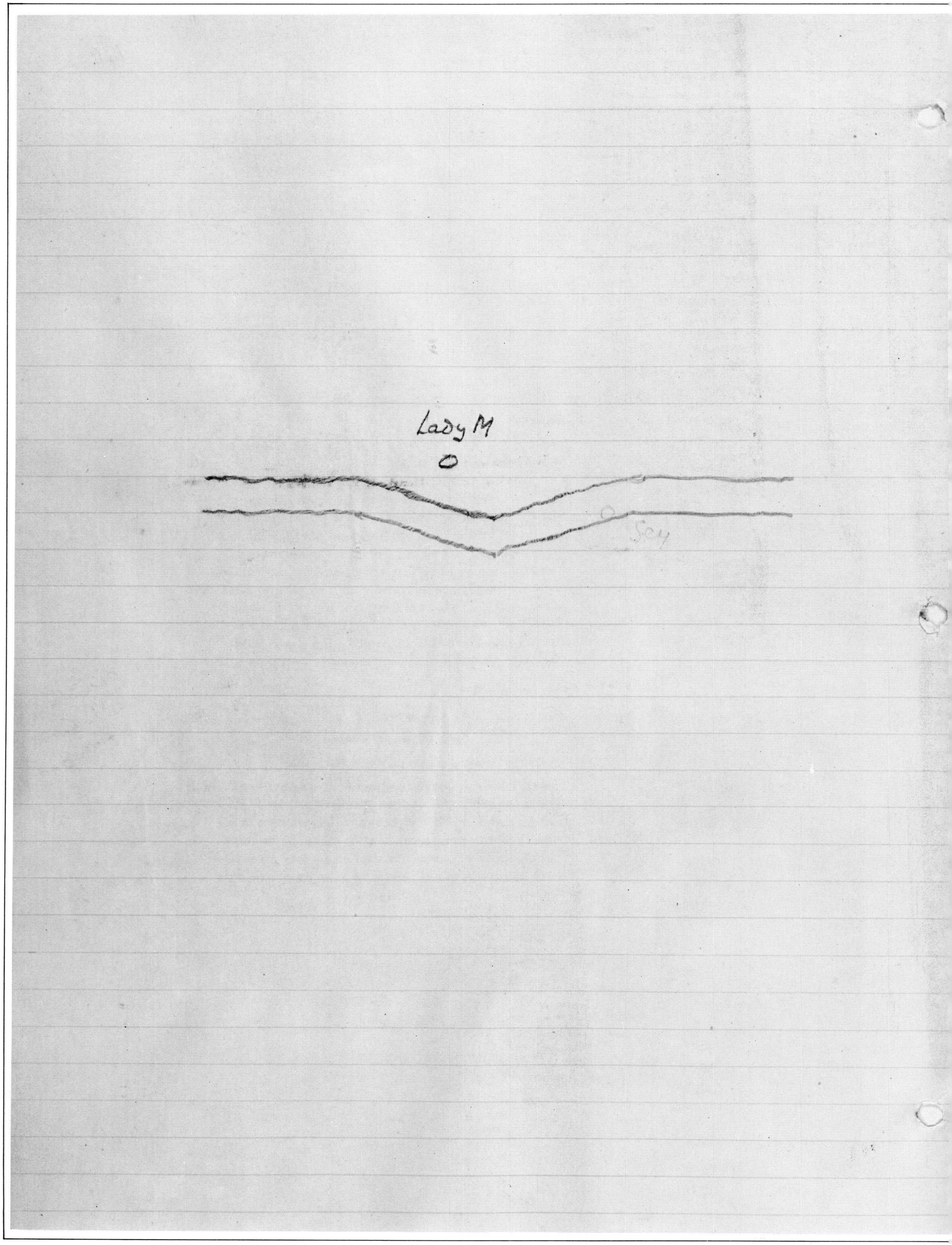

Macbeth, Act I, Scene v

Lady M

O

Sc 4

(17)

Act I Sc. v

To have thee crown'd withal.

Enter ~~Messenger~~ Seyton

What is your tidings?
Mes. The king comes here to-night.
L.M. Thou 'rt mad to say it:
Is not thy master with him? who, were 't so,
Would have inform'd for preparation.
Mes. So please you, it is true: our thane is coming:
One of my fellows had the speed of him,
Who, almost dead for breath, had scarcely more
Than would make up his message.
L.M. Give him tending,
He brings great news, *Exit* ~~Messenger~~ Seyton
the raven himself is hoarse
That croaks the fatal entrance of Duncan
Under my battlements. Come, you spirits
That tend on mortal thoughts, unsex me here,
And fill me, from the crown to the toe, top-full
Of direst cruelty: make thick my blood,
Stop up the access and passage to remorse,
That no compunctious visitings of nature
Shake my fell purpose, nor keep peace between
The effect and it! Come to my woman's breasts,
And take my milk for gall, you murdering ministers,
Wherever, in your sightless substances,

17

OP Door & Comes to OP of Lady M without turning to him

turning slightly away from Seyton

turns to Seyton

Seyton bows

OP Door

Light Fade to evening

moving C stage

Seyton. 30 [years old].
Lee Montague.

The head manservant of the Macbeth household. He is trusted absolutely, by his employers. When they become King & Queen he goes with them to the Royal Palace. Macbeth uses him as his personal servant & armourer. He is, completely, in the know.

Seyton the head manservant comes to tell her that the King will stay at her castle that night. The news is startling & seems like the hand of fate. She calls on the Spirits of evil to help her, which is, of course, exactly what they are waiting to do.

(18)

MACBETH

You wait on nature's mischief! Come, thick night,
And pall thee in the dunnest smoke of hell,
That my keen knife see not the wound it makes,
Nor heaven peep through the blanket of the dark,
To cry 'Hold, hold!'

Enter Macbeth

Great Glamis! worthy Cawdor!
Greater than both, by the all-hail hereafter!
Thy letters have transported me beyond
This ignorant present, and I feel now
The future in the instant.

Mac. My dearest love,
Duncan comes here to-night.

L.M. And when goes hence?

Mac. To-morrow, as he purposes.

L.M. O, never
Shall sun that morrow see!
Your face, my thane, is as a book, where men
May read strange matters. To beguile the time,
Look like the time, bear welcome in your eye,
Your hand, your tongue: look like the innocent flower,
But be the serpent under 't. He that 's coming
Must be provided for: and you shall put
This night's great business into my dispatch,
Which shall to all our nights and days to come

18

OP & through C arch & stands in archway. Lady M turns to face him

They meet mid C stage & embrace. M on OP side of her

he turns slightly away from her

Act I, Scene v. "Great Glamis! worthy Cawdor!" Sir Laurence Olivier (Macbeth), Vivien Leigh (Lady Macbeth).

Act I, Scene v. "My dearest love, Duncan comes here tonight." Sir Laurence Olivier (Macbeth), Vivien Leigh (Lady Macbeth) (see opposite page).

From then [when the Spirits come] on, she is possessed by the Devil & uses every means in her power to overcome her husband's instincts of honour & righteousness.

Macbeth arrives. They only have time for a short but terrifying conversation together before the arrival of the King.

Macbeth is deeply in love with her. It is a well-known fact. Duncan mentions it, in the most charming way, when he arrives at their Castle.

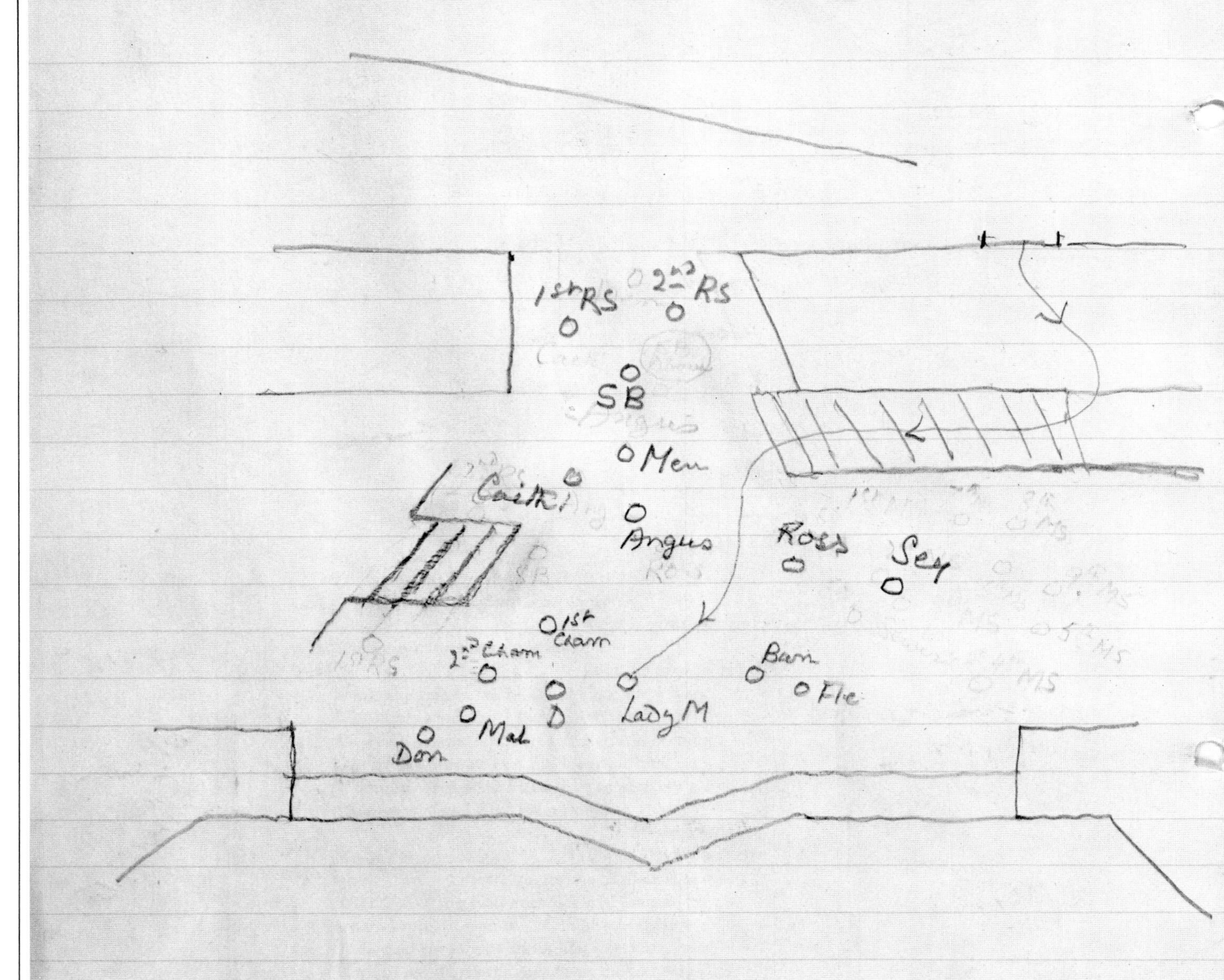

It is a beautiful evening. The Castle looks serene & calm & peaceful. The King greets his hostess with great courtesy & charm & the whole party go into the banquet hall.

Macbeth Servants & The Royal Servants.

They should not behave like footmen with powdered wigs. They are far more rough & open-air than that. One should feel that if they don't behave themselves they are flogged.

(19)

Entrance — C arch.

Seyton (walking backwards)
Duncan & Banquo & Fleance
Malcolm & Donalbain
1st & 2nd Chamberlains
Ross & Angus
Caithness & Menteith
Standard Bearer (Geoffrey Sasse)
1st & 2nd Royal Servants.
(Richard Coe & Peter Van Greenaway)

Act I Sc. vi

Give solely sovereign sway, and masterdom.

Mac. We will speak further.

L.M. Only look up clear;
To alter favour ever is to fear:
Leave all the rest to me. *Exeunt*

~~SCENE VI~~

~~Before~~ *Macbeth's castle*

~~Hautboys and torches.~~ *Enter Duncan, Malcolm, Donalbain,* Fleance *Banquo,* ~~Lennox~~, ~~Macduff~~, *Ross, Angus,* ~~and Attendants~~ Menteith Caithness

Dun. This castle hath a pleasant seat, the air
Nimbly and sweetly recommends itself
Unto our gentle senses.

Ban. This guest of summer,
The temple-haunting martlet, does approve,
By his loved mansionry, that the heaven's breath
Smells wooingly here: no jutty, frieze,
Buttress, nor coign of vantage, but this bird
Hath made his pendant bed and procreant cradle:
Where they most breed and haunt, I have observ'd
The air is delicate.

Enter Lady Macbeth

Dun. See, see, our honour'd hostess!

19

Slight move away OP

TRUMPETS NEARER

TRUMPETS LOUD.

FADE TO NIGHT DURING SCENE

Exit Lady M up PS steps

TRUMPETS in far distance

They both listen

Lady M moves U.S.

M OP PS after steps & trumpets

Turret door & downsteps U.S PS & moves to PS of D.

Act I, Scene vi. Duncan's arrival. "See, see our honour'd hostess!" Ian Holm (Donalbain), Trader Faulkner (Malcolm, with coronet), Geoffrey Bayldon (Duncan), John Springett (Angus, center of arch), Ralph Michael (Banquo, back to camera), William Devlin (Ross, with cape), Vivien Leigh (Lady Macbeth), others unidentified.

She is, obviously, beautiful. A man of Duncan's breeding & sensitivity would never call her "Fair & noble hostess" if she was a plain woman.

Exit

OP Ass.

Duncan & Lady M
Malcolm & Donalbain
1st & 2nd Chamberlains
Banquo & Fleance
Ross & Angus
Menteith & Caithness
Standard Bearer
1 & 2 Royal Servants
Seyton

(20)

MACBETH

The love that follows us sometime is our trouble,
Which still we thank as love. Herein I teach you
How you shall bid God 'ild us for your pains,
And thank us for your trouble.

L.M. All our service,
In every point twice done, and then done double,
Were poor and single business, to contend
Against those honours deep and broad wherewith
Your majesty loads our house: for those of old,
And the late dignities heap'd up to them,
We rest your hermits.

Dun. Where 's the thane of Cawdor?
We cours'd him at the heels, and had a purpose
To be his purveyor: but he rides well,
And his great love, sharp as his spur, hath holp him
To his home before us. Fair and noble hostess,
We are your guest to-night.

L.M. Your servants ever
Have theirs, themselves, and what is theirs, in compt,
To make their audit at your highness' pleasure,
Still to return your own.

Dun. Give me your hand;
Conduct me to mine host: we love him highly,
And shall continue our graces towards him.
By your leave, hostess. *Exeunt*

20

Lady M curtseys

Lady M rises

Lady M accepts the compliment

OP ASS FADE IN WARM LIGHT

in

MUSIC

After exit of Royal Party. Seyton makes sign off stage

'PS mid. to' Sewer?

Macbeth, Act I, Scene vi

Night has fallen. Servants carrying torches cross the court yard with food & wine & the musicians play.

Sewer. 45 [years old].
Mervyn Blake.

The head serving man of the Castle.

Then there is silence in the Court yard as the banquet starts & Macbeth comes out of the over-heated room into the moonlight, unable to sit & eat or drink with the thought of the ghastly murder in his mind.

Entrance PS Pros
cross the forestage
& exit OP Ass

Sewer with Torch (Mervyn Blake)
2nd & 3rd M.S with Wines Leon Eagles, Emrys James
1st with Torch Hugh Cross
4th & 5th MS with Food Kevin Miles, Robert Arnold
8th with Torch Ron Haddrick
6th & 7th MS with Food John Southworth, Alan Haywood
9th with Torch David King

Act I Sc. vii

SCENE VII

Macbeth's castle

Hautboys and torches. Enter a Sewer, and divers Servants with dishes and service, and pass over the stage. Then enter Macbeth

OP Ass

Mac. If it were done, when 'tis done, then 'twere well
It were done quickly : if the assassination
Could trammel up the consequence, and catch,
With his surcease, success ; that but this blow
Might be the be-all and the end-all, here,
But here, upon this bank and shoal of time,
We 'ld jump the life to come. But in these cases
We still have judgement here ; that we but teach
Bloody instructions, which being taught, return
To plague the inventor. This even-handed justice
Commends the ingredience of our poison'd chalice
To our own lips. He 's here in double trust ;
First, as I am his kinsman, and his subject,
Strong both against the deed ; then, as his host,
Who should against his murderer shut the door,
Not bear the knife myself. Besides, this Duncan
Hath borne his faculties so meek, hath been
So clear in his great office, that his virtues

21

MACBETH

Will plead like angels, trumpet-tongu'd against
The deep damnation of his taking-off;
And pity, like a naked new-born babe,
Striding the blast, or heaven's cherubin, hors'd
Upon the sightless couriers of the air,
Shall blow the horrid deed in every eye,
That tears shall drown the wind. I have no spur
To prick the sides of my intent, but only
Vaulting ambition, which o'erleaps itself,
And falls on the other.

Enter Lady Macbeth

How now? what news?

L.M. He has almost supp'd: why have you left the chamber?

Mac. Hath he ask'd for me?

L.M. Know you not he has?

Mac. We will proceed no further in this business:
He hath honour'd me of late, and I have bought
Golden opinions from all sorts of people,
Which would be worn now in their newest gloss,
Not cast aside so soon.

L.M. Was the hope drunk,
Wherein you dress'd yourself? hath it slept since?
And wakes it now to look so green, and pale,
At what it did so freely? From this time,

22

moving slightly PS.

Lady M moves quickly to OP

The King asks what has happened to his host & Lady Macbeth comes to look for her husband. He tells her that it is impossible for them to murder Duncan & that he refuses to do it.

Act I, Scene vii. "We will proceed no further in this business." Sir Laurence Oliver (Macbeth), Vivien Leigh (Lady Macbeth) (see opposite page).

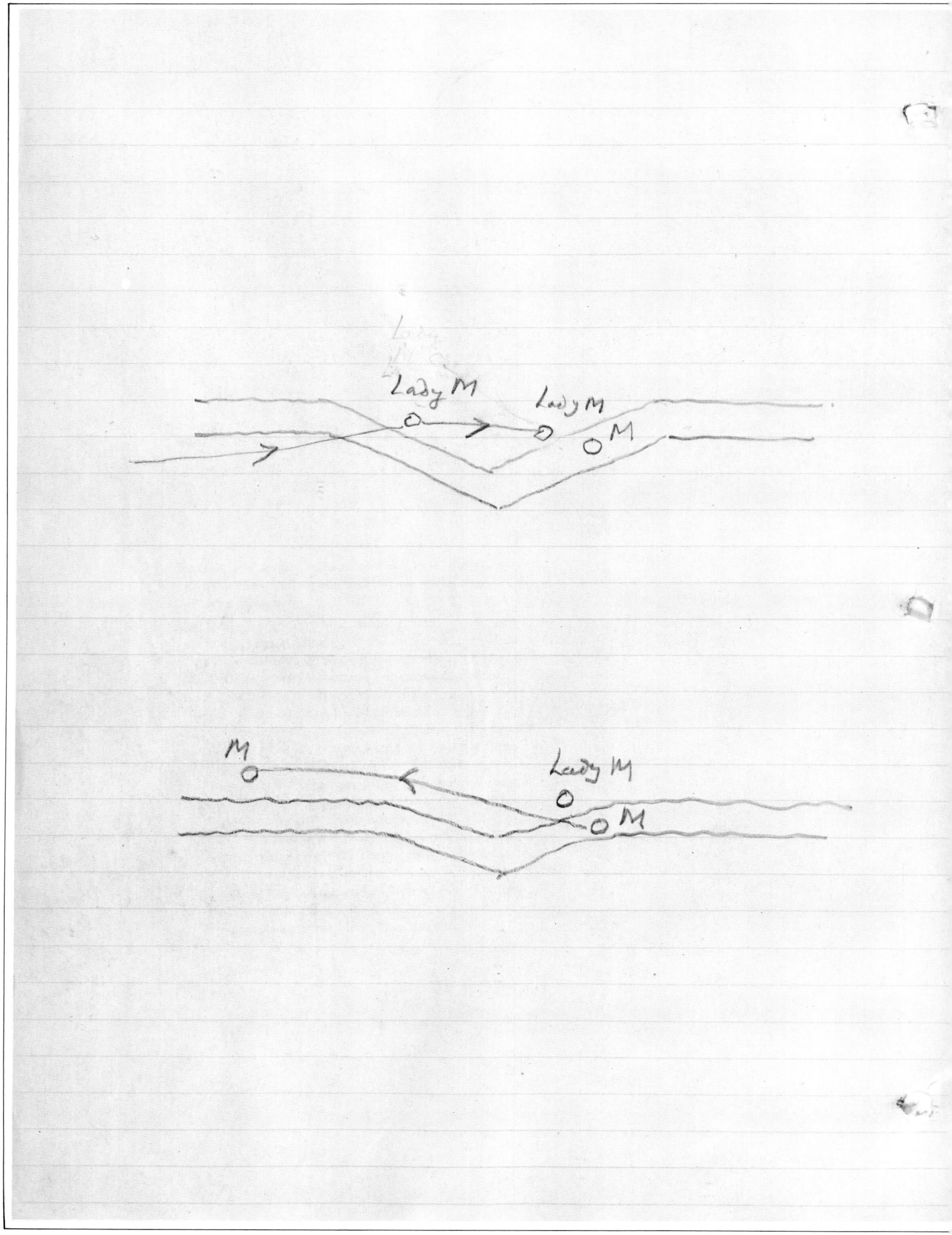

Apart from his burning ambition I feel he has a deep sorrow that gnaws at his heart & I think it is due to the fact that his only son died soon after it was born. He never speaks of it, & we only know about it through what his wife says in the terrible scene they have together before the murder.

Macbeth, Act I, Scene vii

Act I Sc. vii

Such I account thy love. Art thou afeard
To be the same in thine own act and valour
As thou art in desire? Wouldst thou have that
Which thou esteem'st the ornament of life,
And live a coward in thine own esteem?
Letting 'I dare not' wait upon 'I would,'
Like the poor cat i' the adage. †

he looks at her

Mac. Prithee peace:
I dare do all that may become a man,
Who dares do more, is none.

moves to PS down one step

L.M. What beast was 't then
That made you break this enterprize to me?
When you durst do it, then you were a man;
And, to be more than what you were, you would
Be so much more the man. Nor time, nor place,
Did then adhere, and yet you would make both:
They have made themselves, and that their fitness now
Does unmake you. I have given suck, and know
How tender 'tis to love the babe that milks me:
I would, while it was smiling in my face,
Have pluck'd my nipple from his boneless gums,
And dash'd the brains out, had I so sworn
As you have done to this. — *Pause*

moving to OP of him

he turns to her & takes her hand without looking at her

Mac. If we should fail?

X's in front of Lady M to OP

23

She attacks him violently, calls him a coward & refers to their son—who has died when a baby—in the most ghastly way.

MACBETH

L.M. We fail?
But screw your courage to the sticking-place,
And we'll not fail: when Duncan is asleep,
(Whereto the rather shall his day's hard journey
Soundly invite him) his two chamberlains
Will I with wine and wassail so convince,
That memory, the warder of the brain,
Shall be a fume, and the receipt of reason
A limbec only: when in swinish sleep
Their drenched natures lie as in a death,
What cannot you and I perform upon
The unguarded Duncan? what not put upon
His spongy officers, who shall bear the guilt
Of our great quell?
Mac. Bring forth men-children only;
For thy undaunted mettle should compose
Nothing but males. Will it not be receiv'd,
When we have mark'd with blood those sleepy two
Of his own chamber, and us'd their very daggers,
That they have done 't?
L.M. Who dares receive it other,
As we shall make our griefs and clamour roar
Upon his death?
Mac. I am settled, and bend up

24

Macbeth gives in, changes his mind, against all his natural feelings of humanity & nobility, & decides to commit the murder.

Act I, Scene vii. "But screw your courage." Vivien Leigh (Lady Macbeth), Sir Laurence Olivier (Macbeth) (see opposite page).

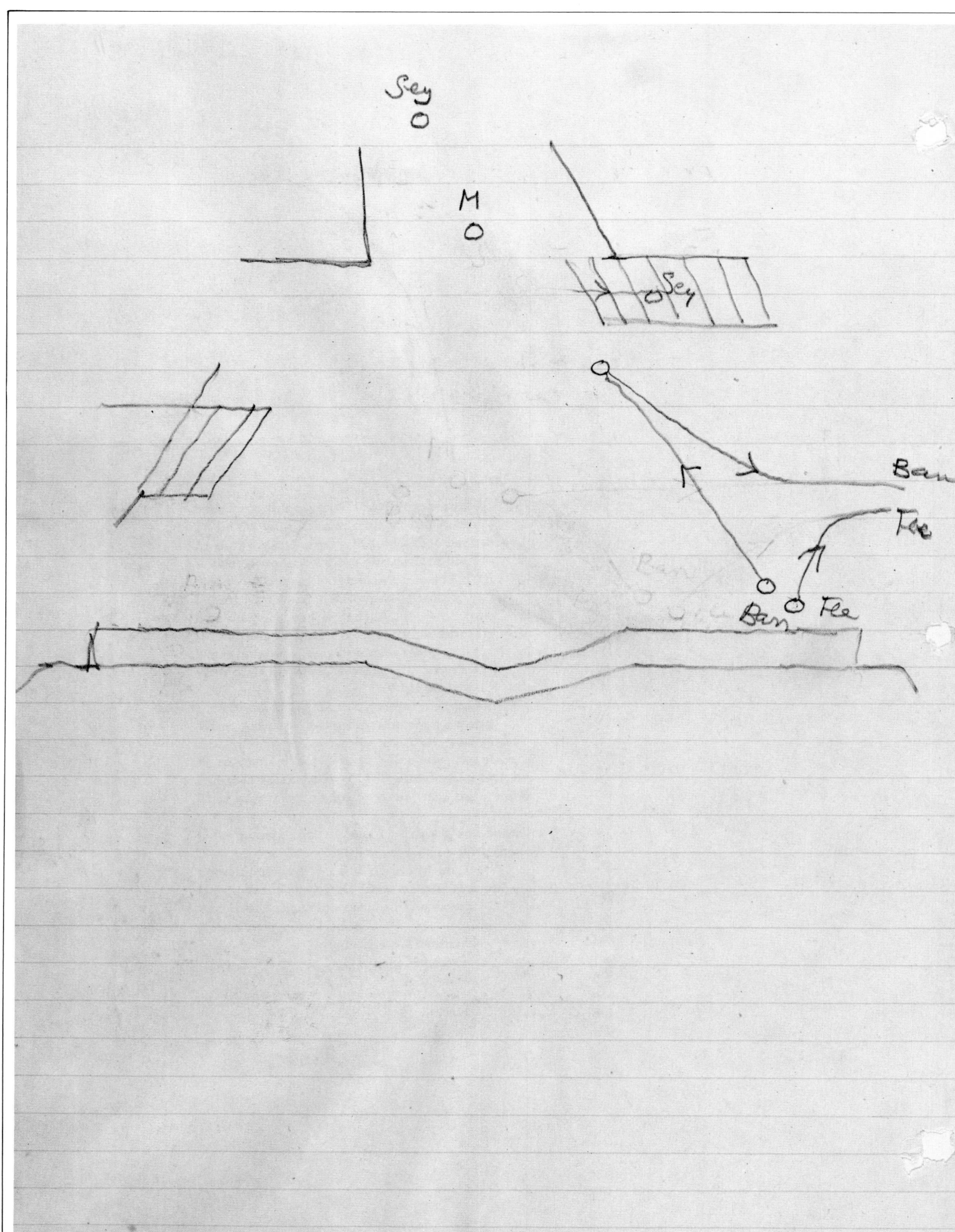

The moon goes down & the courtyard is silent & eerie. The King & his Court have gone to bed. Banquo & Fleance come from the Royal apartments & cross the Courtyard on their way to their own room. Banquo is troubled in his mind. He already feels the evil insinuations of the Witches tormenting him at night. He suddenly hears a sound & is frightened for his son & himself, but it is only his Host & his servant Seyton going on their rounds.

Fleance. 16 [years old]. Paul Vieyra.

Banquo's son, whom he uses as his page. A sensible, pleasant boy.

Seyton watches his Master like a dog. Macbeth is his God & can do no wrong.

Macbeth, Act II, Scene i

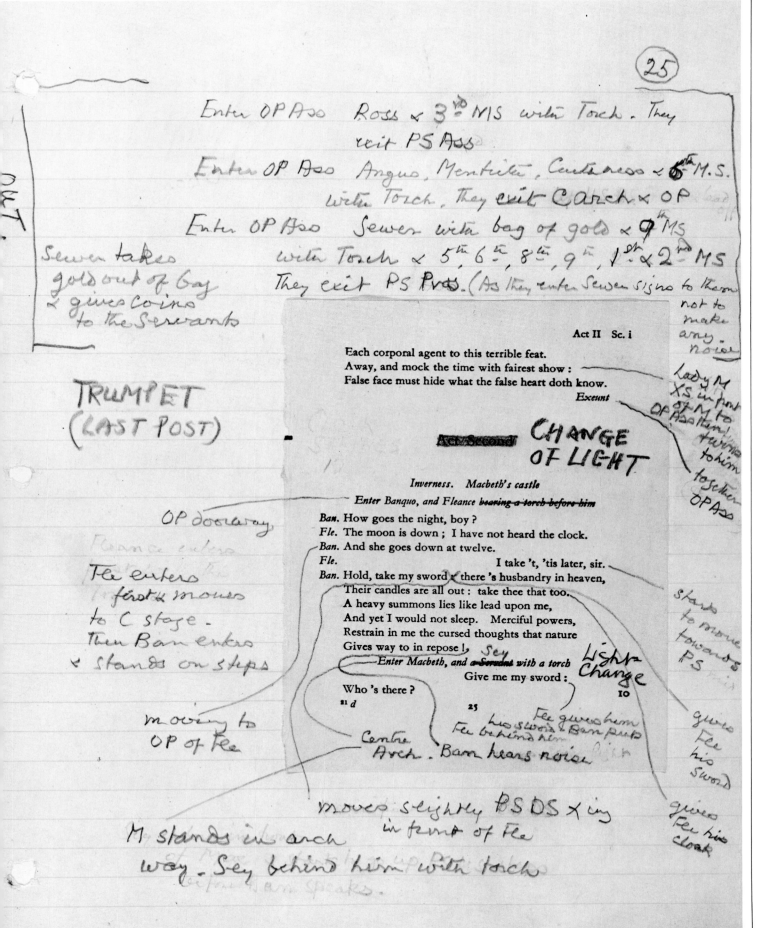

25

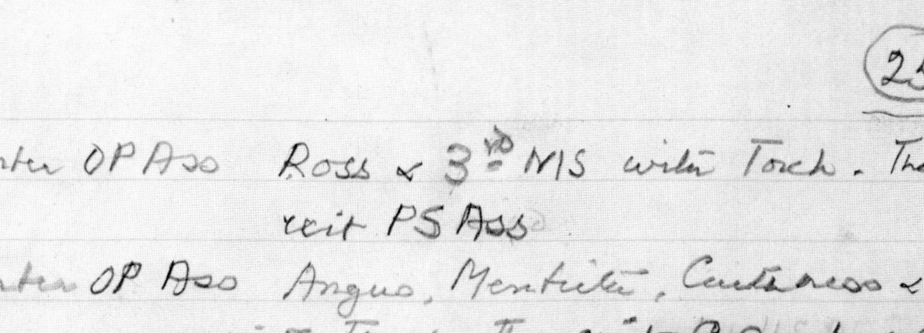

Enter OP Aso Ross & 3rd MS with Torch. They exit PS Ass
Enter OP Aso Angus, Menteith, Caithness & 8th M.S. with Torch. They exit C Arch & OP
Enter OP Aso Sewer with bag of gold & 9th MS with Torch & 5th, 6th, 8th, 9th, 1st & 2nd MS They exit PS Pros. (As they enter Sewer signs to them not to make any noise

Sewer takes gold out of bag & gives coins to the Servants

TRUMPET (LAST POST)

Act II Sc. i

Each corporal agent to this terrible feat.
Away, and mock the time with fairest show :
False face must hide what the false heart doth know.

Exeunt

Lady M XS in front of M to OP Aso then turns to him together OP Aso

~~Act Second~~ CHANGE OF LIGHT

Inverness. Macbeth's castle

Enter Banquo, and Fleance ~~bearing a torch before him~~

OP doorway

Fle enters first & moves to C stage. Then Ban enters & stands on steps

Ban. How goes the night, boy ?
Fle. The moon is down ; I have not heard the clock.
Ban. And she goes down at twelve.
Fle. I take 't, 'tis later, sir.
Ban. Hold, take my sword : there 's husbandry in heaven,
Their candles are all out : take thee that too.
A heavy summons lies like lead upon me,
And yet I would not sleep. Merciful powers,
Restrain in me the cursed thoughts that nature
Gives way to in repose !
Enter Macbeth, and a ~~Servant~~ Sey with a torch
Give me my sword :
Who 's there ?

11 d 25

starts to move towards PS

Light Change

Fle gives him his sword & Ban puts Fle behind him

gives Fle his sword

gives Fle his cloak

moving to OP of Fle

Centre Arch. Ban hears noise

moves slightly PS DS & in in front of Fle

M stands in arch way. Sey behind him with torch

Macbeth, Act II, Scene i

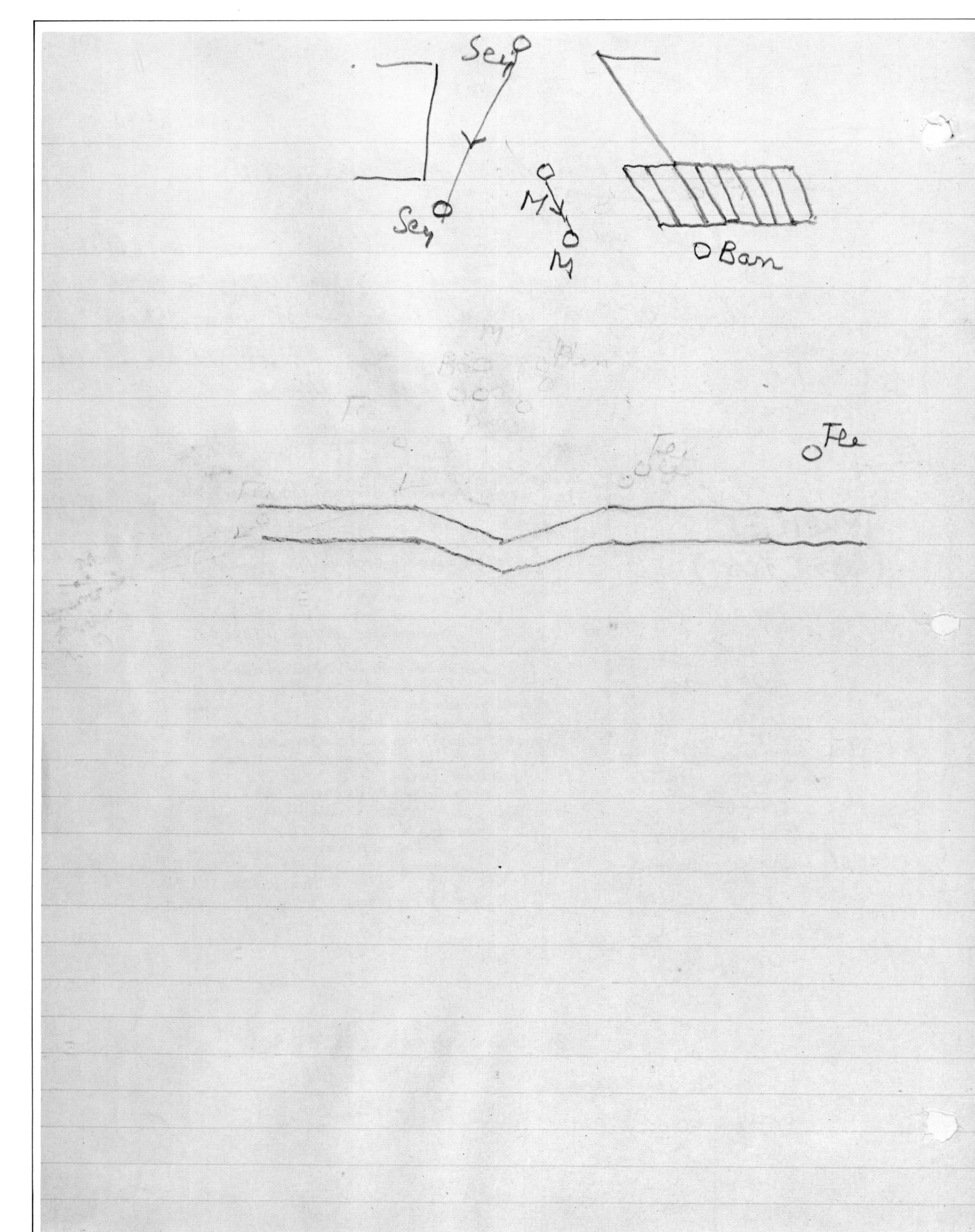
Sey
Sey
M
M
O Ban
Fle

(26)

M moves forward to OP of Ban
Sey OP of M

MACBETH

Mac. A friend.
Ban. What, sir, not yet at rest? The king's a-bed:
He hath been in unusual pleasure, and
Sent forth great largess to your offices:
This diamond he greets your wife withal,
By the name of most kind hostess, and shut up
In measureless content.
Mac. Being unprepar'd,
Our will became the servant to defect,
Which else should free have wrought.
Ban. All 's well.
I dreamt last night of the three weird sisters:
To you they have show'd some truth.
Mac. I think not of them:
Yet when we can entreat an hour to serve,
We would spend it in some words upon that business,
If you would grant the time.
Ban. At your kind'st leisure.
Mac. If you shall cleave to my consent, when 'tis,
It shall make honour for you.
Ban. So I lose none,
In seeking to augment it, but still keep
My bosom franchis'd, and allegiance clear,
I shall be counsell'd.
Mac. Good repose the while!

26

M hands ring to Sey

takes ring out of pocket & gives it to M

He mentions the Witches to Macbeth, but gets a curt reply followed by a guarded suggestion that they shall stand together in the future. He gives an equally guarded answer & he & his son go off to bed.

(27)

Act II Sc. i

Ban. Thanks, sir : the like to you !

Exeunt Banquo and Fleance

Mac. Go bid thy mistress, when my drink is ready,
She strike upon the bell. Get thee to bed.

Exit ~~*Servant*~~ Sey

Is this a dagger, which I see before me,
The handle toward my hand ? Come, let me clutch
thee.
I have thee not, and yet I see thee still.
Art thou not, fatal vision, sensible
To feeling, as to sight ? or art thou but
A dagger of the mind, a false creation,
Proceeding from the heat-oppressed brain ?
I see thee yet, in form as palpable
As this which now I draw.
Thou marshall'st me the way that I was going,
And such an instrument I was to use.
Mine eyes are made the fools o' the other senses,
Or else worth all the rest : I see thee still ;
And on thy blade, and dudgeon, gouts of blood,
Which was not so before. There 's no such thing :
It is the bloody business, which informs
Thus to mine eyes. Now o'er the one half-world
Nature seems dead, and wicked dreams abuse
The curtain'd sleep ; witchcraft celebrates

27

PS Pros
Sey moves a few steps up PS steps to light his way
Light change
OP left
Slight move DS
draws his dagger
Sey goes up last PS steps & moves to C of arch then stops –
M moves slightly PS DS
turning towards OP
turns away DS & shuts his eyes

Macbeth tells Seyton to ask Lady Macbeth to ring a bell when his drink is ready. This is, of course, a pre-arranged signal between them.

Macbeth dismisses Seyton & knows that the terrible moment has almost arrived. His brain is so over-wrought that he has his first hallucination. Or maybe it is a reality. His wife tells him later that it was an "air-drawn dagger" & he himself can't make out whether his eyes are deceiving him or not.

Act II, Scene i. "Come, let me clutch thee!" Sir Laurence Olivier (Macbeth) (see opposite page).

Act II, Scene i.
"I go, and it is done."
Sir Laurence Olivier (Macbeth).

For the first time we see a physical weakness in Lady Macbeth. She has found it necessary to give herself courage by drinking wine. She knows her husband is actually committing the murder & it fills her with suppressed excitement & she resents the fact that she was not able to bring herself to do it.

(28)

MACBETH

Pale Hecat's offerings ; and wither'd murder,
Alarum'd by his sentinel, the wolf,
Whose howl 's his watch, thus with his stealthy pace,
With Tarquin's ravishing strides, towards his design †
Moves like a ghost. Thou sure and firm-set earth,
Hear not my steps, which way they walk, for fear
Thy very stones prate of my whereabout,
And take the present horror from the time,
Which now suits with it. Whiles I threat, he lives :
Words to the heat of deeds too cold breath gives.

A bell rings

I go, and it is done : the bell invites me.
Hear it not, Duncan, for it is a knell
That summons thee to heaven, or to hell. *Exit*

Owl cries in distance

Enter Lady Macbeth — OP lift & comes to C of Arch

L.M. That which hath made them drunk hath made me bold ;
What hath quench'd them hath given me fire. Hark !
Peace !
It was the owl that shriek'd, the fatal bellman,
Which gives the stern'st good-night. He is about it,

28

moves to PS US steps & starts coming down them - stops on steps

Act II Sc. ii

The doors are open: and the surfeited grooms
Do mock their charge with snores: I have drugg'd
their possets,
That death and nature do contend about them,
Whether they live or die.

Mac. (*within*) Who 's there? what ho!

L.M. Alack, I am afraid they have awak'd,
And 'tis not done: the attempt, and not the deed,
Confounds us. Hark! I laid their daggers ready,
He could not miss 'em. Had he not resembled
My father as he slept, I had done 't.

Enter Macbeth OP doorway

My husband?

Mac. I have done the deed. Didst thou not hear a noise?

L.M. I heard the owl scream and the crickets cry.
Did not you speak?

Mac. When?

L.M. Now.

Mac. As I descended?

L.M. Ay.

Mac. Hark!
Who lies i' the second chamber?

L.M. Donalbain.

Mac. This is a sorry sight. *Looking ~~on his hands~~* at his left hand

L.M. A foolish thought, to say a sorry sight.

29

Off stage OP

coming down steps & moving to C stage

comes to OP of Lady M

moves slightly US OP

moves to OP of Lady M again

turns to listen

slight move DS PS

Macbeth appears. He has committed the crime & immediately the appalling horror of it takes possession of him.

MACBETH

Mac. There 's one did laugh in 's sleep, and one cried
'Murder !'
That they did wake each other : I stood and heard
them :
But they did say their prayers, and address'd them
Again to sleep.
L.M. There are two lodg'd together.
Mac. One cried, 'God bless us !', and 'Amen' the
other,
As they had seen me with these hangman's hands :
Listening their fear, I could not say 'Amen,'
When they did say 'God bless us !'
L.M. Consider it not so deeply.
Mac. But wherefore could not I pronounce 'Amen' ?
I had most need of blessing, and 'Amen'
Stuck in my throat.
L.M. These deeds must not be thought
After these ways ; so, it will make us mad.
Mac. Methought I heard a voice cry 'Sleep no more !
Macbeth does murder sleep '—the innocent sleep,
Sleep that knits up the ravell'd sleeve of care,
The death of each day's life, sore labour's bath,
Balm of hurt minds, great nature's second course,
Chief nourisher in life's feast,—
L.M. What do you mean ?

30

Slight move OP DS.

moving to PS of M

Slight move away from M

The nightmare has started & he has already felt the fire of hell drying up his throat so that he couldn't say "Amen" when one of the Royal Servants said a prayer to God.

(31)

Act II Sc. ii

Mac. Still it cried ' Sleep no more ! ' to all the house :
' Glamis hath murder'd sleep, and therefore Cawdor
Shall sleep no more : Macbeth shall sleep no more.'
L.M. Who was it, that thus cried ? Why, worthy thane,
You do unbend your noble strength, to think
So brainsickly of things. Go get some water,
And wash this filthy witness from your hand.
Why did you bring these daggers from the place ?
They must lie there : go carry them, and smear
The sleepy grooms with blood.
Mac. I 'll go no more :
I am afraid, to think what I have done ;
Look on 't again I dare not.
L.M. Infirm of purpose !
Give me the daggers : the sleeping, and the dead,
Are but as pictures : 'tis the eye of childhood,
That fears a painted devil. If he do bleed,
I 'll gild the faces of the grooms withal,
For it must seem their guilt.
Exit. Knocking within
Mac. Whence is that knocking ?
How is 't with me, when every noise appals me ?
What hands are here ? ha ! they pluck out mine eyes !
Will all great Neptune's ocean wash this blood
Clean from my hand ? No ; this my hand will rather

31

Slight move DS

moving round US of him to OP of him

Lady M takes hold of his right hand with daggers

moving RS away from her

takes the daggers from his right hand

OP doorway

move US—to OP slightly

Act II, Scene ii. "Give me the daggers." Vivien Leigh (Lady Macbeth), Sir Laurence Olivier (Macbeth).

He has lost his nerve & even forgotten to leave the daggers behind, & refuses to take them back. Macbeth is never a coward but the thought of what he has done is terrible torture & he can't look at that murdered old King again.

Act II, Scene ii. "The sleeping, and the dead." Vivien Leigh (Lady Macbeth) (see opposite page).

His wife takes the daggers back herself, but it seems to me that the supreme effort needed to do so undermines her mental & physical strength for ever. Suddenly there is the sound of knocking at the South Gate of the castle. To Macbeth it has an unearthly significance, but to his wife who is still, just, in command of the situation, it means the danger of detection & she forces her husband to retire.

Macbeth, Act II, Scene ii

MACBETH

The multitudinous seas incarnadine,
Making the green one red. †

Re-enter Lady Macbeth

L.M. My hands are of your colour : but I shame
To wear a heart so white. (*Knocking within.*) I hear
a knocking
At the south entry ! retire we to our chamber :
A little water clears us of this deed :
How easy is it then ! Your constancy
Hath left you unattended. (*Knocking within.*) Hark !
more knocking :
Get on your nightgown, lest occasion call us
And show us to be watchers : be not lost
So poorly in your thoughts.

Mac. To know my deed, 'twere best not know myself.

Knocking within

Wake Duncan with thy knocking ! I would thou
could'st !

Exeunt

Start of FADE IN OF MORNING

Enter a Porter. Knocking within

Por. Here's a knocking indeed ! If a man were porter
of hell-gate, he should have old turning the key.
(*Knocking within.*) Knock, knock, knock ! Who 's

32

M moves OP looking at OP doorway

X-ing in front of M to OP of him & pushing him towards PS steps turns & looks at OP doorway

OP doorway & comes to OP of M

X-ing in front of M to PS

Lady M X's in front of M & goes up PS steps followed by M

OP & C arch

putting on his clothes & carrying his boots & keys –

Sits on OP steps & puts on one boot

Porter. 50 [years old].
Patrick Wymark.

One wonders why Macbeth & Lady Macbeth should have such a man as this for the Porter of their Castle, but I believe one should think of him as an old soldier—an old sweat—who is past fighting & whose coarse barrack room humour amuses the General. He has a strange imagination, too, which would appeal to Macbeth.

When we see him first he is semi-drunk & half-asleep. He is not a comic character but a real person.

The Porter of the Castle comes to open the Gate, still half-drunk & half-asleep. He is gross and bestial (a Porter of Hell), full of drink & lust.

He opens the gate & lets in Macduff. This is the first time that we have seen him & we must recognise at once in him the strength & power & determination of goodness. Nothing sentimental or sweet or comfortable. The inflexible nature of a man of God.

Macduff. [35 years old].
Keith Michell.

He is a very big man & enormously strong. A real Scot. He is generally quiet, but when he is roused he can be extremely passionate. He is very determined & is incapable of pretending. He is a man who has a simple and true belief in God.

Mac
Port
Len

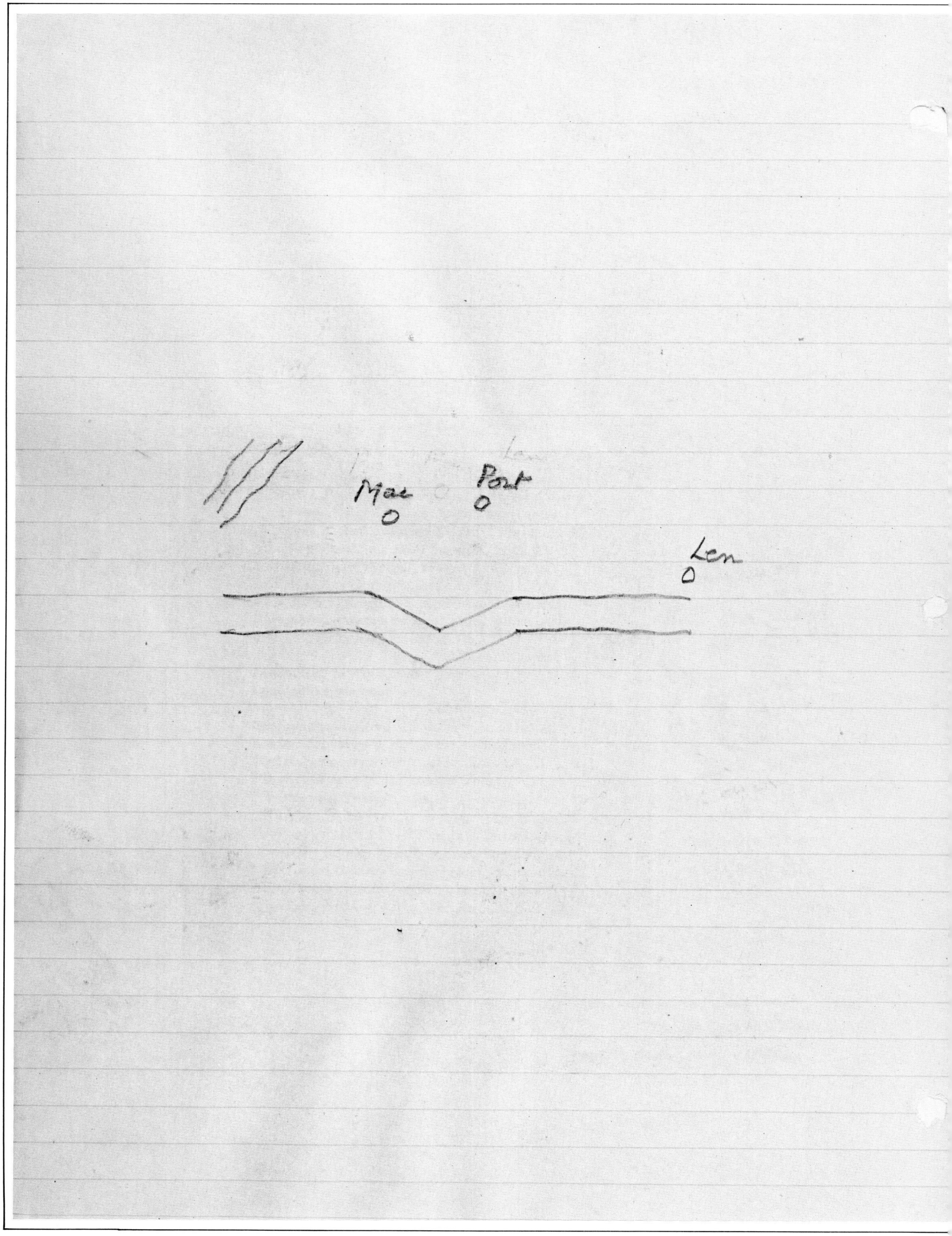

Act II Sc. iii

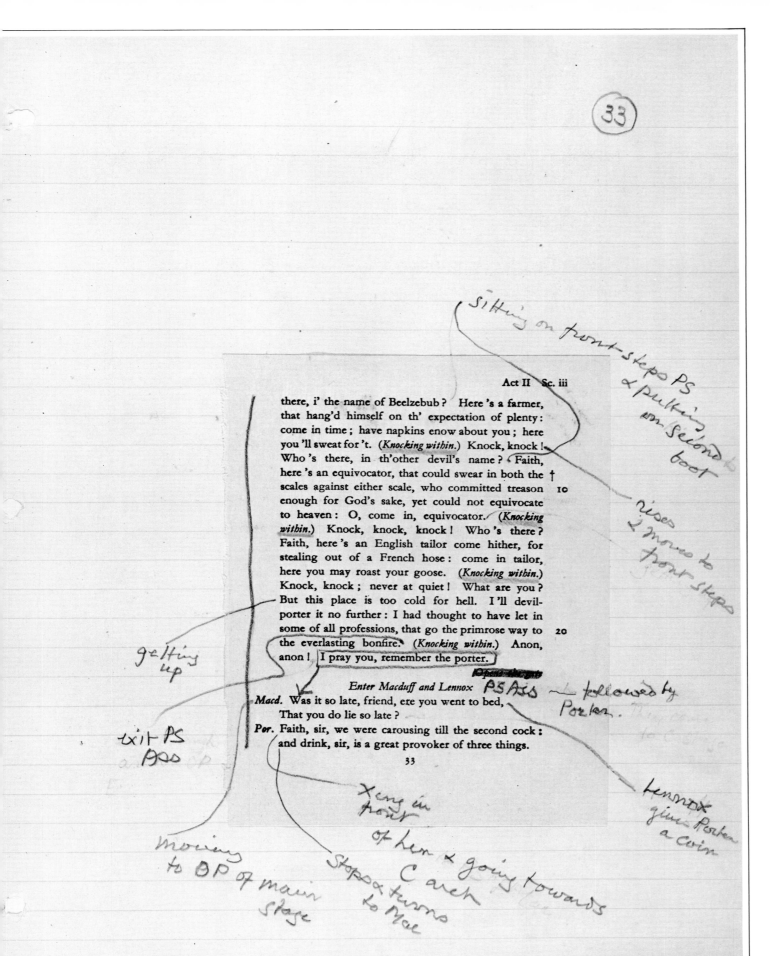

there, i' the name of Beelzebub? Here 's a farmer, that hang'd himself on th' expectation of plenty: come in time; have napkins enow about you; here you 'll sweat for 't. (*Knocking within.*) Knock, knock! Who 's there, in th'other devil's name? Faith, here 's an equivocator, that could swear in both the † scales against either scale, who committed treason enough for God's sake, yet could not equivocate to heaven: O, come in, equivocator. (*Knocking within.*) Knock, knock, knock! Who 's there? Faith, here 's an English tailor come hither, for stealing out of a French hose: come in tailor, here you may roast your goose. (*Knocking within.*) Knock, knock; never at quiet! What are you? But this place is too cold for hell. I'll devil-porter it no further: I had thought to have let in some of all professions, that go the primrose way to the everlasting bonfire. (*Knocking within.*) Anon, anon! I pray you, remember the porter.

~~[*Opens the gate*]~~

Enter Macduff and Lennox PS ASS

Macd. Was it so late, friend, ere you went to bed,
That you do lie so late?

Por. Faith, sir, we were carousing till the second cock: and drink, sir, is a great provoker of three things.

33

sitting on front-steps PS & putting on second boot

rises & moves to front steps

getting up

exit PS ASS

— followed by Porter.

Lennox gives Porter a coin

Xing in front of Len & going towards C arch

moving to OP of main stage

stops & turns to Mac

Act II, Scene iii. "Here's a farmer." Patrick Wymark (Porter).

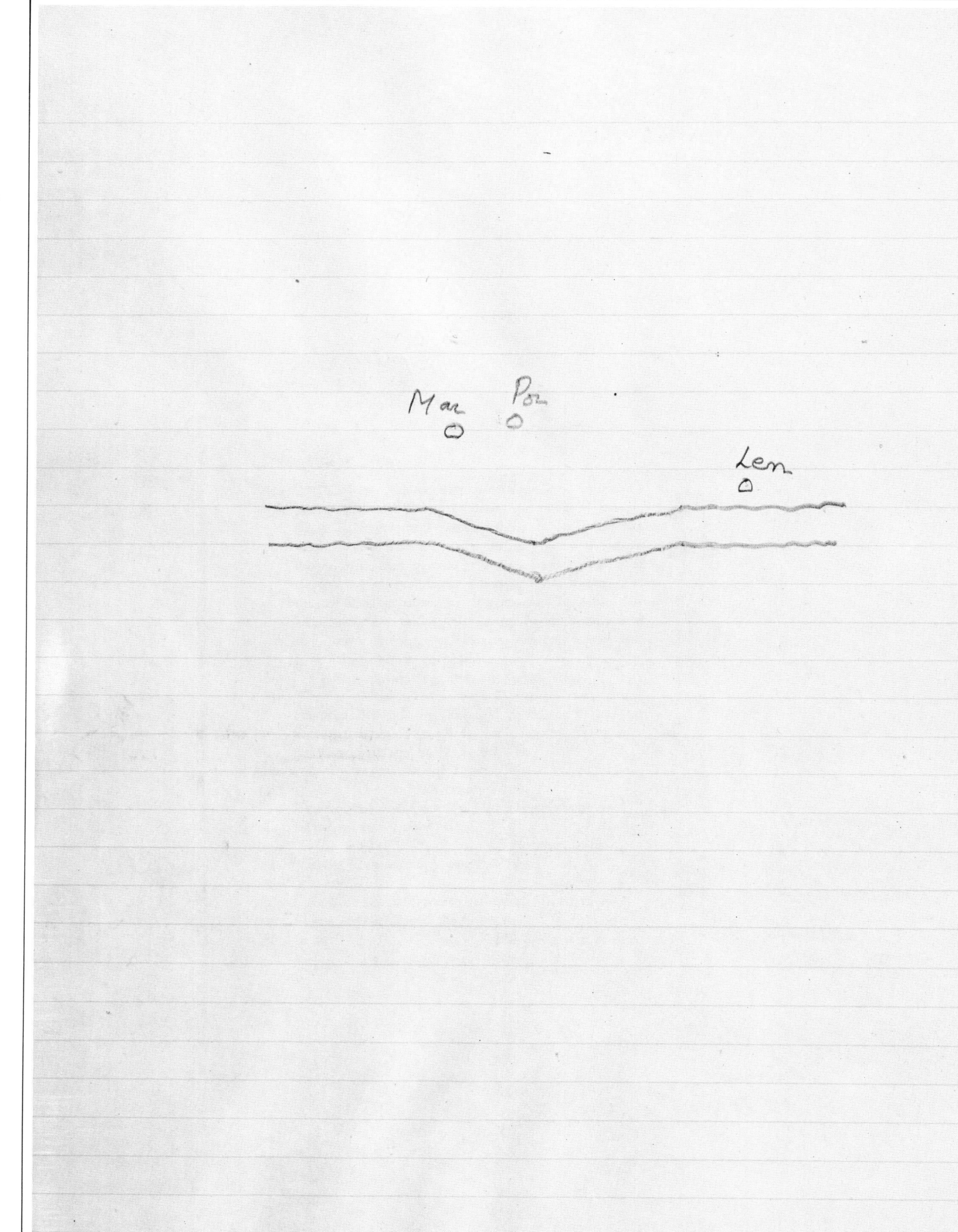
Mar
Por
Len

(34)

MACBETH

Macd. What three things does drink especially provoke?

Por. Marry, sir, nose-painting, sleep, and urine. Lechery, sir, it provokes and unprovokes; it provokes the desire, but it takes away the performance: therefore much drink may be said to be an equivocator with lechery: it makes him and it mars him; it sets him on and it takes him off; it persuades him and disheartens him; makes him stand to, and not stand to; in conclusion, equivocates him in a sleep, and giving him the lie, leaves him.

Macd. I believe drink gave thee the lie last night.

Por. That it did, sir, i' the very throat on me: but I requited him for his lie, and, I think, being too strong for him, though he took up my legs sometime, yet I made a shift to cast him.

Macd. Is thy master stirring?

Enter Macbeth

Our knocking has awak'd him; here he comes.

Len. Good morrow, noble sir.

Mac. Good morrow, both.

Macd. Is the king stirring, worthy thane?

Mac. Not yet.

Macd. He did command me to call timely on him;
I have almost slipp'd the hour.

Mac. I'll bring you to him.

34

Porter starts to go towards PS US steps

Turret door & comes down US PS steps

Porter exit C arch & OP

Macbeth enters. He has recovered his nerve; from now on until his second hallucination he is completely in command of the situation.

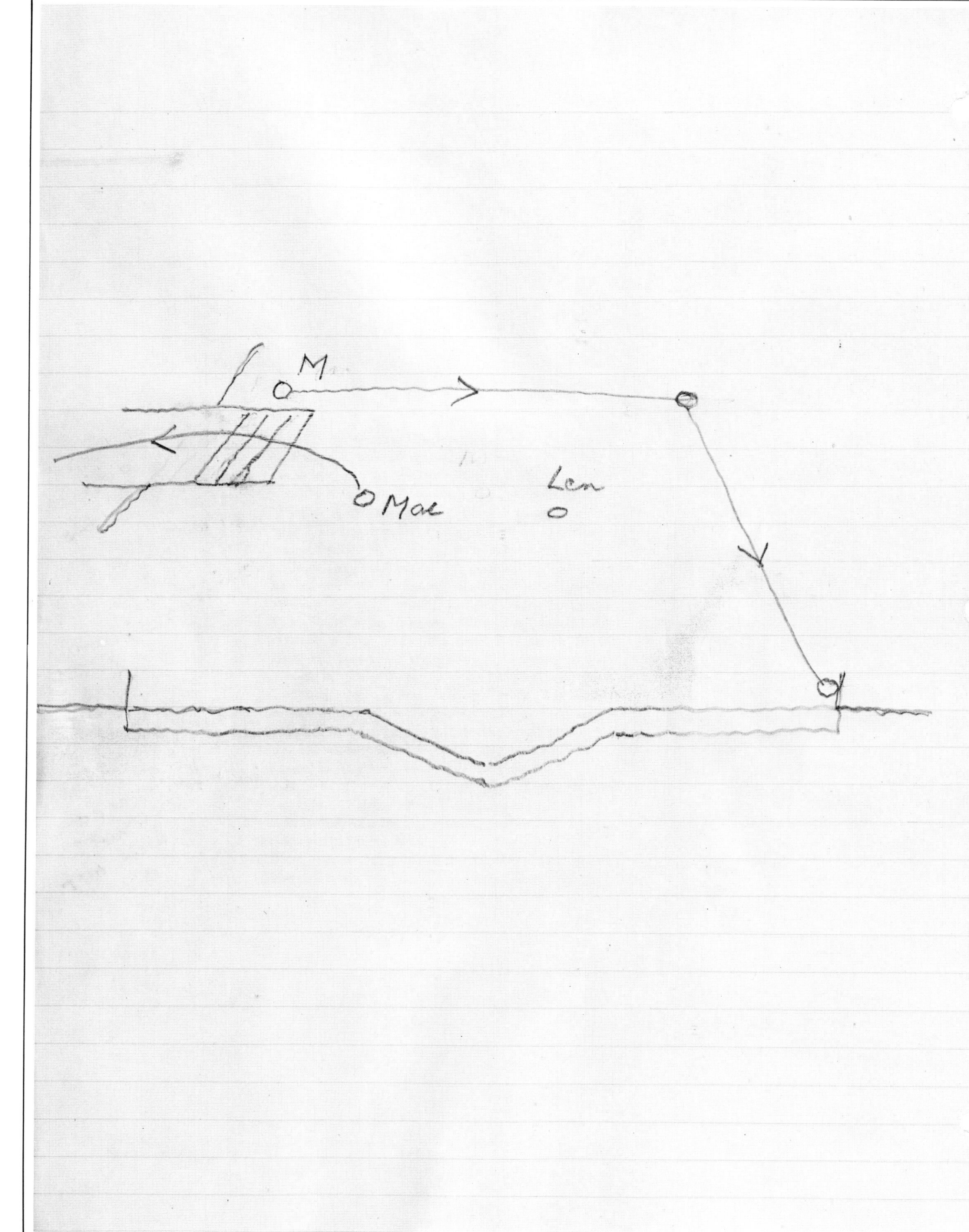

Macduff goes into the King's apartment; there are a few agonising moments of suspense which should seem like an eternity & then the appalling crime is discovered.

Macbeth, Act II, Scene iii

(35)

Macd. I know this is a joyful trouble to you;
But yet 'tis one.
Mac. The labour we delight in physics pain:
This is the door.
Macd. I 'll make so bold to call,
For 'tis my limited service. *Exit*
Len. Goes the king hence to-day?
Mac. He does: he did appoint so.
Len. The night has been unruly: where we lay,
Our chimneys were blown down, and, as they say,
Lamentings heard i' the air, strange screams of death,
And prophesying, with accents terrible,
Of dire combustion, and confus'd events,
New hatch'd to the woful time: the obscure bird
Clamour'd the livelong night: some say, the earth
Was feverous, and did shake.
Mac. 'Twas a rough night.
Len. My young remembrance cannot parallel
A fellow to it.

Re-enter Macduff

Macd. O horror, horror, horror! Tongue nor heart
Cannot conceive nor name thee.
Mac.
Len. } What 's the matter?
Macd. Confusion now hath made his masterpiece.

XS US of Mac to US of OP steps
OP doorway
Slight move US
moving to PS US of Len then DS to PS Pros
OP doorway & stands on steps

The whole castle is in an up-roar. The Alarum Bell crashes out & half-naked figures stand about in the Courtyard confused & terrified.

Lady Macbeth enters & tries to take command but she makes a dangerous mistake & begins to understand, for the first time, the horror that such a crime will have on the ordinary human beings around her.

1st Lady in Waiting Jill Dixon

2nd Lady in Waiting Ann Firbank

Two ladies who attend on Lady Macbeth, & go the the Royal Palace with her when she becomes Queen.

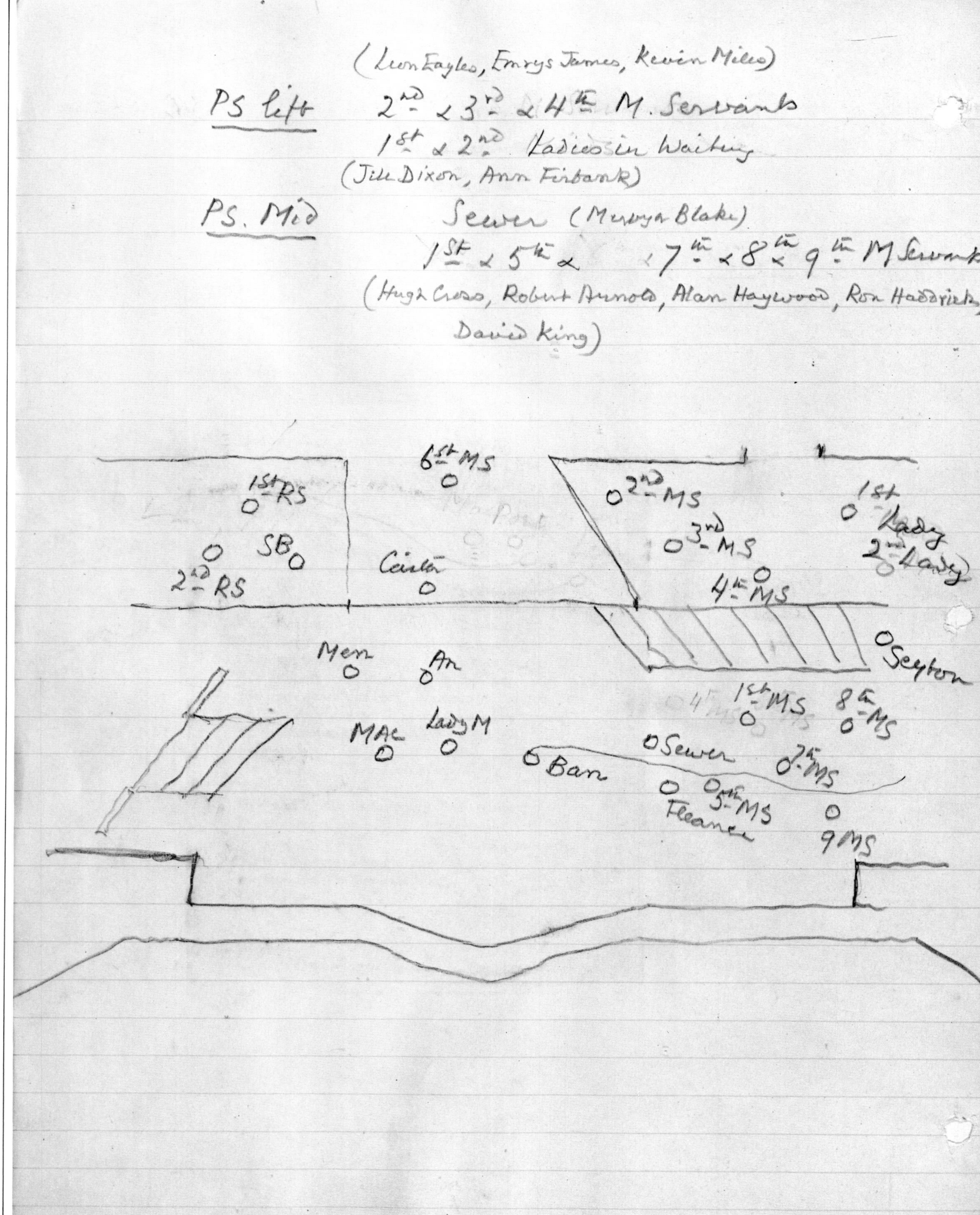

Macbeth, Act II, Scene iii

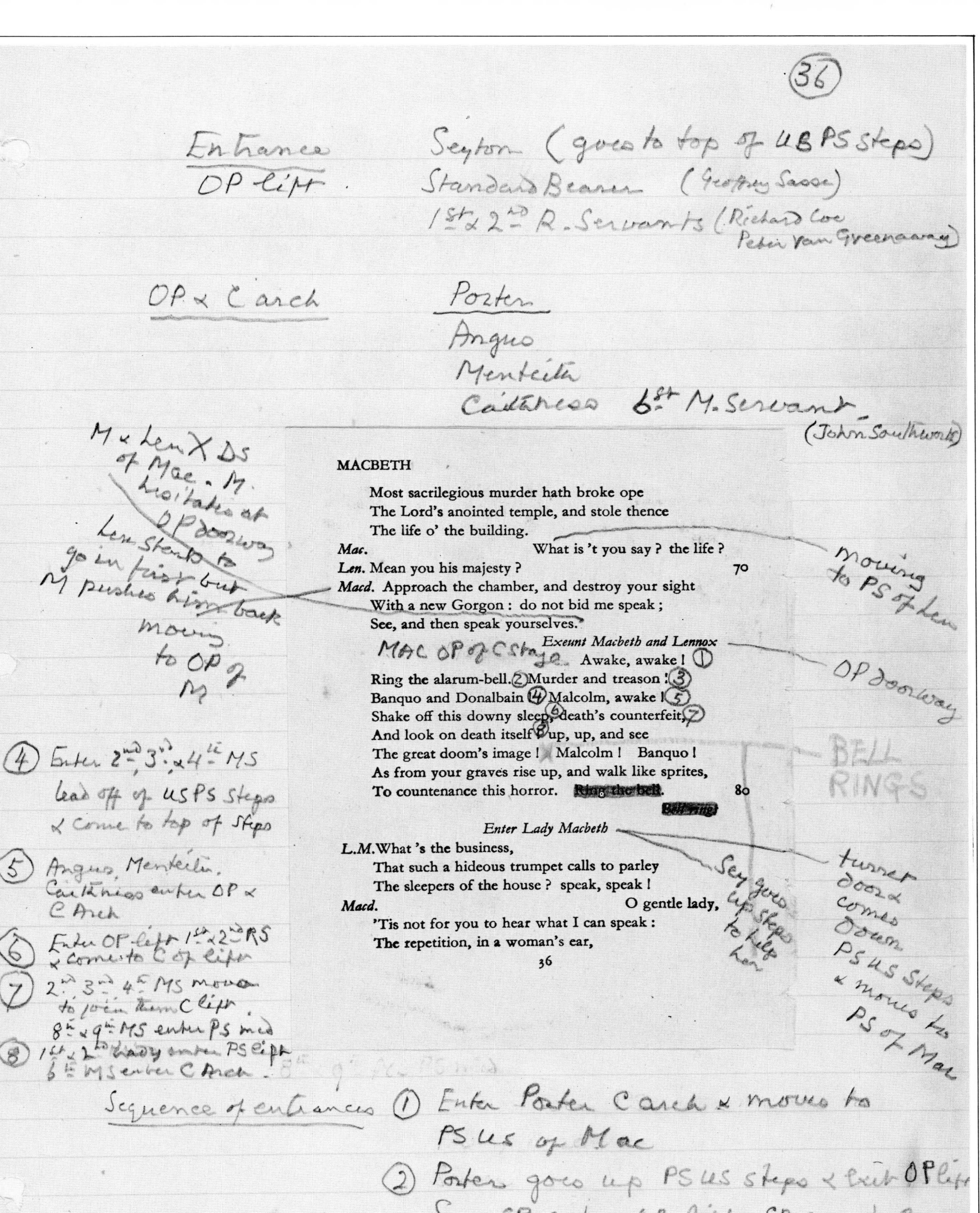

(36)

Entrance OP lift — Seyton (goes to top of USPS steps); Standard Bearer (Geoffrey Sasse); 1st & 2nd R. Servants (Richard Coe, Peter Van Greenaway)

OP & C arch — Porter; Angus; Menteith; Caithness; 6th M. Servant (John Southworth)

MACBETH

Most sacrilegious murder hath broke ope
The Lord's anointed temple, and stole thence
The life o' the building.

Mac. What is 't you say? the life?

Len. Mean you his majesty?

Macd. Approach the chamber, and destroy your sight
With a new Gorgon: do not bid me speak;
See, and then speak yourselves.

Exeunt Macbeth and Lennox

Awake, awake! (1)
Ring the alarum-bell. (2) Murder and treason! (3)
Banquo and Donalbain (4) Malcolm, awake! (5)
Shake off this downy sleep, (6) death's counterfeit, (7)
And look on death itself (8) up, up, and see
The great doom's image! Malcolm! Banquo!
As from your graves rise up, and walk like sprites,
To countenance this horror. ~~Ring the bell.~~

Bell rings

Enter Lady Macbeth

L.M. What 's the business,
That such a hideous trumpet calls to parley
The sleepers of the house? speak, speak!

Macd. O gentle lady,
'Tis not for you to hear what I can speak:
The repetition, in a woman's ear,

36

M & Len X DS of Mac. M. hesitates at OP doorway. Len starts to go in first but M pushes him back moving to OP of M

MAC OP of C stage

moving to PS of Len

OP doorway

BELL RINGS

turret door & comes down PS US steps & moves to PS of Mac

Sey goes up steps to help her

(4) Enter 2nd, 3rd & 4th MS lead off of USPS steps & come to top of steps

(5) Angus, Menteith, Caithness enter OP & C Arch

(6) Enter OP lift 1st & 2nd RS & come to C of lift

(7) 2nd 3rd 4th MS move to join them C lift. 8th & 9th MS enter PS mid

(8) 1st & 2nd Lady enter PS lift, 6th MS enter C Arch.

Sequence of entrances (1) Enter Porter C arch & moves to PS US of Mac

(2) Porter goes up PS US steps & exit OP lift. Sey & SB enter OP lift. SB goes to C of lift, Sey goes to half way down US PS steps

(3) Sewer 1st 5th & 7th MS enter PS mid

Macbeth, Act II, Scene iii

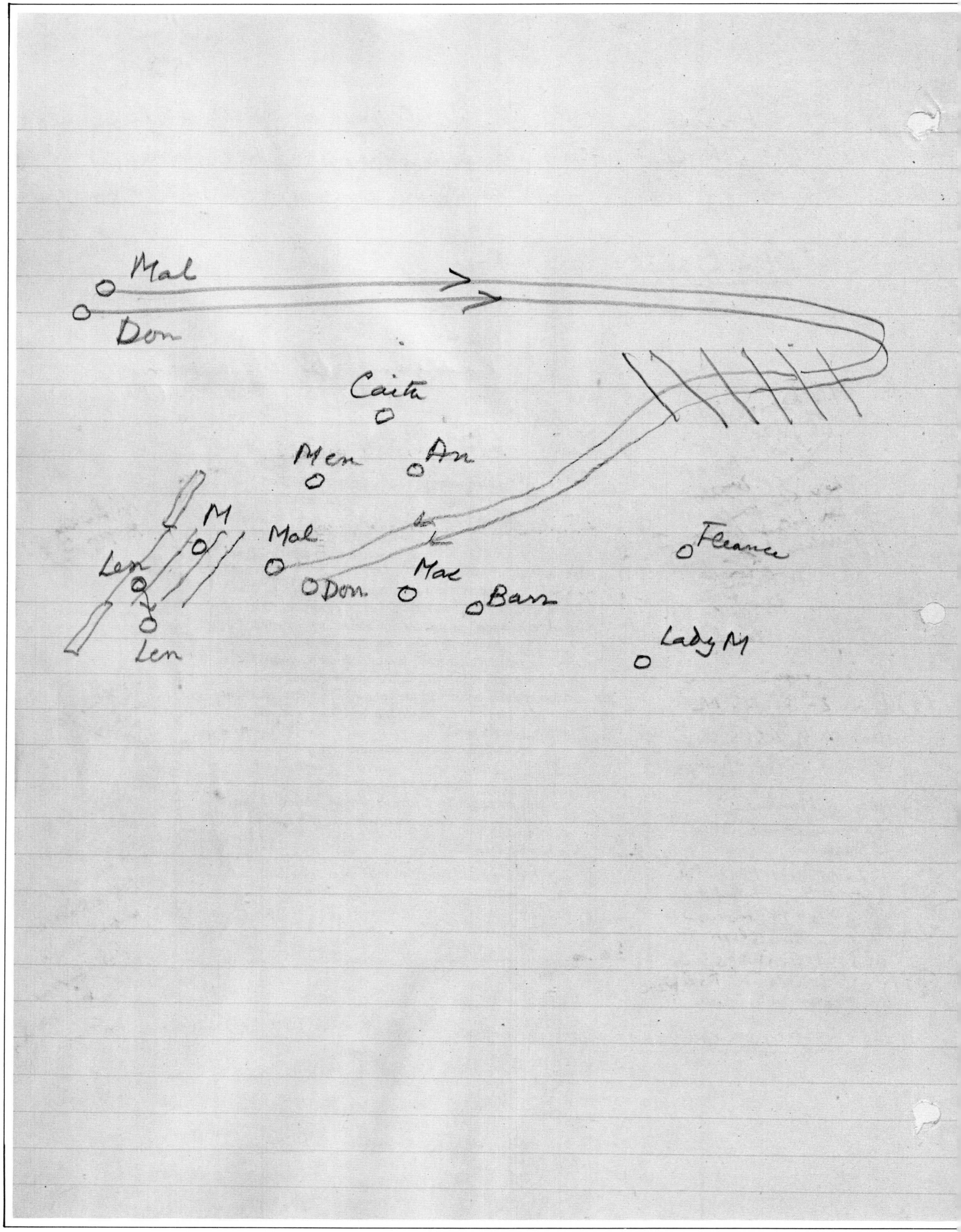

Suddenly Macbeth comes back from the King's apartment & the white faces staring out of the darkness are focused on him. Everyone is completely silent. The alarum bell stops. What he says is not insincere. It is, as if for the moment, he loathes the murder as much as anyone present.

Act II Sc. iii

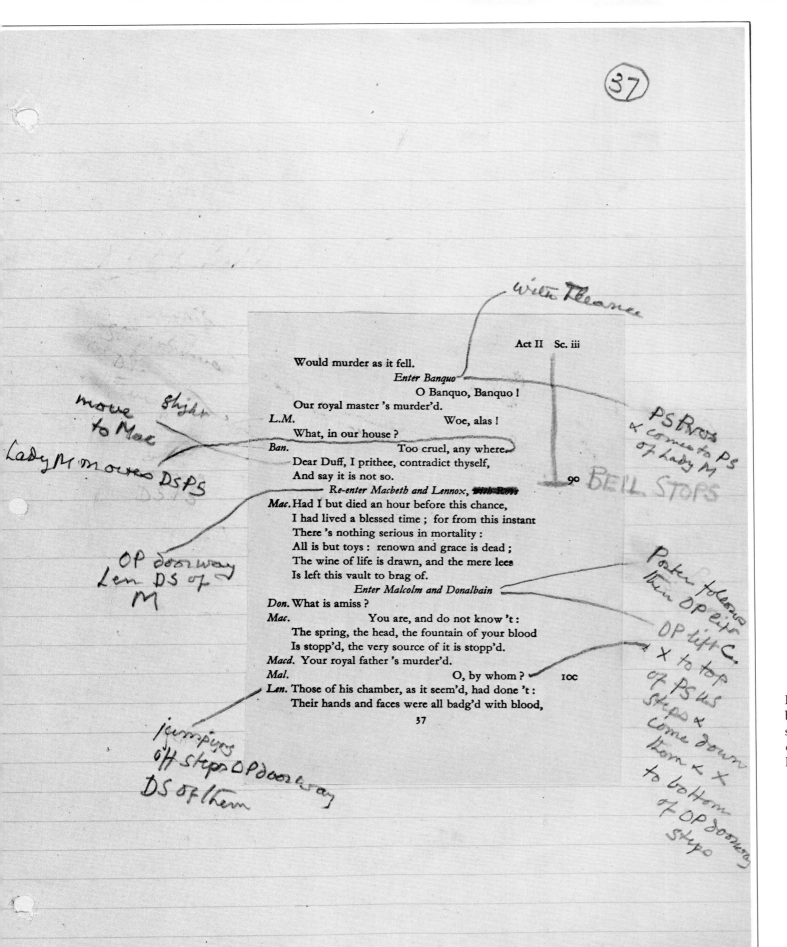

Would murder as it fell.

Enter Banquo

O Banquo, Banquo!
Our royal master 's murder'd.

L.M. Woe, alas!
What, in our house?

Ban. Too cruel, any where.
Dear Duff, I prithee, contradict thyself,
And say it is not so.

Re-enter Macbeth and Lennox, ~~with Ross~~

Mac. Had I but died an hour before this chance,
I had lived a blessed time; for from this instant
There 's nothing serious in mortality:
All is but toys: renown and grace is dead;
The wine of life is drawn, and the mere lees
Is left this vault to brag of.

Enter Malcolm and Donalbain

Don. What is amiss?

Mac. You are, and do not know 't:
The spring, the head, the fountain of your blood
Is stopp'd, the very source of it is stopp'd.

Macd. Your royal father 's murder'd.

Mal. O, by whom?

Len. Those of his chamber, as it seem'd, had done 't:
Their hands and faces were all badg'd with blood,

37

The Royal Princes Malcolm & Donalbain come into the Courtyard, bewildered & terrified. The focus is suddenly switched on to them. Macbeth chooses this moment to tell how he has killed the Grooms.

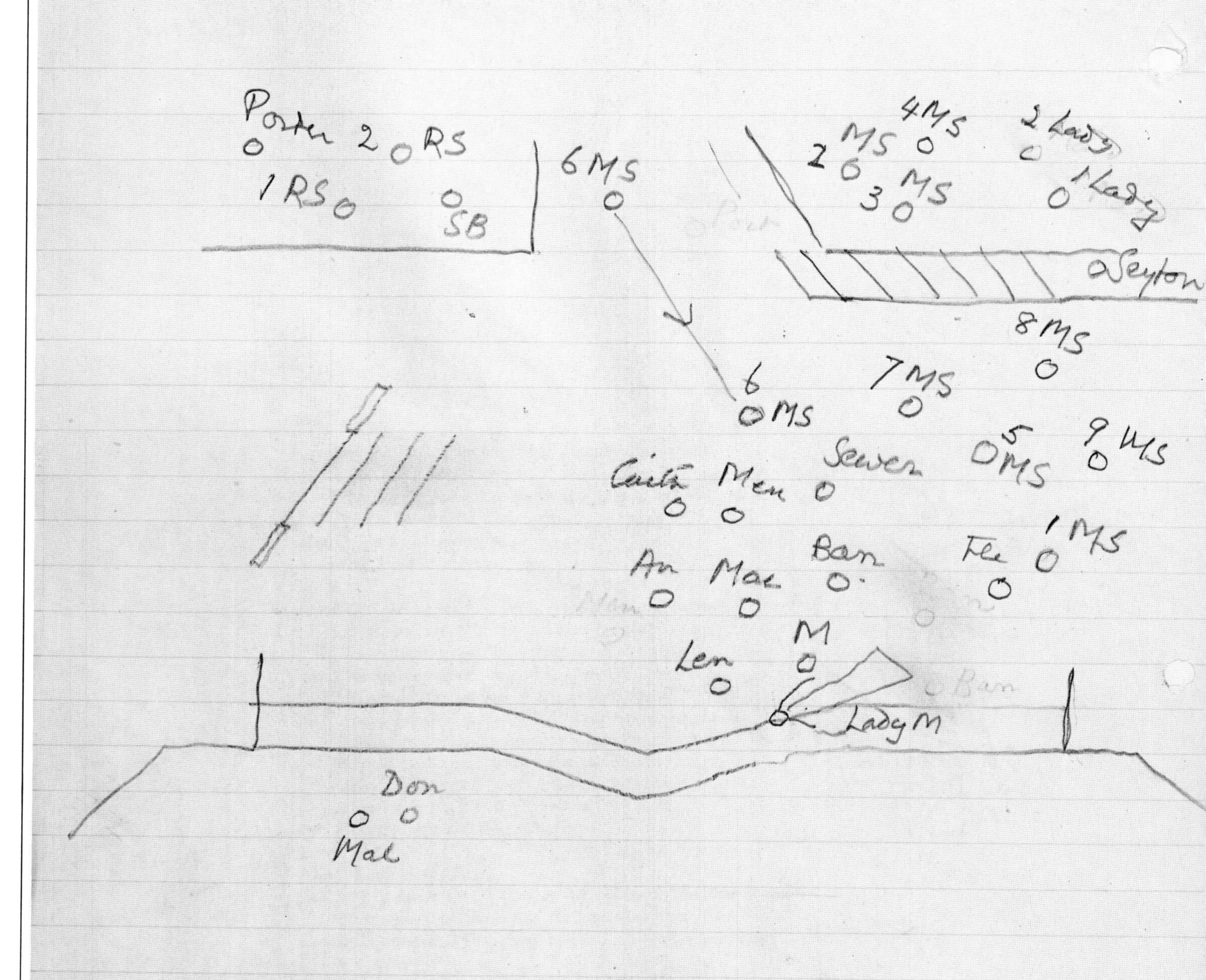
Porter 2 RS
1 RS
SB
6 MS
4 MS
MS
2
3
MS
2 Lady
1 Lady
Seyton
8 MS
6
MS
7 MS
5
MS
9 MS
Sewer
Caith
Men
Ban
1 MS
An
Mac
Fle
M
Len
Lady M
Don
Mal

MACBETH

So were their daggers, which unwip'd we found
Upon their pillows :
They star'd, and were distracted ; no man's life
Was to be trusted with them.
Mac. O, yet I dò repent me of my fury,
That I did kill them.
Macd. Wherefore did you so ?
Mac. Who can be wise, amaz'd, temperate, and furious,
Loyal, and neutral, in a moment ? No man :
The expedition of my violent love
Outran the pauser, reason. Here lay Duncan,
His silver skin lac'd with his golden blood,
And his gash'd stabs look'd like a breach in nature
For ruin's wasteful entrance : there the murderers,
Steep'd in the colours of their trade ; their daggers
Unmannerly breech'd with gore : who could refrain,
That had a heart to love, and in that heart
Courage to make 's love known ?
L.M. Help me hence, ho !
Macd. Look to the lady.
Mal. (*aside to Don.*) Why do we hold our tongues,
That most may claim this argument for ours ?
Don. (*aside to Mal.*) What should be spoken here, where our fate,
Hid in an auger-hole, may rush, and seize us ?

38

moving down off steps & coming to PS of C Stage

She staggers forward

Macbeth L lifts her up & she recovers slowly

positions as shown on opposite page

(Lady M moves to PS Pros arch) turns to Mac she faints on top of C steps PS.

He almost takes a ghastly pleasure in describing the horror of the scene in full detail. His wife cannot stand the strain & she loses consciousness. Immediately, the focus, if not suspicion, centre on her. Her husband goes to her at once & as she recovers they are face to face with the knowledge of their guilt & surrounded by those strained, white faces peering at them out of the darkness.

Act II, Scene iii. "Look to the Lady." Trader Faulkner (Malcolm), Ian Holm (Donalbain), James Grout (Lennox, kneeling, white shirt), Keith Michell (Macduff), John Springett (Angus, wearing mantle), Sir Laurence Olivier (Macbeth), Vivien Leigh (Lady Macbeth), Ralph Michael (Banquo, with beard), Gabriel Woolf (Caithness, barefoot), Paul Vieyra (Fleance), Lee Montague (Seyton, kneeling), others unidentified (see following pages).

The Royal Princes begin to panic.

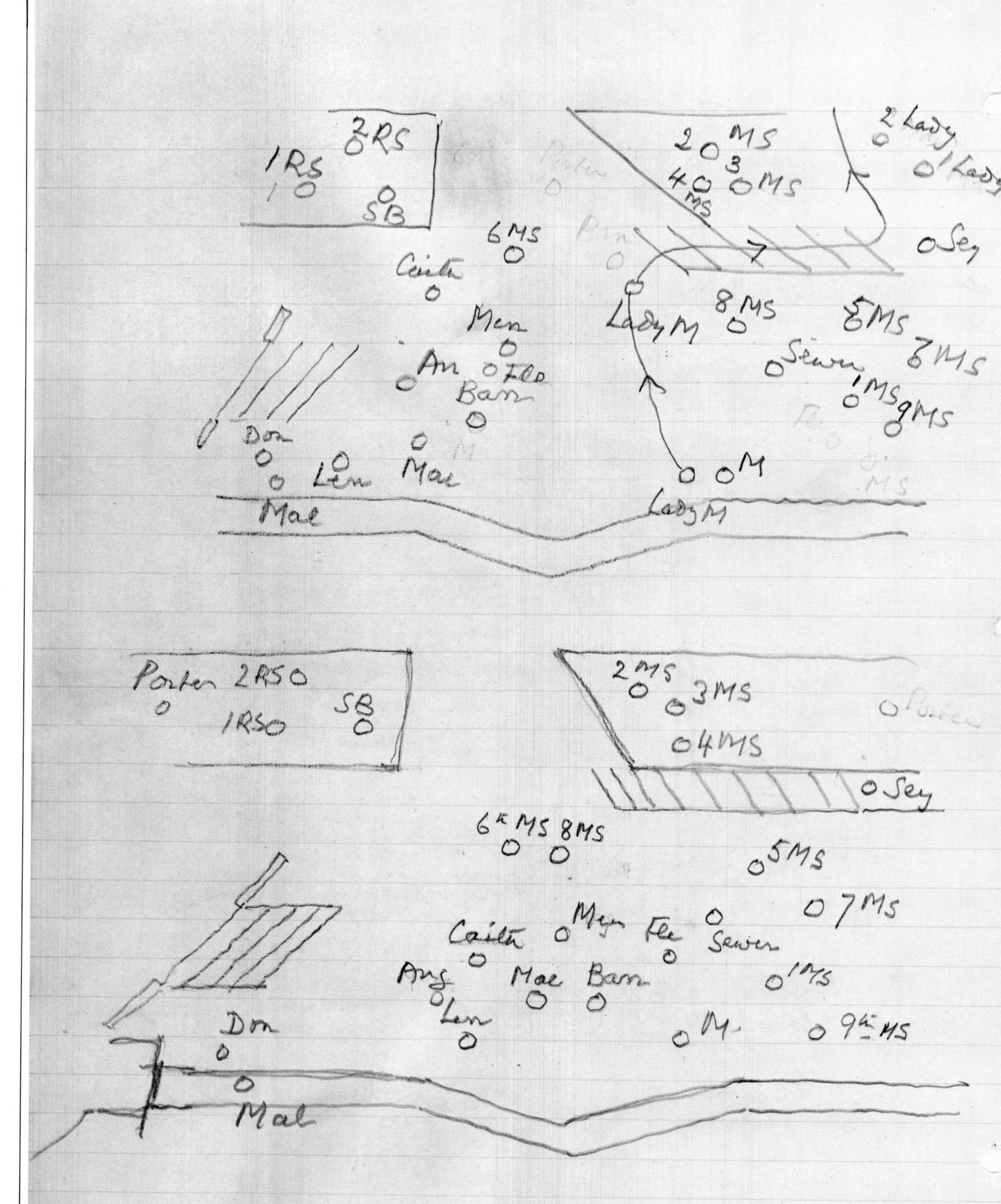

Macbeth, Act II, Scene iii

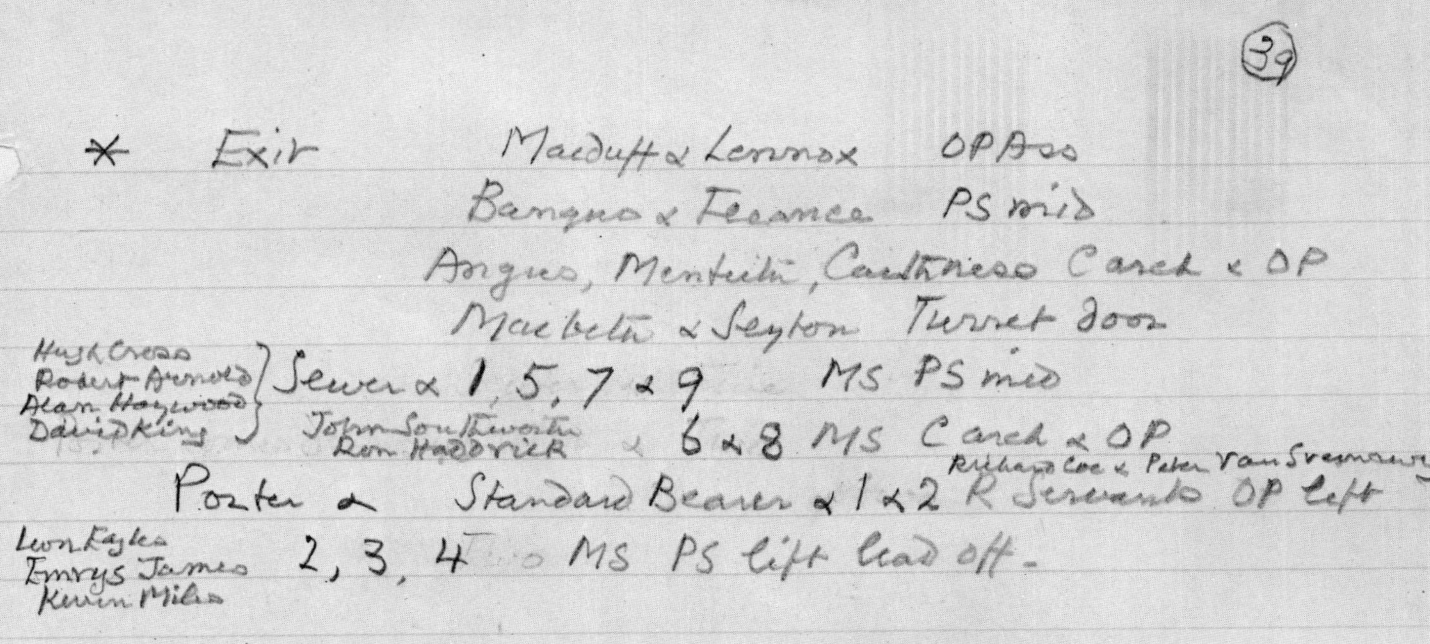

39

* Exit Macduff & Lennox OP Ass

Banquo & Fleance PS mid

Angus, Menteith, Caithness C arch & OP

Macbeth & Seyton Turret door

Hugh Cross, Robert Arnold, Alan Haywood, David King } Sewer & 1, 5, 7 & 9 MS PS mid

John Southworth, Don Hadrick & 6 & 8 MS C arch & OP

Porter & Standard Bearer & 1 & 2 R Servants OP left (Richard Coe & Peter van Greenaway)

Leon Eagles, Emrys James, Kevin Miles 2, 3, 4 MS PS left lead off.

Act II Sc. iii

Let 's away ;
Our tears are not yet brew'd.

Mal. (*aside to Don.*) Nor our strong sorrow
Upon the foot of motion.

Ban. Look to the lady :

Lady Macbeth ~~*is carried out*~~ goes up PS US steps & exit Turret door assisted by two ladies

And when we have our naked frailties hid,
That suffer in exposure, let us meet,
And question this most bloody piece of work,
To know it further. Fears and scruples shake us :
In the great hand of God I stand, and thence
Against the undivulg'd pretence I fight
Of treasonous malice.

Macd. And so do I.

All. So all.

Mac. Let 's briefly put on manly readiness,
And meet i' the hall together.

~~*All.*~~ BAN. Well contented.

* *Exeunt all but Malcolm and Donalbain* — Don moves C looking US.

Mal. What will you do ? Let 's not consort with them : — moves to OP of Don
To show an unfelt sorrow is an office
Which the false man does easy. I 'll to England.

Don. To Ireland, I ; our separated fortune
Shall keep us both the safer : where we are,
There 's daggers in men's smiles : the near in blood,

39

Lady Macbeth is helped to her own apartments & Banquo takes charge & calls for a conference of all the chieftains. It is agreed that they put on "manly readiness" & meet in the hall.

The Princes are left alone. They realise the danger of their position & being young & inexperienced they do the worst possible thing & decide to fly the country.

An old hermit & Ross enter. The old man is deeply religious & knows that a terrible thing has happened, & that God is angry.

Old Man. 80 [years old].
John MacGregor.

An old hermit. There is something wise & detached about him. I think that he lives entirely alone in the highlands & only comes to the Castle because he has had a presentiment that something terrible has happened.

MACBETH

The nearer bloody.
Mal. This murderous shaft that 's shot
Hath not yet lighted, and our safest way
Is to avoid the aim. Therefore to horse;
And let us not be dainty of leave-taking,
But shift away: there 's warrant in that theft
Which steals itself, when there 's no mercy left.
Exeunt

Enter Macbeth from Turret door. He sees them going. Moves to C of lift then comes down UP PS steps.

Catch & OP.

Ban enter PS Pros as M is at bottom of steps They look at each other & exit OP Ass.

LAMENT *Enter Ross with an old Man*

PS Ass.

Old Man. Threescore and ten I can remember well,
Within the volume of which time I have seen
Hours dreadful and things strange: but this sore
night
Hath trifled former knowings.
Ross. Ah, good father,
Thou seest the heavens, as troubled with man's act,
Threatens his bloody stage: by the clock 'tis day,
And yet dark night strangles the travelling lamp:
Is 't night's predominance, or the day's shame,
That darkness does the face of earth entomb
When living light should kiss it?

moving to PS of Old man

Looking up at the sky

40

As they go Macbeth sees them & realises that he can plant the crime on them.

As he goes into the hall he meets Banquo. Nothing is said.

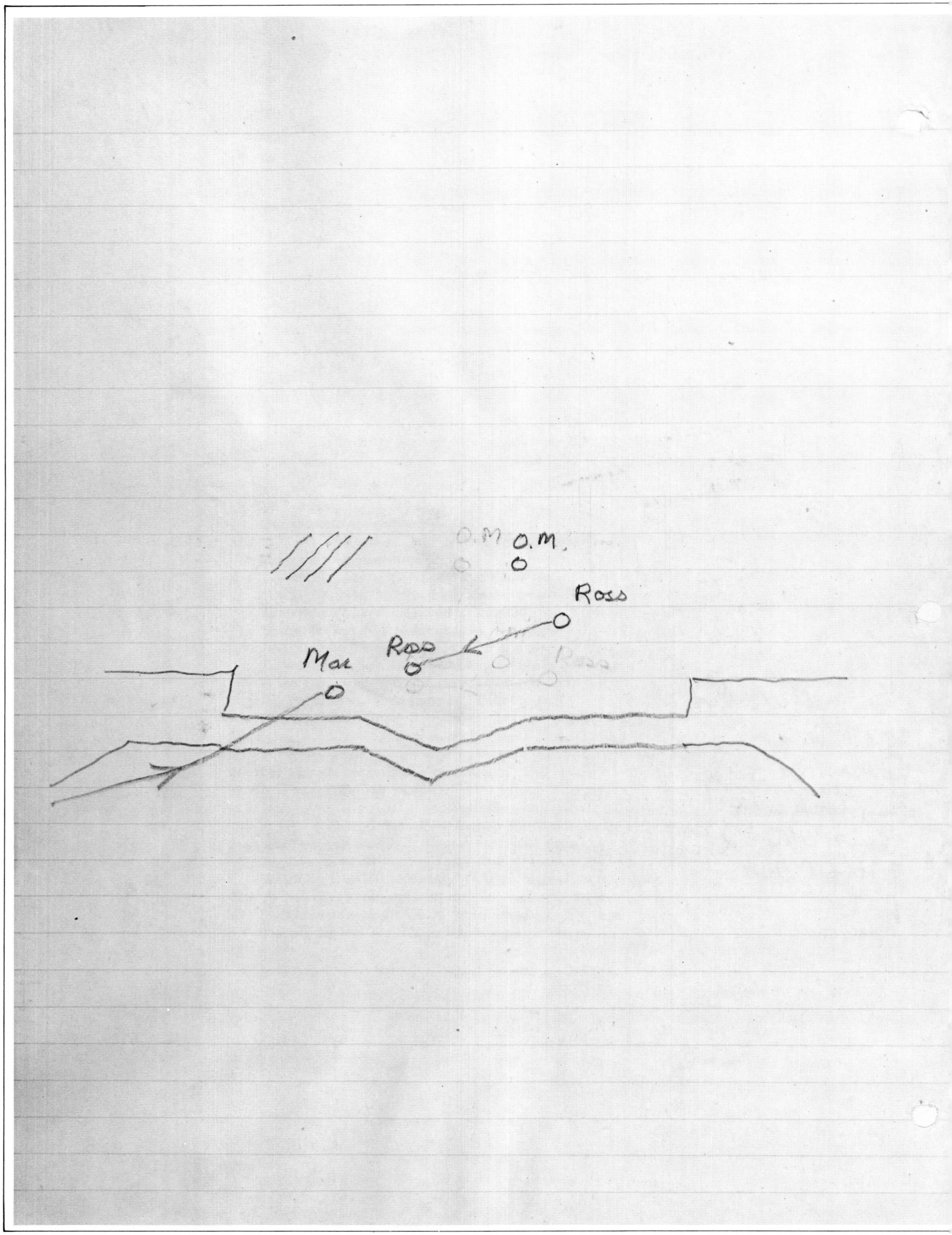

Macduff comes from the conference. Macbeth has been chosen as the next King. The Powers of Evil seem to have triumphed, but Macduff has already decided that he won't go to the Coronation. The fight between evil & good has started.

moving US to look at OP doorway

Old Man. 'Tis unnatural,
Even like the deed that 's done. On Tuesday last,
A falcon towering in her pride of place
Was by a mousing owl hawk'd at, and kill'd.
Ross. And Duncan's horses (a thing most strange and certain)
Beauteous, and swift, the minions of their race,
Turn'd wild in nature, broke their stalls, flung out,
Contending 'gainst obedience, as they would
Make war with mankind.
Old Man. 'Tis said they ate each other.
Ross. They did so; to the amazement of mine eyes,
That look'd upon 't.

turning to look PS Aso

Enter Macduff

OP Aso

Here comes the good Macduff.
How goes the world, sir, now?
Macd. Why, see you not?
Ross. Is 't known who did this more than bloody deed?
Macd. Those that Macbeth hath slain.
Ross. Alas, the day!
What good could they pretend?
Macd. They were suborn'd:
Malcolm and Donalbain, the king's two sons,
Are stol'n away and fled, which puts upon them
Suspicion of the deed.

XS in front of Old man

21 e

(42)

MACBETH

Ross. 'Gainst nature still:
Thriftless ambition, that wilt ravin up
Thine own lives' means! Then 'tis most like
The sovereignty will fall upon Macbeth.
Macd. He is already nam'd, and gone to Scone
To be invested.
Ross. Where is Duncan's body?
Macd. Carried to Colme-kill,
The sacred storehouse of his predecessors,
And guardian of their bones.
Ross. Will you to Scone?
Macd. No, cousin, I'll to Fife.
Ross. Well, I will thither.
Macd. Well, may you see things well done there: adieu
Lest our old robes sit easier than our new!
Ross. Farewell, father.
Old Man. God's benison go with you, and with those
That would make good of bad and friends of foes!
~~Exeunt~~

turning to look at OP Ass

X s in front of R & OM & exit PS Ass

Ross exit OP Ass

turns & walks slowly US towards C arch as Curtain falls

SLOW CURTAIN

42

END OF PART I

Macbeth, Act II, Scene iv

PART II (III, i to III, iv; v and vi, omitted). 26:00

Scene 1 (III, i and ii), Palace Scene. 10:30.

During the fourteen-minute interval, behind the curtain stagehands strike the Courtyard set and set up the Palace, changing the heights of the lifts, moving rostrums and wings, flying cloths and borders in, and setting up the palace frame (see theatre plans, p. 14). This set was used for Macbeth's presence chamber and banquet hall, Banquo's murder being played on the forestage in front of the runners, while stagehands brought in the banquet furniture and props.

The houselights dim to blackout, and before the curtain rises, trumpets ring out, announcing the coming of Macbeth as King. Banquo comes on and, as the trumpets grow nearer, he sums up his suspicions. Then with a flourish of trumpets, the King and Queen enter, leading a train of courtiers. Banquo and Fleance kneel. The Court is magnificent: Macbeth now wears Duncan's crown, his gold embossed belt, a green tunic and breeches, a red cloak and a plum velvet drape; Lady Macbeth, also crowned, now wears green satin, her bracelets are jewelled, and over her shoulders she wears a blue and gold tweed cloak, lined in red shot with gold. Where before Lady Macbeth was active, Macbeth slow to move, they have now changed. She sits in state while Macbeth moves among the courtiers, questioning Banquo, who backs away slightly, as the courtiers look on. One senses a greater vigor in this King than in Duncan, who let others speak for him. Seyton, who "watches his master like a dog," jumps to his side when the others leave, and goes to fetch the murderers. Alone, Macbeth reveals the private doubts and fears that press him to action. When the murderers come, "ruthless, callous, and cruel"; he goes down to them, Seyton standing to one side. Richard David describes their meeting:

> The murderers, half-scared, half-fascinated by the now evil magnetism of the King. shrank back each time he approached them in a swirl of robes, while he, pacing the stage between and around them continuously spun a web of bewildering words about their understandings, about his own conscience, about the crime that between them they were to commit.

When they agree, Macbeth "moves close to them," as if actually to embrace them. Seyton leads them out, and Macbeth follows. Into the empty throne room comes Lady Macbeth, followed by a watchful Seyton, whom she sends to call Macbeth. She stands between the thrones, flanked by the symbols of kingship, then sits just before Macbeth comes in to join her. His dark grimace and menacing words, his writhing as he sits on his throne, and Lady Macbeth's frail, worried look clash with the ease and dignity represented by their crowns, by their royal robes, and by the seat of state. As a dramatic image, the scene demonstrates what others report—Macbeth's physical discomfort with the trappings of kingship. Through his obliquity in speech and the aversion of his eyes, we see enacted the estrangement that now isolates him from his wife. While they confer, the lights begin to fade, so that, when Macbeth says that light thickens, it actually has grown nearly dark. They step deeper into the gloom, "his arm around her," as the lights fade to blackout.

Scene 2 (III, iii), Banquo's Murder Scene. 1:30.

As the runners close, the clock begins to strike, and the murderers come in, accompanied by Seyton, who is the third murderer (thus solving the old conundrum about his identity). From offstage comes the thudding of horses' hooves. Tense, the murderers "draw their daggers." Banquo and Fleance come in downstage right, and the murderers set on them from behind, one dousing Fleance's torch, the other two stabbing Banquo with their daggers.

Scene 3 (III, iv), Banquet Scene. 9:00.

After the murderers rush off with Banquo's corpse, trumpets sound, and the runners part to reveal the Banquet Hall. In the great vaulted hall where Macbeth had earlier held his court there are now tables laden with food, royal servants with torches stand ready to serve. The company assembles as the trumpets ring out. The Queen sits on her throne. The King, his arms open wide, signals his guests to take their places. It is as if we have entered that banquet hall that earlier appeared to be just offstage right, and Macbeth's vision of himself as King has been fulfilled. He wears Duncan's crown, he sits in his seat of power, and the guests await his command. Even as we gaze, however, the idealized *tableau vivant* begins to shift. Unlike Duncan, who held himself back, Macbeth descends to mix with his company. The others are seated, only he stands. Seyton comes, and draws him aside downstage, away from his guests. Like the asymmetrical setting with its oblique angles and its oddly shaped furniture, things are awry from the start: the empty throne, the absent host, the servant with blood on his face. Lady Macbeth senses the tension in the guests, calls her husband back, and one of the Lords offers him a seat. He instead ascends the royal dais to propose a toast. Strange music, a dimmer light, and the hunched figure on the stool straightens up. Facing the guests and the audience, Macbeth backs up the steps to the throne. The Ghost grows brighter, its bloodied head and pale shoulders picked out by spotlights, and Macbeth flees from it around the table (see Shaw's stage map, p. 144). "Ghost turns on stool & follows him round with eyes." Lady Macbeth rises, the guests stir and start to get up, then, sitting at her command, they watch her taunt Macbeth, who looks in terror at the Ghost. Order has departed. The thrones are both empty, the King has gone mad, and the Queen cannot bring him out of it. The Ghost rises, as if summoned by Macbeth's frenzied question, "Prithee, see here! behold! look! lo! how say you?" It walks toward him, and he cringes downstage away from it, as it passes between him and Lady Macbeth, and thence offstage. The Queen backs away "with her eye on Lords," who "turn and look at Macbeth" while he speaks of blood that hath been shed ere now. Slowly, he calms down and goes back to the table.

The tension begins to build again at once. He goes back to the empty stool, "turns with cup to Sewer" to renew the toast. They all rise and drink. Again strange music sounds, and again the Ghost appears, standing this time between the two empty thrones. Macbeth turns to sit and sees the Ghost. The cup falls from his hand. He backs away from the Ghost. Lady Macbeth goes to him, soothing, trying to reassure her guests. "M pushes her aside," and, shouting, he rushes at the Ghost, leaping on the table amidst the clatter of tableware, shouting at it, sweeping his scarlet cloak up in front of him to hide from it. As if by magic, the Ghost sinks from sight, obeying Macbeth's command: "Unreal mockery, hence!" Although Macbeth tries to smooth things over, Lady Macbeth brusquely dismisses the guests, who file out, attended by the servants. King and Queen are alone in the Banquet Hall, the ruins of the feast scattered around the table. Macbeth first sits on the stool—

as if proving to himself that he can. She leans across the table to him, then he circles around it to stop next to her at the throne steps, looking and thinking. He leaves her. She "sinks down on her knees leaning against the King's throne," then begins to move up the stairs as the curtain falls.

As the audience went out for the interval, they took with them powerful visual images, carefully composed by Shaw, depicting Macbeth's ruined kingship: the empty thrones with the hideous Ghost between them, the frozen terror of the guests, Macbeth's frenzied leap up onto the table, and the desolation of the empty hall, the wasted wine and meat. Behind these images lies a solution to the scene's practical problems of blocking: how to manage the Ghost's entries and exits, and how to properly direct attention from the Ghost to Macbeth, thence to the guests and to Lady Macbeth without having one point of focus obscure others. To bring the Ghost on and off, Shaw used a trap, shielded by the table. And, making virtue of necessity, he made the Ghost's first exit a demonstration of its invisibility to Lady Macbeth and of its visible terror for Macbeth as it passed between the two.

We need to see not only the Ghost, however, but also Macbeth's reaction to it, and, in turn, the reactions of his wife and of the guests. By moving Macbeth, Lady Macbeth, and the Ghost, Shaw keeps the guests always in view. Macbeth's reaction is clearly seen because he is upstage of the Ghost when it first appears, and he is clearly heard because he moves down to the forestage in terror, thereby permitting us to see the Ghost as it turns and also drawing his wife to his side, where their speech is semiprivate, and more credible than if shouted to Macbeth from her throne. At the same time, Macbeth's violent running and leaping—particularly the leap up onto the table—sets off another display of theatrical fireworks (like the alarums, the shouting, and running when Duncan's murder is discovered), and it releases the tension that has been building since the act began.

[Banquo] is the first person, I think, to suspect the truth about the murder of Duncan, but he says nothing. Why? Is it out of loyalty to his friend, or fear of the consequences, or because he feels that he is, to quite a considerable degree, mixed up in the business? Judging by what he says, first in the Courtyard just before the murder & secondly when he is entirely alone in the throne room waiting for Macbeth & his wife, now King & Queen, to enter, I think his silence about the Witches is mostly on account of his own interest in the future of the Crown. In which case he is a guilty man & to some extent gets what he deserves.

I don't think that it is possible to believe that he remains silent only out of friendship for Macbeth; & if it is fear that prevents him from telling the truth, & he is completely honest, then he could leave the country.

Of course he is not a villain but is not a simple honest man either. He has his own particular form of ambition.

Macbeth, Act III, Scene i

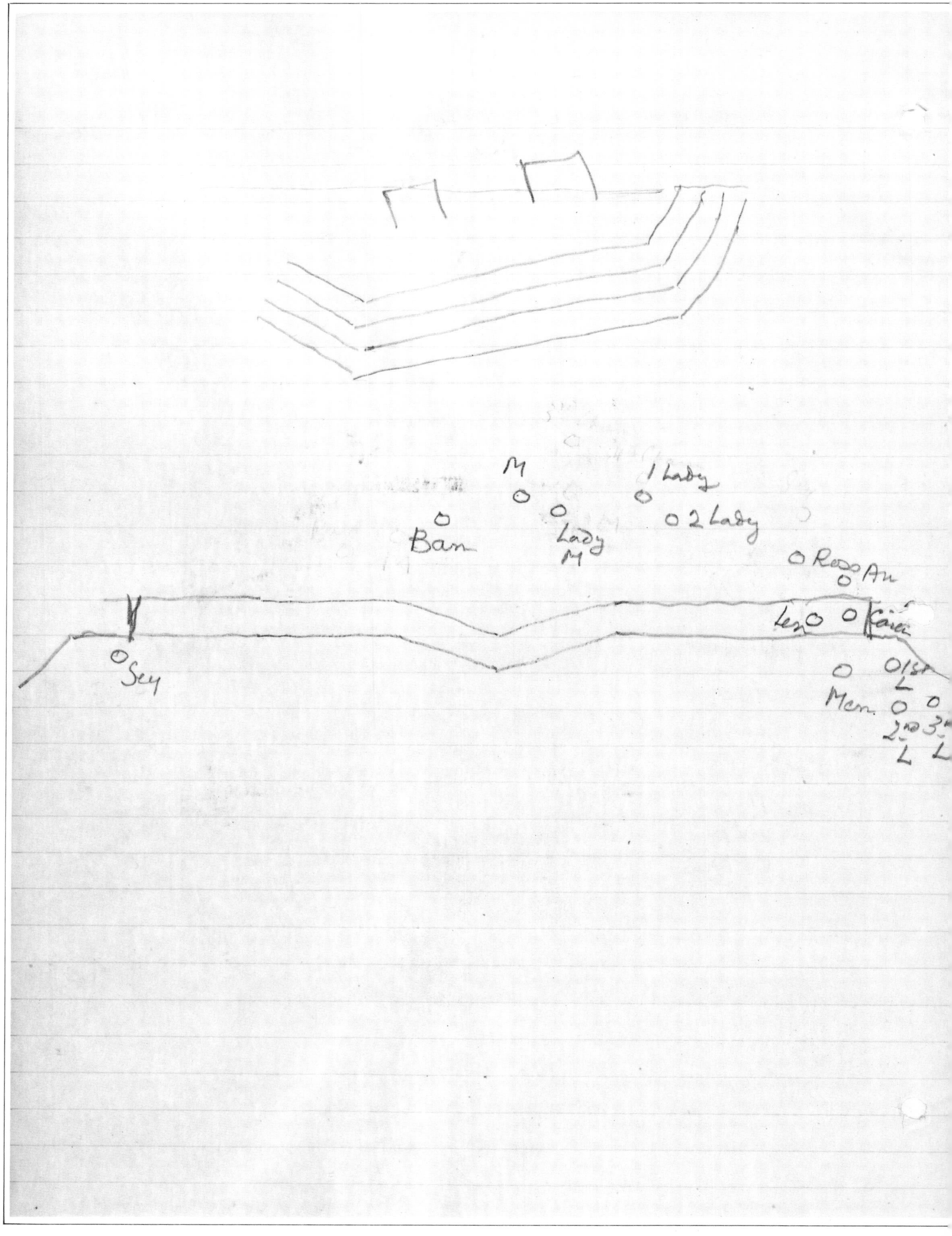

* Order of entrance Scyton OP Ass & stands on Front Steps OP
PS Ass Macbeth & Lady Macbeth
1st & 2nd Ladies
Ross, Angus, Lennox, Menteith
Caithness, 1st, 2nd, & 3rd Lords.

HOUSE LIGHTS FADE OUT

TRUMPETS CURTAIN UP

TRUMPETS in distance

TRUMPETS nearer

PART II

~~Act Third~~

SCENE I ~~[struck out]~~ Palace 5PM

Forres. The palace

~~Enter~~ *Banquo*

Ban. Thou hast it now, king, Cawdor, Glamis, all,
As the weird women promis'd, and I fear
Thou play'dst most foully for 't: yet it was said
It should not stand in thy posterity,
But that myself should be the root and father
Of many kings. If there come truth from them,
As upon thee, Macbeth, their speeches shine,
Why, by the verities on thee made good,
May they not be my oracles as well
And set me up in hope? But hush, no more.

* *Sennet sounded. Enter Macbeth, as king, Lady Macbeth, as queen, Lennox, Ross,* ~~*Lords*~~, ~~*Ladies*~~, *and* ~~*Attendants*~~ 3rd, 4th Angus Menteith Caith Chamberlains 1, 2, 3 Lords

Mac. Here 's our chief guest.
L.M. If he had been forgotten,
It had been as a gap in our great feast,
And all-thing unbecoming.
Mac. To-night we hold a solemn supper, sir,

43

Standing PS of C stage looking at thrones. He hears trumpets & turns to look towards PS Ass moving OP DS

Ban kisses M hand then Lady M's hand

Palace Scene. 5 pm.

I imagine that approximately three months have elapsed since the end of Part I. We are, again, in the Royal Palace at Forres. Banquo, in spite of very grave suspicions, has accepted the situation & has become Macbeth's chief counsellor.

The new King & his Queen enter with their nobles & Banquo is invited to the banquet that they are giving that night.

Act III, Scene i. "Is 't far you ride?" Ralph Michael (Banquo), Paul Vieyra (Fleance), Sir Laurence Olivier (Macbeth). Although Shaw's promptbook excludes Fleance from this scene, the Stratford promptbook has him onstage, and apparently a change was made late in rehearsals.

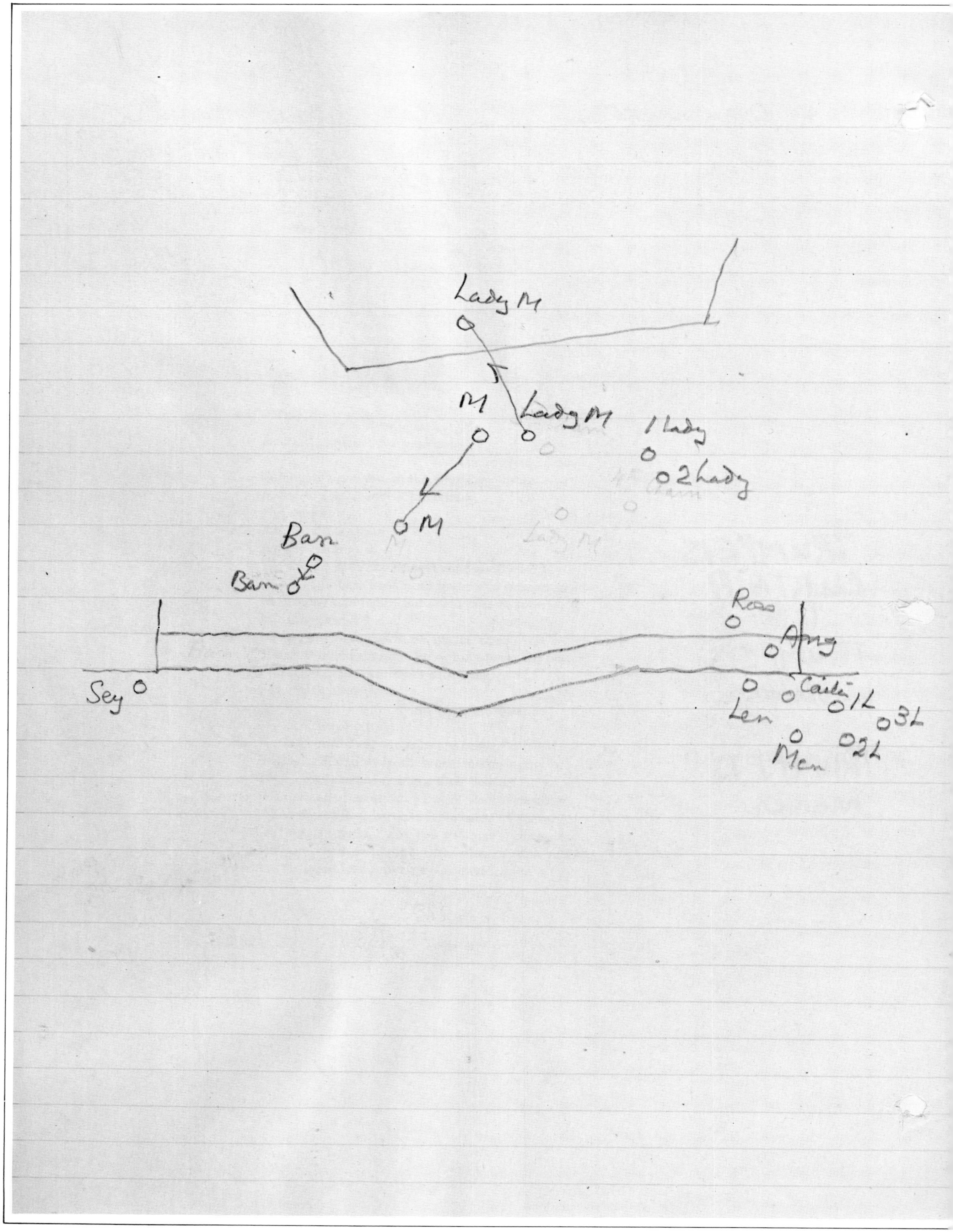

Lady M
M
Lady M
1 Lady
2 Lady
M
Ban
Ban
Ross
Ang
Sey
Caith
1L
3L
Len
2L
Men

MACBETH

And I 'll request your presence.
Ban. Let your highness
Command upon me, to the which my duties
Are with a most indissoluble tie
For ever knit.
Mac. Ride you this afternoon?
Ban. Ay, my good lord.
Mac. We should have else desir'd your good advice,
~~(Which still hath been both grave and prosperous)~~
In this day's council; but we 'll take to-morrow.
Is 't far you ride?
Ban. As far, my lord, as will fill up the time
'Twixt this and supper: go not my horse the better,
I must become a borrower of the night,
For a dark hour or twain.
Mac. Fail not our feast.
Ban. My lord, I will not.
Mac. We hear our bloody cousins are bestow'd
In England, and in Ireland, not confessing
Their cruel parricide, filling their hearers
With strange invention. But of that to-morrow,
When therewithal we shall have cause of state
Craving us jointly. Hie you to horse: adieu,
Till you return at night. Goes Fleance with you?
Ban. Ay, my good lord: our time does call upon 's.

44

Stops & turns DS to look at Ban
Lady M moves on to Throne Steps & Stops

moving US with Lady M & 1 & 2 Ladies

Ban bows & turns towards OP Arch

Macbeth comes to DS US of Ban

Macbeth, subtly, gets Banquo to tell him what he is going to do before the time of the Banquet; he also refers to Malcolm & Donalbain, saying that he has heard that, having murdered their father, they have fled to England & Ireland respectively. Banquo leaves the Court & as he is going Macbeth makes sure that his son is going riding with him.

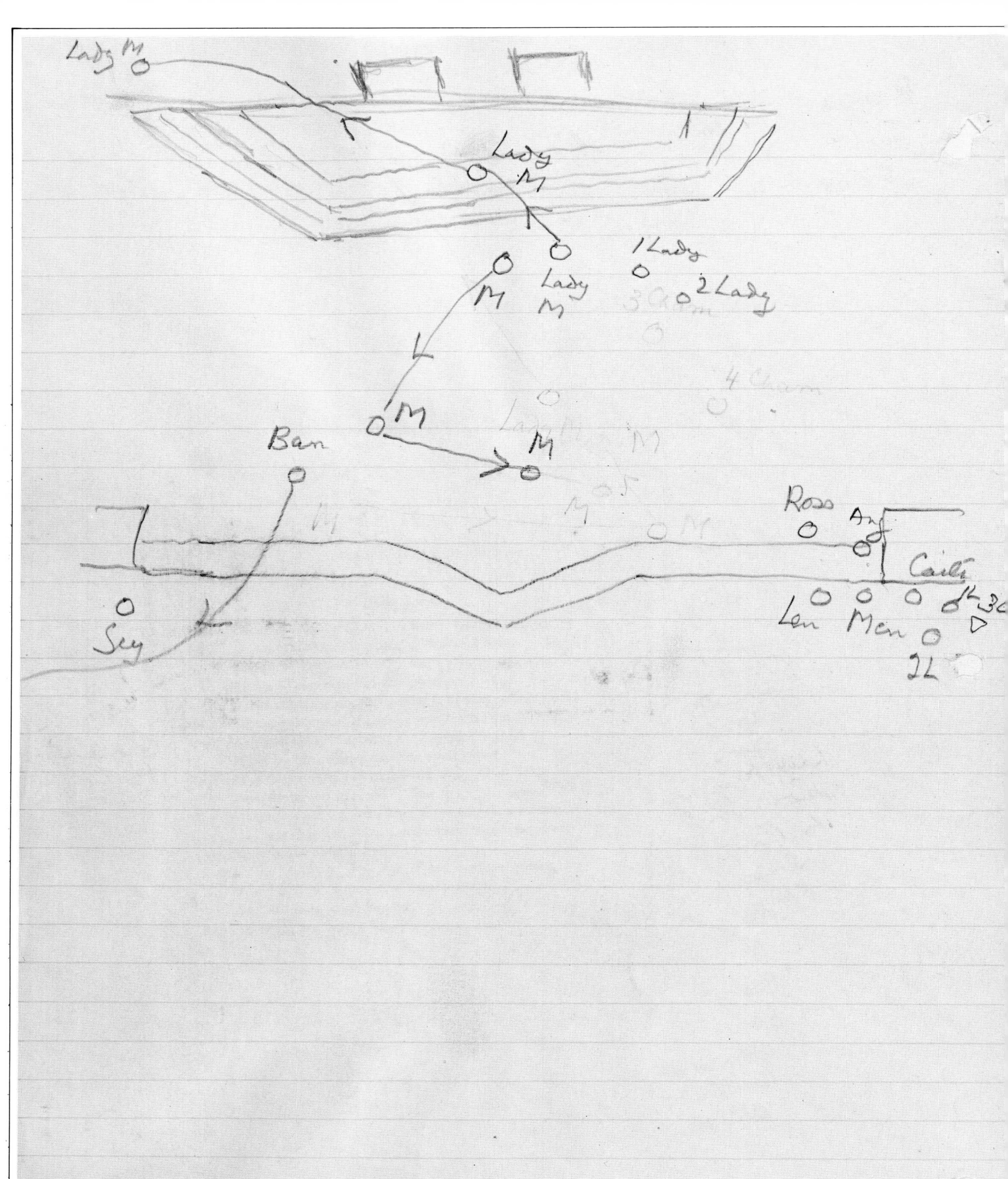

The Queen goes to her apartments & the King dismisses the Court & orders his head Steward—Seyton—to bring in two men who are waiting to see him.

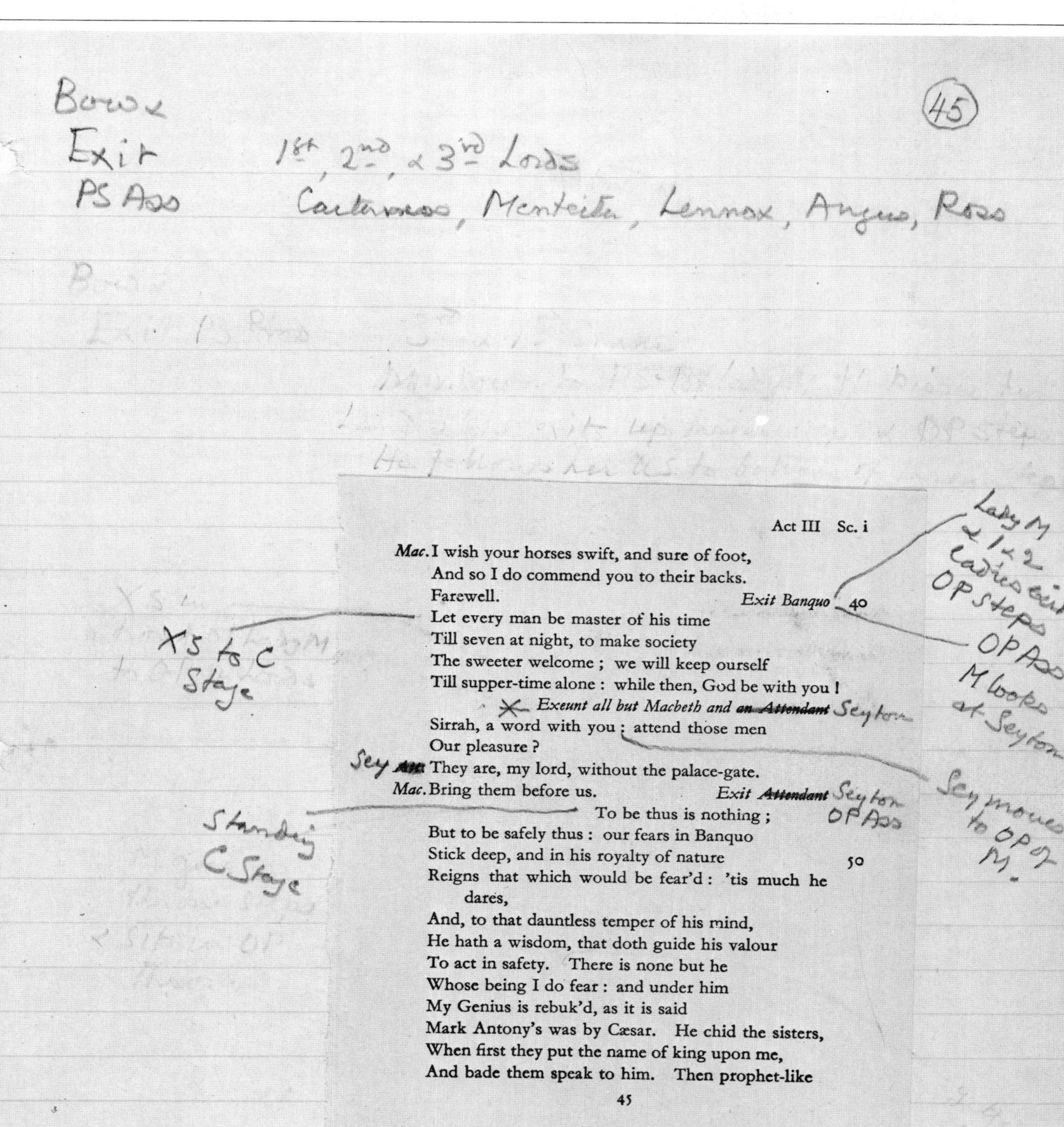

Bows
Exit
PS Ass

1st, 2nd, & 3rd Lords
Caithness, Menteith, Lennox, Angus, Ross

(45)

Act III Sc. i

Mac. I wish your horses swift, and sure of foot,
And so I do commend you to their backs.
Farewell. *Exit Banquo*
Let every man be master of his time
Till seven at night, to make society
The sweeter welcome; we will keep ourself
Till supper-time alone: while then, God be with you!
Exeunt all but Macbeth and ~~an Attendant~~ Seyton
Sirrah, a word with you: attend those men
Our pleasure?
Sey ~~*Att.*~~ They are, my lord, without the palace-gate.
Mac. Bring them before us. *Exit ~~Attendant~~* Seyton OP Ass
To be thus is nothing;
But to be safely thus: our fears in Banquo
Stick deep, and in his royalty of nature
Reigns that which would be fear'd: 'tis much he
dares,
And, to that dauntless temper of his mind,
He hath a wisdom, that doth guide his valour
To act in safety. There is none but he
Whose being I do fear: and under him
My Genius is rebuk'd, as it is said
Mark Antony's was by Cæsar. He chid the sisters,
When first they put the name of king upon me,
And bade them speak to him. Then prophet-like

45

XS to C Stage

Standing C Stage

Lady M & 1 & 2 Ladies exit OP steps

OP Ass

M looks at Seyton

Sey moves to OP of M.

Seyton comes back with two brutish looking men. They have been soldiers under Macbeth's command but have obviously got themselves into considerable trouble in the past.

1st Murderer. Ron Haddrick.
2nd Murderer. Hugh Cross.
They are terrifying brutes. Almost like savage animals. They are utterly ruthless, callous, & cruel. Their faces should express the bestiality of their natures.

As soon as Macbeth is alone we realise why he was so interested in Banquo & his son. Banquo knows too much, he is a danger, & furthermore the Witches fore-told that Banquo's issue should be Kings. He determines to get rid of him & his son.

MACBETH

They hail'd him father to a line of kings.
Upon my head they plac'd a fruitless crown,
And put a barren sceptre in my gripe,
Thence to be wrench'd with an unlineal hand,
No son of mine succeeding. If 't be so,
For Banquo's issue have I fil'd my mind,
For them the gracious Duncan have I murder'd,
Put rancours in the vessel of my peace
Only for them, and mine eternal jewel
Given to the common enemy of man,
To make them kings, the seed of Banquo kings!
Rather than so, come fate into the list,
And champion me to the utterance! Who 's there?

Re-enter ~~Attendant~~ Seyton*, with two Murderers* OP Pros

Now go to the door, and stay there till we call.

~~*Exit Attendant*~~

Was it not yesterday we spoke together?
1.*M.* It was, so please your highness.
Mac. Well then, now
Have you consider'd of my speeches? Know
That it was he in the times past which held you
So under fortune, which you thought had been
Our innocent self: this I made good to you,
In our last conference, ~~pass'd in probation with you~~;

46

Sey goes to C steps OP
1st & 2nd Mur on forestage OP

moves to PS of 1st M

Slight move DS

Sey xs US of 1st & 2nd Murds to OP Pros & stands in entrance

M beckons 1st & 2nd Murds to him

Macbeth plays on their feelings & pretends that it was Banquo who was responsible for their misfortunes. He is not a bully but his discipline with men is obviously very severe & his two ex-soldiers, whom he turns into murderers, have suffered from it. He urges them to murder, not only Banquo, but also his son.

(47)

~~How you were borne in hand, how cross'd; the instruments;~~
~~Who wrought with them~~; and all things else that might
To half a soul, and to a notion craz'd,
Say 'Thus did Banquo.'

1.M. You made it known to us.

Mac. I did so; and went further, which is now
Our point of second meeting. Do you find
Your patience so predominant in your nature,
That you can let this go? Are you so gospell'd,
To pray for this good man, and for his issue,
Whose heavy hand hath bow'd you to the grave,
And beggar'd yours for ever?

1.M. We are men, my liege.

Mac. Ay, in the catalogue ye go for men,
As hounds, and greyhounds, mongrels, spaniels, curs,
Shoughs, water-rugs, and demi-wolves, are clept
All by the name of dogs: the valued file
Distinguishes the swift, the slow, the subtle,
The housekeeper, the hunter, every one
According to the gift which bounteous nature
Hath in him clos'd, whereby he does receive
Particular addition, from the bill
That writes them all alike: and so of men.

Slight restless move

Macbeth, Act III, Scene i

Now if you have a station in the file,
Not i' the worst rank of manhood, say it,
And I will put that business in your bosoms,
Whose execution takes your enemy off,
Grapples you to the heart and love of us,
Who wear our health but sickly in his life,
Which in his death were perfect.

2.M. I am one, my liege,
Whom the vile blows and buffets of the world
Hath so incens'd, that I am reckless what
I do to spite the world.

1.M. And I another,
So weary with disasters, tugg'd with fortune,
That I would set my life on any chance,
To mend it, or be rid on 't.

Mac. Both of you
Know Banquo was your enemy.

1 ~~*Both*~~ *M.* True, my lord.

Mac. So is he mine; and in such bloody distance,
That every minute of his being thrusts
Against my near'st of life: and though I could
With barefac'd power sweep him from my sight,
And bid my will avouch it, yet I must not,
For certain friends that are both his, and mine,
Whose loves I may not drop, but wail his fall

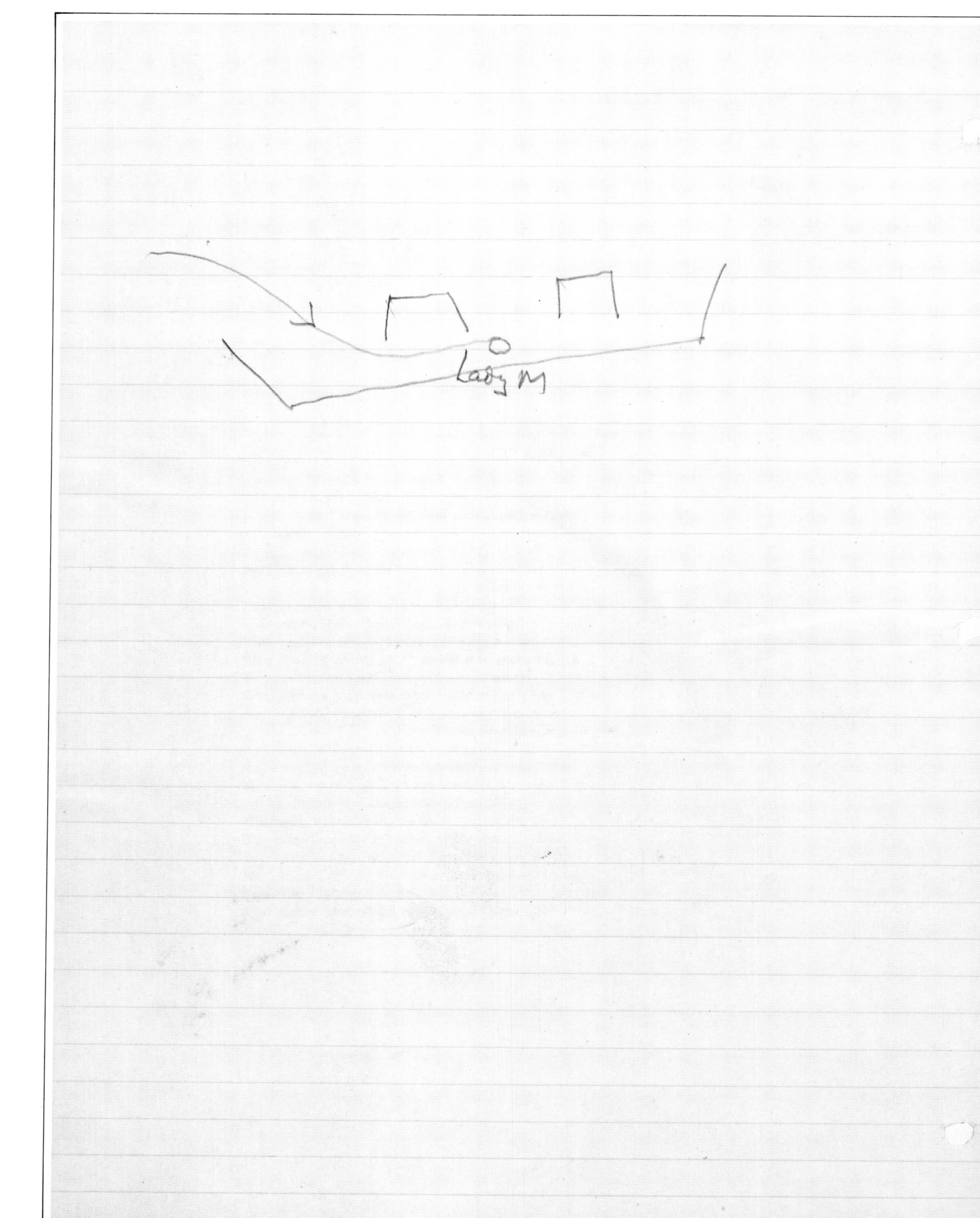
Lady M

(49)

Who I myself struck down: and thence it is
That I to your assistance do make love,
Masking the business from the common eye,
For sundry weighty reasons.

2.M. We shall, my lord,
Perform what you command us.

1.M. Though our lives—

Mac. Your spirits shine through you. Within this hour, at most,
I will advise you where to plant yourselves,
Acquaint you with the perfect spy o' the time, †
The moment on 't, for 't must be done to-night,
And something from the palace; ~~always thought,~~
~~That I require a clearness~~; and with him,
To leave no rubs nor botches in the work,
Fleance, his son, that keeps him company,
Whose absence is no less material to me
Than is his father's, must embrace the fate
Of that dark hour: resolve yourselves apart,
I 'll come to you anon.

1 ~~*Both*~~ *M.* We are resolv'd, my lord.

Mac. I 'll call upon you straight: abide within,

Exeunt Murderers & Seyton

It is concluded: Banquo, thy soul's flight,
If it find heaven, must find it out to-night. *Exit*

49

moves close to them

OP Ass.

PS Ass.
Enter Lady M
OP lift & sees
M going. She
OP of Kingst
throne & comes
to between
the thrones

They agree & the interview ends.

Macbeth, Act III, Scene ii

Start of FADE

MACBETH

~~Enter Lady Macbeth and a Servant~~

L.M. Is Banquo gone from court?
Sey ~~*Ser.*~~ Ay, madam, but returns again to-night.
L.M. Say to the king, I would attend his leisure
For a few words.
Sey ~~*Ser.*~~ Madam, I will. PS Ass *Exit*
L.M. Nought 's had, all 's spent,
Where our desire is got without content:
'Tis safer to be that which we destroy
Than by destruction dwell in doubtful joy.
Enter Macbeth PS Ass
How now, my lord, why do you keep alone,
Of sorriest fancies your companions making,
Using those thoughts which should indeed have died
With them they think on? Things without all remedy
Should be without regard: what 's done, is done.
Mac. We have scotch'd the snake, not kill'd it: †
She 'll close, and be herself, whilst our poor malice
Remains in danger of her former tooth.
But let the frame of things disjoint, both the worlds suffer,
Ere we will eat our meal in fear, and sleep
In the affliction of these terrible dreams,

50

from top of throne steps

he moves slowly towards her

Sits in her throne

Sits on his throne

Enter Seyton OP Ass

He stops when he sees her

The Queen returns. She feels that something is going on.

Left alone, we realise that she is as tortured & oppressed as her husband. They are drifting apart, he no longer takes her into his confidence.

When Macbeth comes to see her she tries to find out what is the matter with him & what he is planning to do.

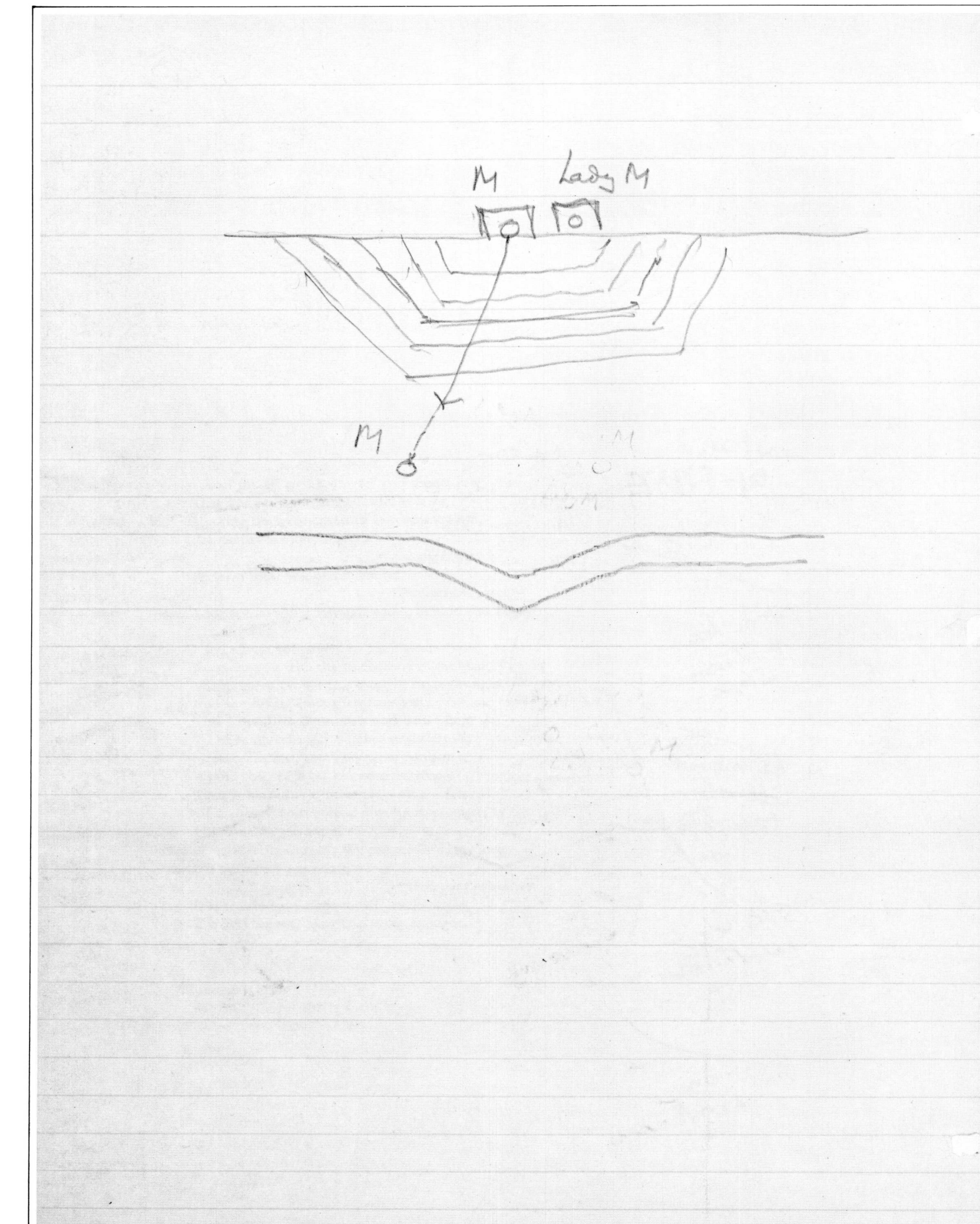

Macbeth, Act III, Scene ii

Act III Sc. ii

That shake us nightly: better be with the dead,
Whom we, to gain our ~~peace~~, have sent to peace,
Than on the torture of the mind to lie
In restless ecstasy. Duncan is in his grave:
After life's fitful fever, he sleeps well,
Treason has done his worst: nor steel, nor poison,
Malice domestic, foreign levy, nothing,
Can touch him further.

L.M. Come on;
Gentle my lord, sleek o'er your rugged looks,
Be bright and jovial among your guests to-night.

Mac. So shall I, love, and so, I pray, be you:
Let your remembrance apply to Banquo,
Present him eminence, both with eye and tongue: †
Unsafe the while, that we
Must lave our honours in these flattering streams,
And make our faces vizards to our hearts,
Disguising what they are.

L.M. You must leave this.

Mac. O, full of scorpions is my mind, dear wife!
Thou know'st that Banquo, and his Fleance, lives.

L.M. But in them nature's copy 's not eterne.

Mac. There 's comfort yet, they are assailable,
Then be thou jocund: ere the bat hath flown
His cloister'd flight, ere to black Hecat's summons

51

place

Puts hand on his arm

rises & moves to PS of M

rising

moving DS OP

Looking towards OP Ass

Act III, Scene ii. "Sleek o'er your rugged looks." Sir Laurence Olivier (Macbeth), Vivien Leigh (Lady Macbeth).

He is not direct with her & hedges her off. She is still his wife but not his companion or confidant.

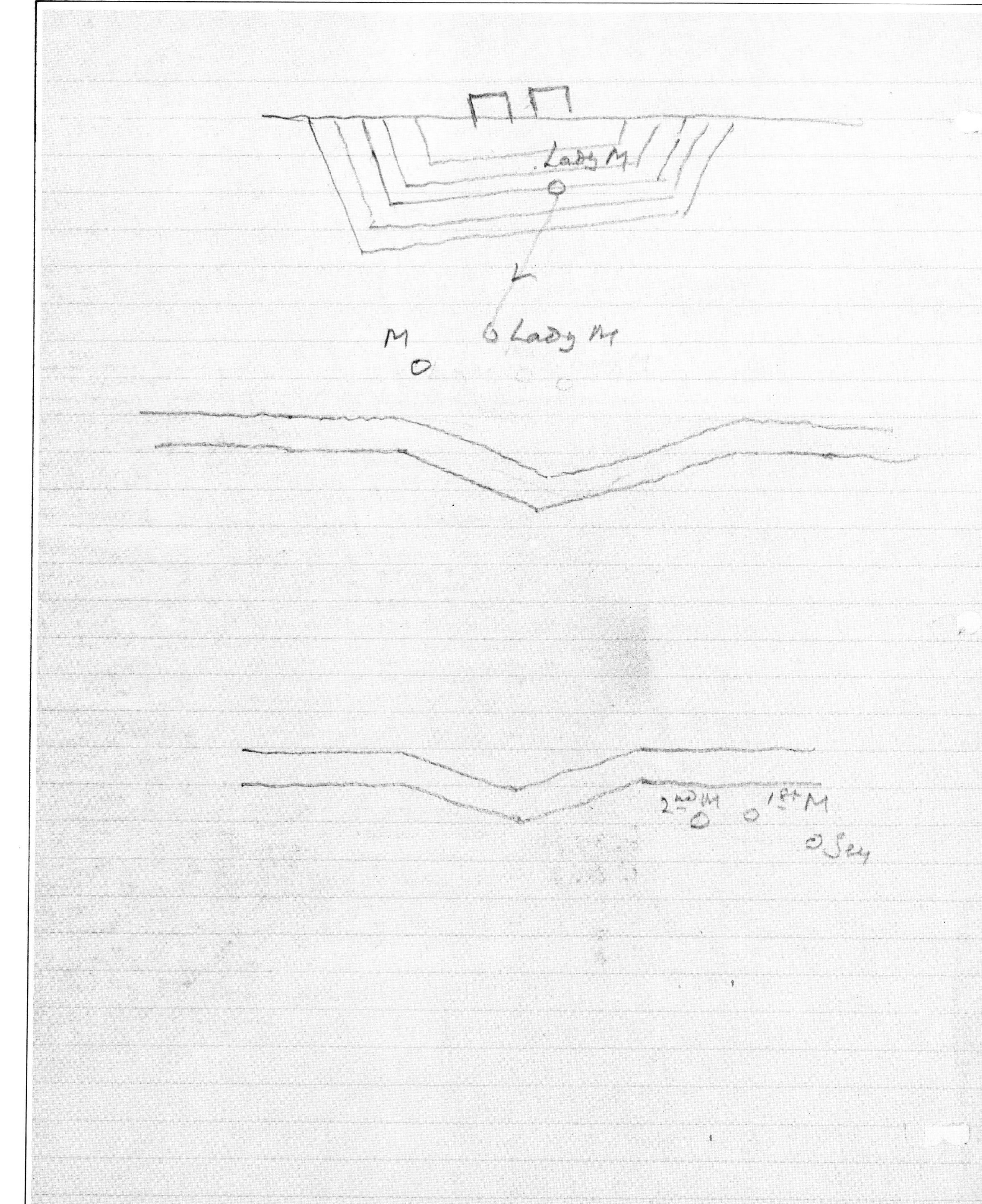

Macbeth, Act III, Scene iii

MACBETH

The shard-borne beetle, with his drowsy hums,
Hath rung night's yawning peal, there shall be done
A deed of dreadful note.

L.M. What 's to be done?

Mac. Be innocent of the knowledge, dearest chuck,
Till thou applaud the deed. Come, seeling night,
Scarf up the tender eye of pitiful day,
And with thy bloody and invisible hand
Cancel and tear to pieces that great bond
Which keeps me pale! Light thickens, and the crow
Makes wing to the rooky wood:
Good things of day begin to droop and drowse,
Whiles night's black agents to their preys do rouse.
Thou marvell'st at my words: but hold thee still;
Things bad begun make strong themselves by ill:
So, prithee go with me. *Exeunt*

FADE to BLACK OUT
RUNNERS CLOSE
FADE IN

SCENE ~~III~~ 2

A park near the palace

Enter ~~three~~ 1 & 2 Murderers & Seyton

1.*M.* But who did bid thee join with us?

~~3.M.~~ Sey Macbeth.

52

turns to her
moves to PS US of M
turning
looking OP ass
turns to her
takes her hand – They move US towards Throne steps OP.
Banquo's Murder 7PM
PS Ass
CLOCK STRIKES 7

Banquo's Murder Scene. 7 pm.

The two murderers have been joined by Seyton, who has been sent by Macbeth to ensure that the job is properly done. They wait for Banquo & his son in the grounds of the Palace.

They hear the horses approach & Banquo & Fleance dismount.

There is a pause & then Banquo & Fleance appear & are set upon. Banquo is murdered but his son escapes.

(53)

Act III Sc. iii

2M. He needs not our mistrust, since he delivers
Our offices, and what we have to do,
To the direction just.

1.M. Then stand with us:
The west yet glimmers with some streaks of day:
Now spurs the lated traveller apace,
To gain the timely inn, and near approaches
The subject of our watch.

~~1.M.~~ 2M Hark! I hear horses.

Ban. (*within*) Give us a light there, ho!

~~2.M.~~ Sey Then 'tis he: the rest,
That are within the note of expectation,
Already are i' the court.

1.M. His horses go about.

~~3.M.~~ Sey Almost a mile: but he does usually—
So all men do—from hence to the palace gate
Make it their walk.

2.M. A light, a light!

Enter Banquo, and Fleance with a torch

~~3.M.~~ Sey 'Tis he.

1.M. Stand to 't.

Ban. It will be rain to-night.

1.M. Let it come down.

They set upon Banquo

Ban. O, treachery! Fly, good Fleance, fly, fly, fly!

53

Xs in front of 2nd M & moving on to top of front steps PS & followed by Seyton

Horses hoofs

Horses gallop away

They take out their daggers

OP Ass

1st Sey move US & slightly C

1st M seizes torch from Fle & puts it out 2nd M & Sey attack Banquo with daggers moving over to PS.

Act III, Scene iii. Banquo's murder. Ron Haddrick (Murderer), Ralph Michael (Banquo), Lee Montague (Seyton), Hugh Cross (Murderer).

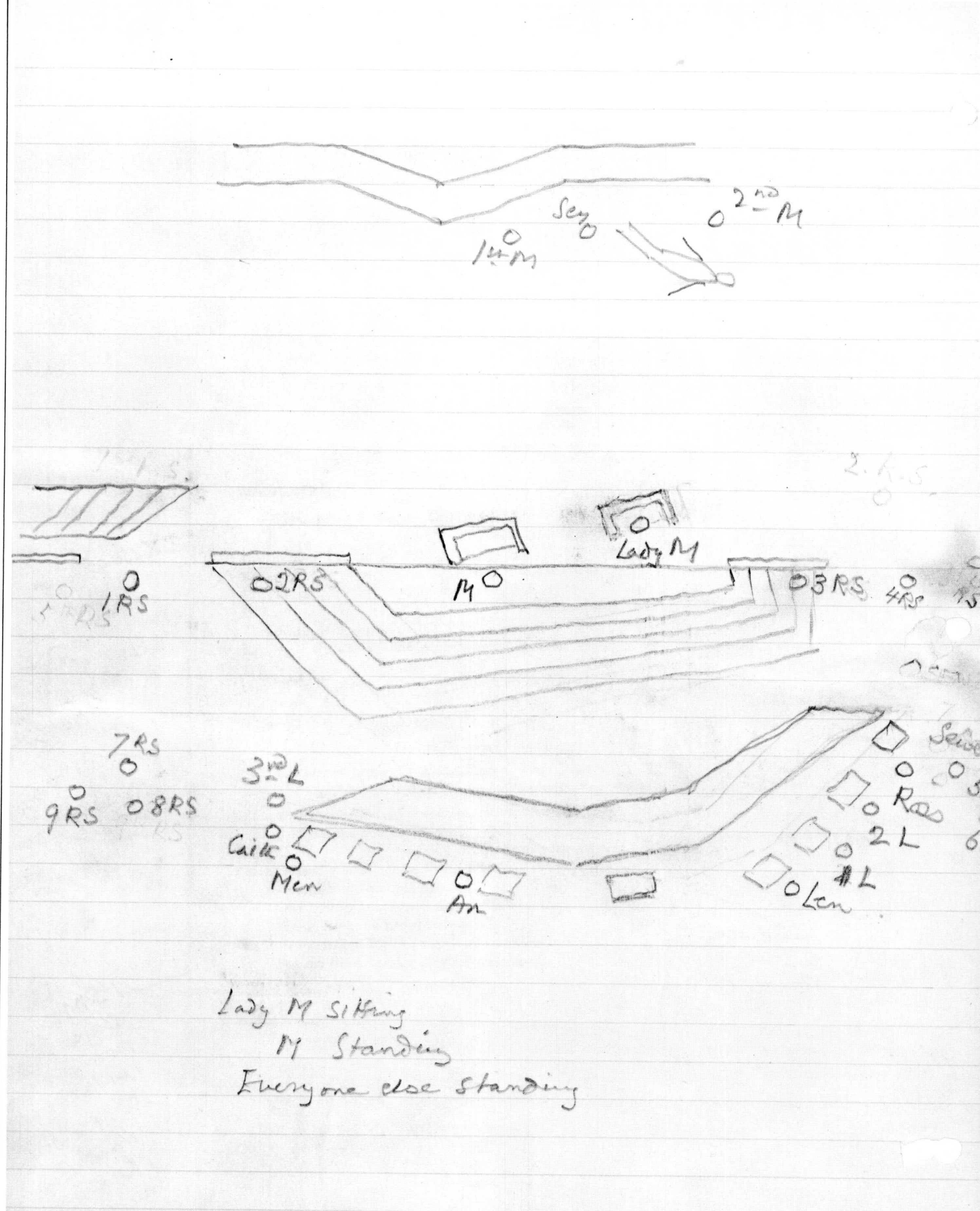

Banquet Scene. 8 pm.

The guests have assembled. The King & Queen receive them & they are told to take their places at the Banquet table. Macbeth tells the Nobles that the Queen will "keep her state" but that he will join them at the table.

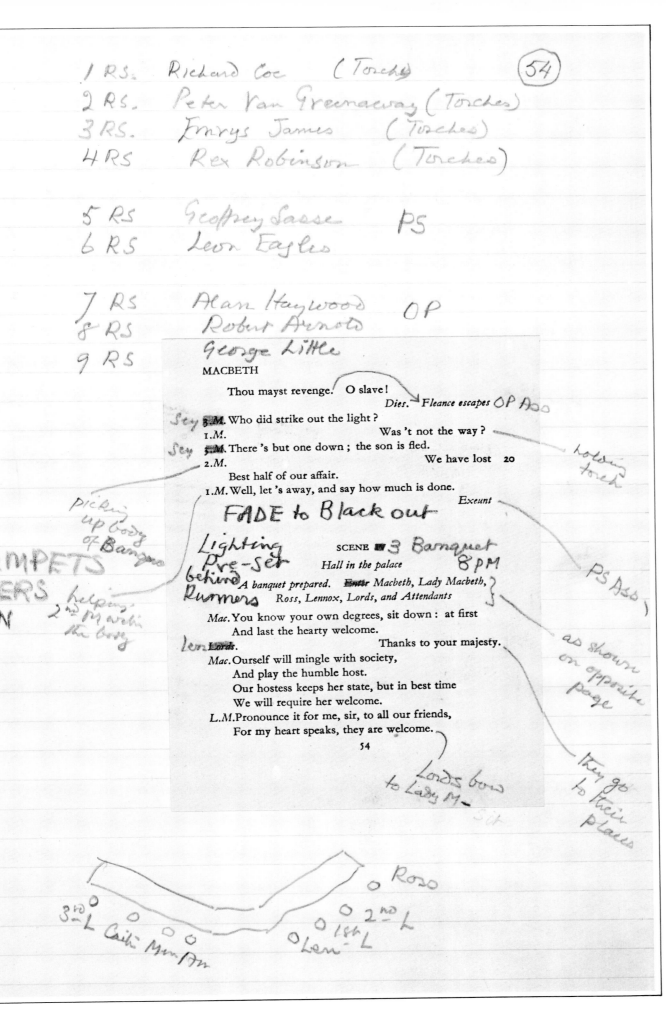

1 RS. Richard Coe (Torches) (54)
2 RS. Peter Van Greenaway (Torches)
3 RS. Emrys James (Torches)
4 RS Rex Robinson (Torches)

5 RS Geoffrey Sasse PS
6 RS Leon Eagles

7 RS Alan Haywood OP
8 RS Robert Arnold
9 RS George Little

MACBETH

Thou mayst revenge. O slave!

Dies. *Fleance escapes* OP Ass

Sey ~~3.M.~~ Who did strike out the light?

1.M. Was 't not the way? — holding torch

Sey ~~3.M.~~ There 's but one down; the son is fled.

2.M. We have lost

Best half of our affair.

1.M. Well, let 's away, and say how much is done.

Exeunt — PS Ass

picking up body of Banquo

FADE to Black out

TRUMPETS

RUNNERS OPEN

helping 2nd M with the body

Lighting Pre-set behind Runners

SCENE ~~II~~ 3 Banquet 8PM

Hall in the palace

A banquet prepared. ~~*Enter*~~ *Macbeth, Lady Macbeth, Ross, Lennox, Lords, and Attendants*

as shown on opposite page

Mac. You know your own degrees, sit down: at first

And last the hearty welcome.

Len ~~*Lords*~~. Thanks to your majesty.

They go to their places

Mac. Ourself will mingle with society,

And play the humble host.

Our hostess keeps her state, but in best time

We will require her welcome.

L.M. Pronounce it for me, sir, to all our friends,

For my heart speaks, they are welcome.

Lords bow to Lady M — Sit

54

Ross

3rd L Caith Men Ang 2nd L 1st L Len

The Royal Palace Banquet Scene.

Act III, Scene iv. "You know your own degrees." John Springett (Angus, just left of empty stools), Sir Laurence Olivier (Macbeth), Vivien Leigh (Lady Macbeth), James Grout (Lennox, just right of stools), others unidentified (see following pages).

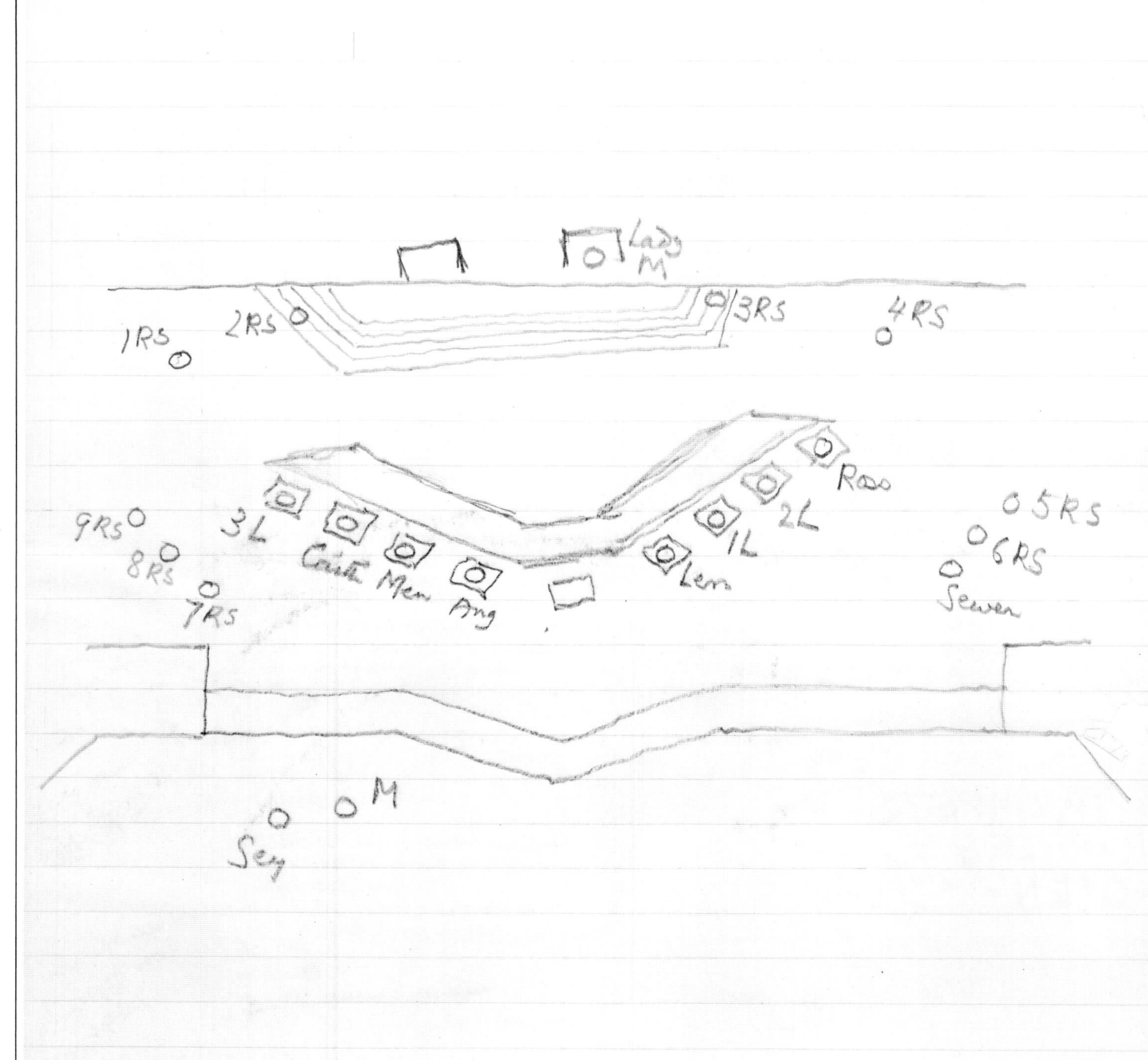

Macbeth, Act III, Scene iv

Act III Sc. iv

Enter ~~First Murderer to the door~~

Mac. See, they encounter thee with their hearts' thanks.
Both sides are even: here I 'll sit i' the midst,
Be large in mirth, anon we 'll drink a measure
The table round. (*Approaching ~~the door~~*) There 's
blood upon thy face.

~~Mur.~~ 'Tis Banquo's then.

Mac. ~~'Tis better thee without than he within.~~
Is he dispatch'd?

~~Mur.~~ My lord, his throat is cut, that I did for him.

Mac. Thou art the best o' the cut-throats, yet he 's good
That did the like for Fleance: if thou didst it,
Thou art the nonpareil.

~~Mur.~~ Most royal sir,
Fleance is 'scap'd.

Mac. (*aside*) Then comes my fit again: I had else been
perfect,
Whole as the marble, founded as the rock,
As broad, and general, as the casing air:
But now I am cabin'd, cribb'd, confin'd, bound in
To saucy doubts and fears.—But Banquo 's safe?

~~Mur.~~ Ay, my good lord: safe in a ditch he bides,
With twenty trenched gashes on his head;
The least a death to nature.

Mac. Thanks for that.

55

Seyton appears. Macbeth tells his guests to drink & he goes to Seyton to hear what has happened. Seyton has Banquo's blood on his face. He tells Macbeth that Banquo is dead but that Fleance has escaped.

MACBETH

(*aside*) There the grown serpent lies, the worm that 's fled
Hath nature that in time will venom breed,
No teeth for the present. Get thee gone, to-morrow
We 'll hear ourselves again. *Exit* ~~Murderer~~

[Sey OP Aso]

L.M. My royal lord,
You do not give the cheer, the feast is sold †
That is not often vouch'd, while 'tis a making:
'Tis given, with welcome: to feed were best at home;
From thence, the sauce to meat is ceremony,
Meeting were bare without it.

The Ghost of Banquo enters, and sits in Macbeth's place

[M moves US round OP end of table & up throne steps to OP of Lady M]

Mac. Sweet remembrancer!
Now good digestion wait on appetite,
And health on both!

Len. May 't please your highness sit.

Mac. Here had we now our country's honour roof'd,
Were the grac'd person of our Banquo present
Who may I rather challenge for unkindness,
Than pity for mischance!

[SOUND]

[OP Aso & sits C stool]

[looking at Lady M]

Ross. His absence, sir,
Lays blame upon his promise. Please 't your highness
To grace us with your royal company?

[Ross sits again]

[rises & moves to PS of throne steps]

56

The news maddens Macbeth but he recovers, dismisses Seyton & is called back to the Banquet table by his wife.

He speaks to his guests & regrets Banquo's absence & as he does so Banquo's Ghost appears & takes Macbeth's place at the table.

Act III, Scene iv. "Never shake thy gory locks at me." Gabriel Woolf (Caithness), Robert Hunter (Menteith), John Springett (Angus), Sir Laurence Olivier (Macbeth), Ralph Michael (Ghost), Vivien Leigh (Lady Macbeth), James Grout (Lennox) (see opposite page).

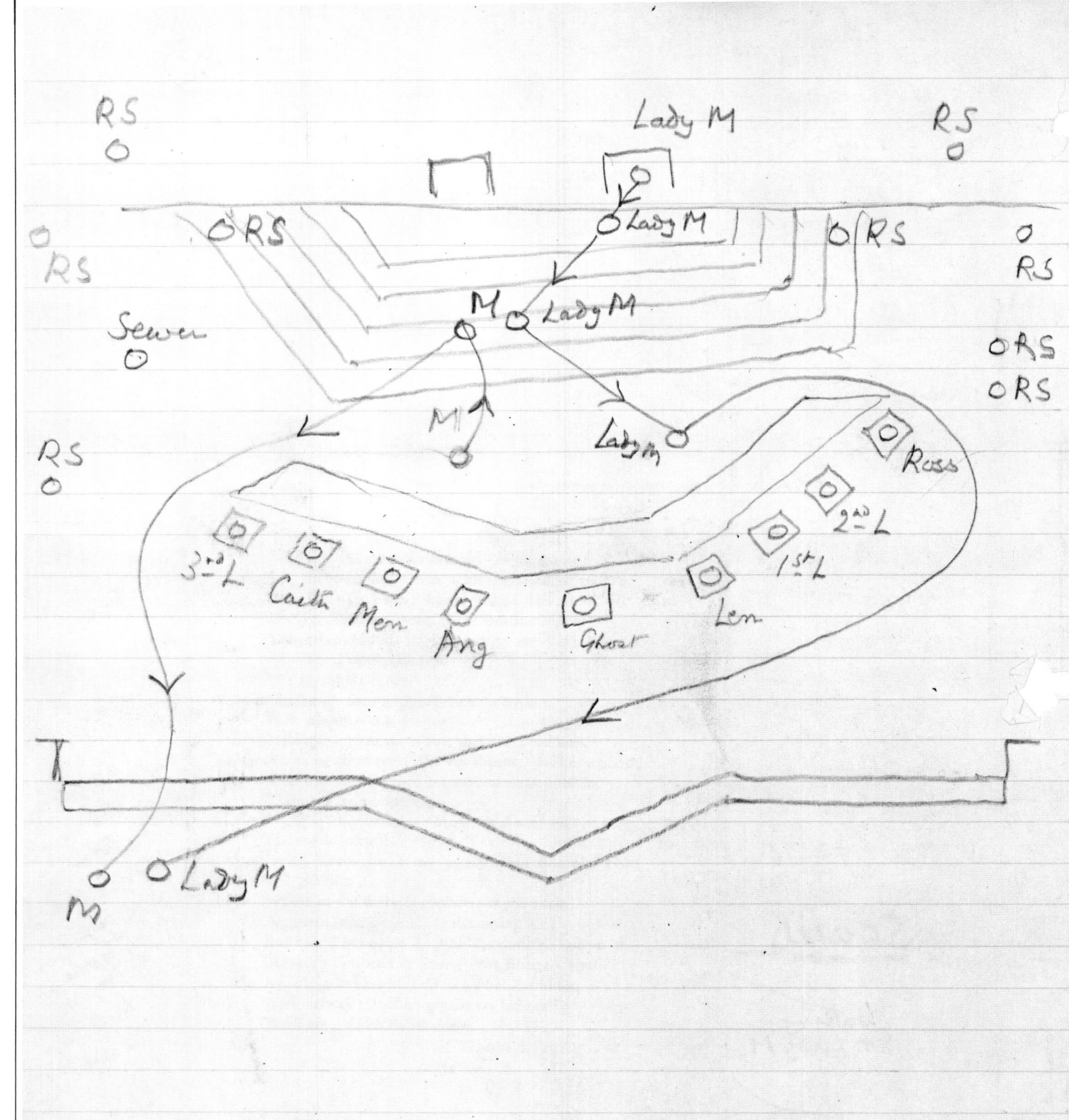

She then does her best to calm her husband, but he still sees the Ghost & even when it disappears he is in a terrible state.

Macbeth, Act III, Scene iv

Act III Sc. iv

Mac. The table 's full.
Len. Here is a place reserv'd, sir.
Mac. Where?
Len. Here, my good lord. What is 't that moves your highness?
Mac. Which of you have done this?
~~*Lords.*~~ LEN. What, my good lord?
Mac. Thou canst not say I did it: never shake
Thy gory locks at me.
Ross. Gentlemen, rise, his highness is not well.
L.M. Sit, worthy friends: my lord is often thus,
And hath been from his youth: pray you, keep seat,
The fit is momentary, upon a thought
He will again be well. If much you note him,
You shall offend him, and extend his passion,
Feed, and regard him not. Are you a man?
Mac. Ay, and a bold one, that dare look on that
Which might appal the devil.
L.M. O proper stuff!
This is the very painting of your fear:
This is the air-drawn dagger which you said
Led you to Duncan. O, these flaws and starts,
(Impostors to true fear) would well become
A woman's story at a winter's fire,
Authoriz'd by her grandam. Shame itself,

21 f 57

coming down steps
sees Ghost
backing up steps
rises other Lords start to rise
Lords sit except Ross
coming to PS of M
coming round PS end of table
indicating C stool
Lady M rises
Ross sits
M suddenly rushes round OP end of table to front steps OP Ghost turns on stool & follows him round with its eyes
Xs to PS of M

Macbeth turns & sees the Ghost & is terrified. No one else sees the Ghost & the Nobles think that Macbeth is going mad. Lady Macbeth tells them that the fit will soon pass & that they should take no notice.

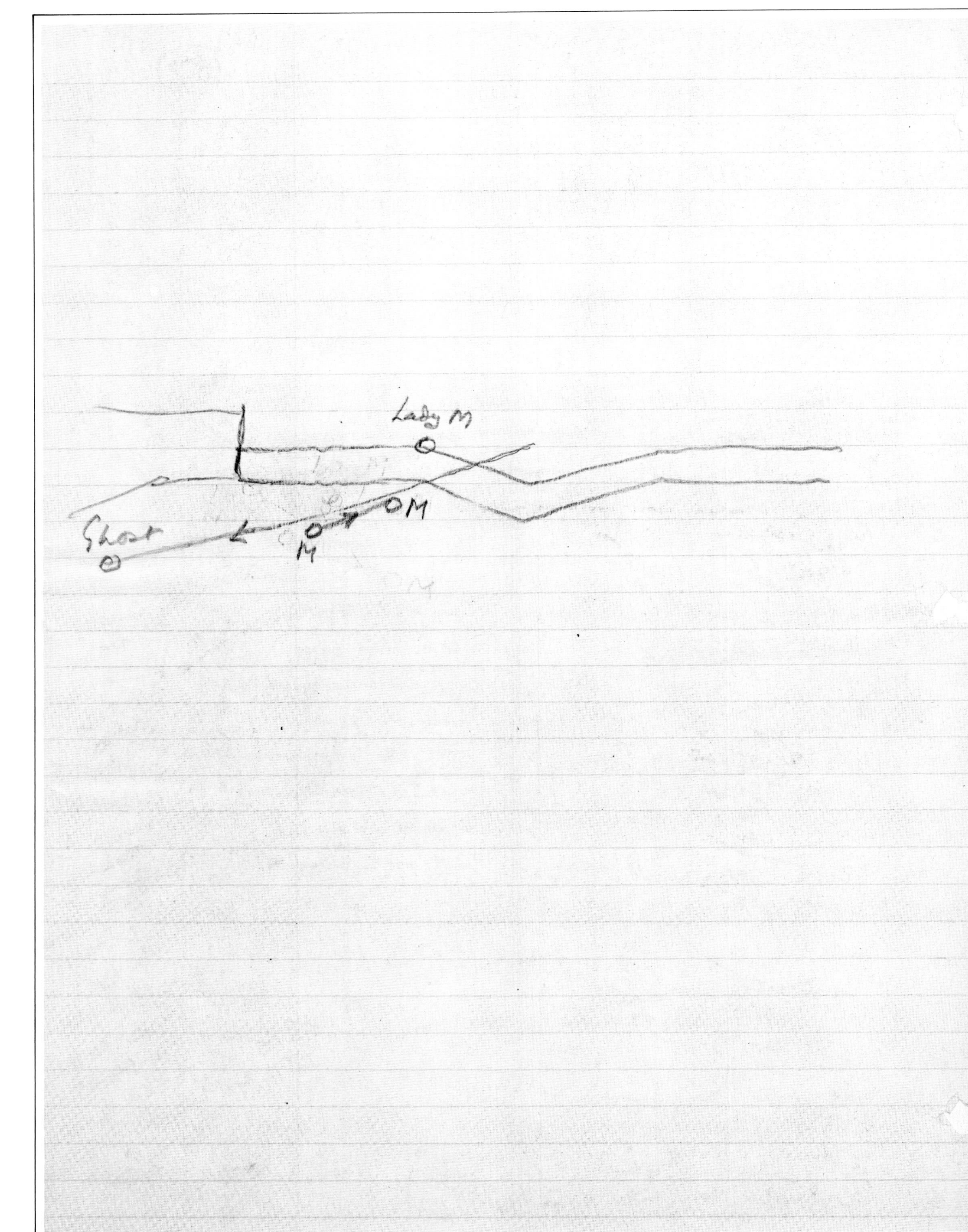

Macbeth, Act III, Scene iv

(58)

MACBETH

Why do you make such faces? When all 's done,
You look but on a stool.
Mac. Prithee see there! behold! look! lo! how say you?
Why, what care I? If thou canst nod, speak too.
If charnel-houses and our graves must send
Those that we bury back, our monuments
Shall be the maws of kites. *Exit Ghost*
L.M. What, quite unmann'd in folly?
Mac. If I stand here, I saw him.
L.M. Fie, for shame!
Mac. Blood hath been shed ere now, i' the olden time,
Ere humane statute purg'd the gentle weal;
Ay, and since too, murders have been perform'd
Too terrible for the ear: the time has been,
That, when the brains were out, the man would die,
And there an end; but now they rise again,
With twenty mortal murders on their crowns,
And push us from our stools: this is more strange
Than such a murder is.
L.M. My worthy lord,
Your noble friends do lack you.
Mac. I do forget.
Do not muse at me, my most worthy friends,
I have a strange infirmity, which is nothing
To those that know me. Come, love and health to all,

58

Ghost rises & moves towards M

Ghost walks between Lady M & M & exit OP Ass

OP Ass

comes to OP of M

Lords start to turn & look at M

M turns to her

moves to PS of Lady M

Xs in front of Lady M & moving to OP C forestage

Lady M moves to OP Pros arch with her eye on Lords – During M's speech Lords turn & look at him

Again his wife reminds him of his guests.

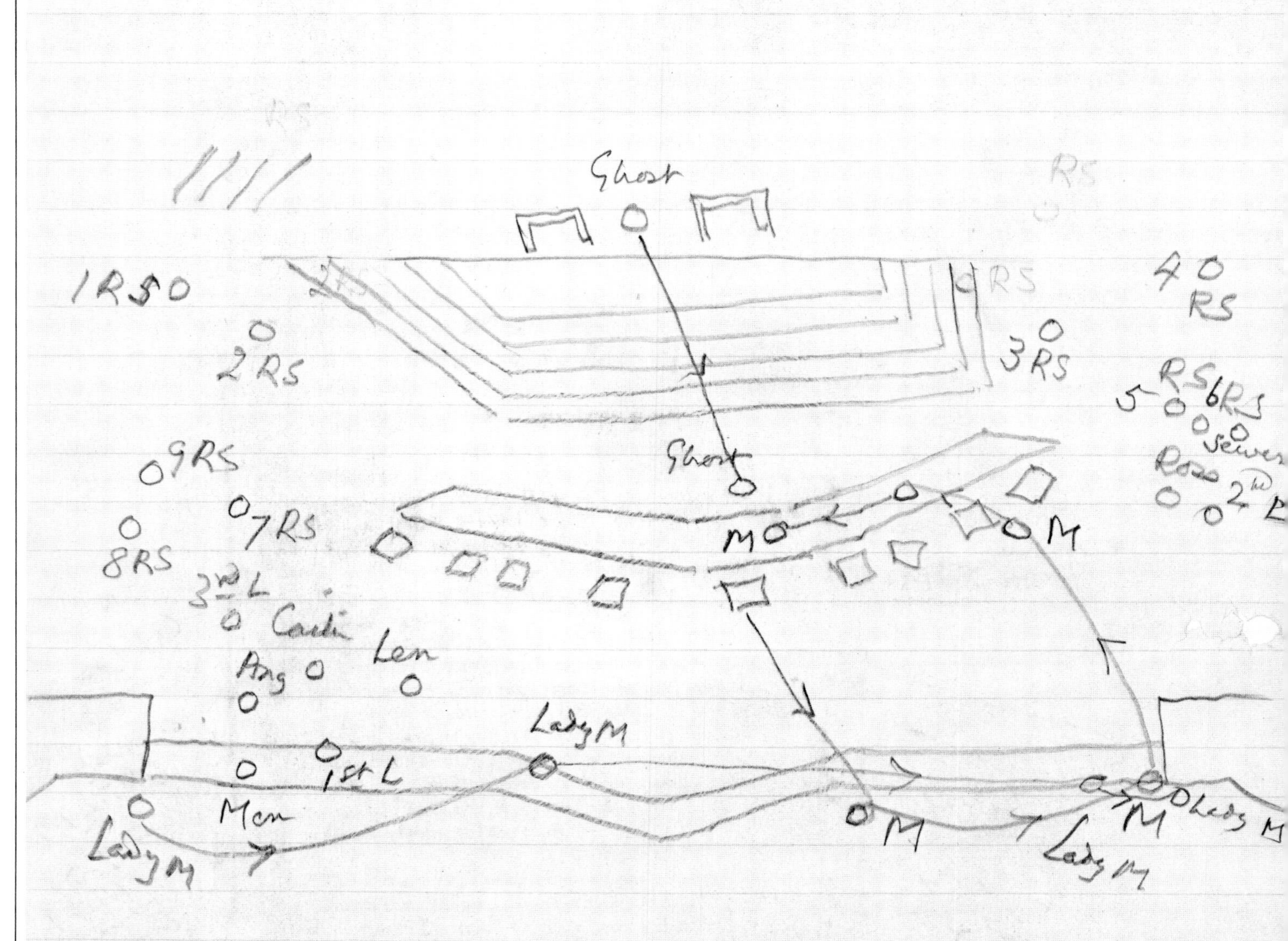

The Ghost appears again, this time standing between the two Royal thrones. Macbeth turns & sees it & practically goes off his head with terror. Again his wife tries to make little of his behavior but by now the nobles are very alarmed & suspicious. Macbeth sees the Ghost approaching. He rushes at it in a mad fury of desperation & it disappears.

Macbeth, Act III, Scene iv

Act III Sc. iv

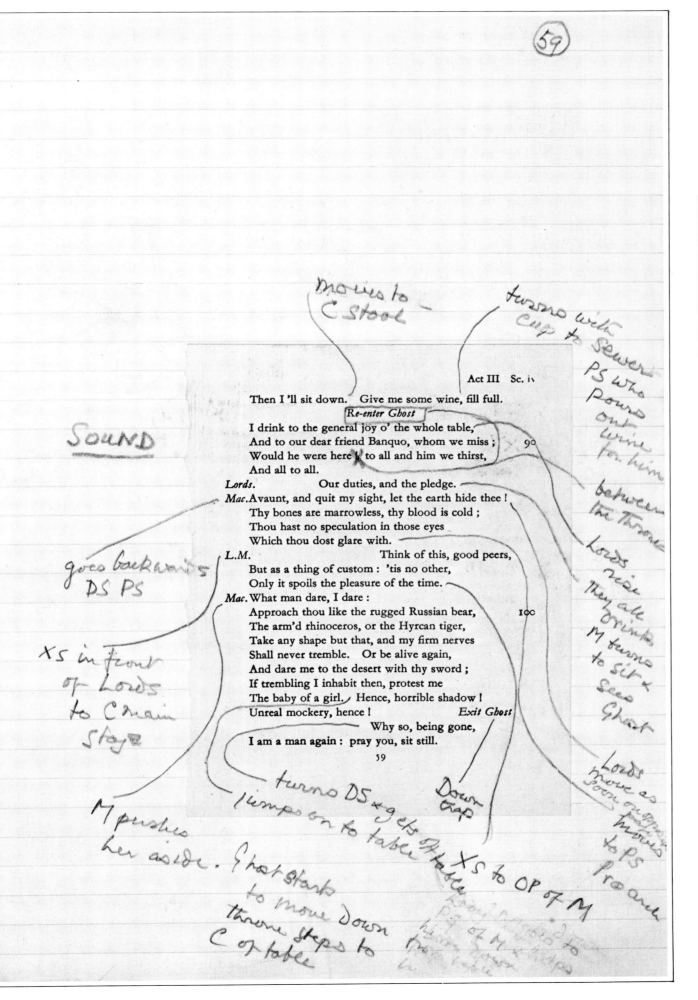

Then I'll sit down. Give me some wine, fill full.

Re-enter Ghost

I drink to the general joy o' the whole table,
And to our dear friend Banquo, whom we miss ;
Would he were here ! to all and him we thirst,
And all to all.

Lords. Our duties, and the pledge.

Mac. Avaunt, and quit my sight, let the earth hide thee !
Thy bones are marrowless, thy blood is cold ;
Thou hast no speculation in those eyes
Which thou dost glare with.

L.M. Think of this, good peers,
But as a thing of custom : 'tis no other,
Only it spoils the pleasure of the time.

Mac. What man dare, I dare :
Approach thou like the rugged Russian bear,
The arm'd rhinoceros, or the Hyrcan tiger,
Take any shape but that, and my firm nerves
Shall never tremble. Or be alive again,
And dare me to the desert with thy sword ;
If trembling I inhabit then, protest me
The baby of a girl. Hence, horrible shadow !
Unreal mockery, hence ! *Exit Ghost*
Why so, being gone,
I am a man again : pray you, sit still.

59

Act III, Scene iv.
"Hence, horrible shadow!"
Ralph Michael (Ghost),
Sir Laurence Olivier (Macbeth).

Act III, Scene iv.
"What man dare, I dare."
Vivien Leigh (Lady Macbeth),
Sir Laurence Olivier (Macbeth).

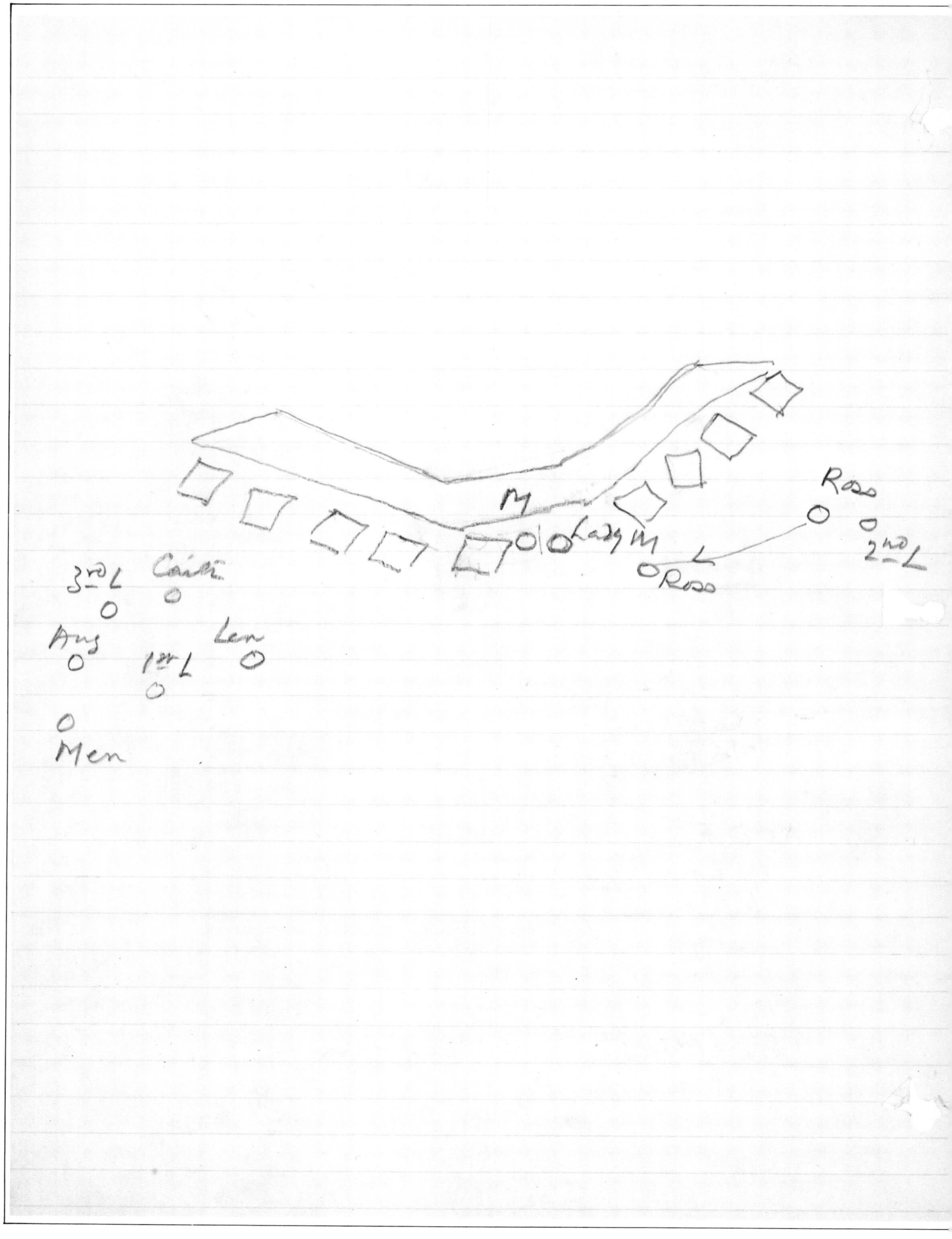

M
Lady M
Ross
2nd L
Ross
3rd L
Caith.
Ang
1st L
Len
Men

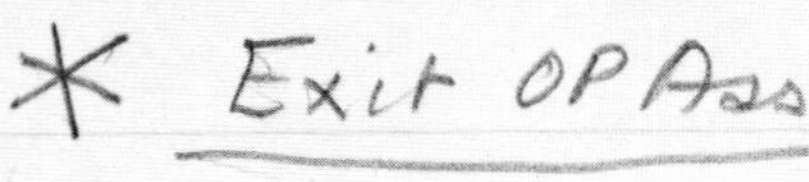

Menteith
1st Lord
Angus
Lennox
3rd Lord
Caithness
2nd Lord } who x in front
Ross } of Lady M & M

(60)

MACBETH

L.M. You have displac'd the mirth, broke the good meeting,
With most admir'd disorder.
Mac. Can such things be,
And overcome us like a summer's cloud,
Without our special wonder? You make me strange
Even to the disposition that I owe,
When now I think you can behold such sights,
And keep the natural ruby of your cheeks,
When mine is blanch'd with fear.
Ross. What sights, my lord?
L.M. I pray you, speak not; he grows worse and worse;
Question enrages him: at once, good night.
Stand not upon the order of your going,
But go at once.
Len. Good night, and better health
Attend his majesty!
L.M. A kind good night to all!
* *Exeunt all but Macbeth and Lady Macbeth*
Mac. It will have blood they say: blood will have blood:
Stones have been known to move, and trees to speak;
Augures and understood relations have
By maggot-pies, and choughs, and rooks brought forth

60

moving to PS of Macbeth

move to OP of Ross

2nd L moving with to PS of Lady M

Change of Lighting

Lady M sits PS of M

OP Ass

Exit PS Mid 3 & 4 R.S.
Exit OP mid 1 & 2 R.S.
Exit PS Pros Sewer & 5 & 6 RS
Exit OP Pros 7, 8 & 9 RS

He is exhausted, but makes a last effort to recover the confidence of his guests. It is no good. He tries to explain & Ross asks him a direct question. Lady Macbeth again protects him from himself & asks the guests to leave. She & Macbeth are left alone.

She is utterly worn out & can hardly answer his questions, but he has recovered & with fantastic energy begins to think of new crimes to commit. He decides to go & visit the Witches. He is charging further & further into crime & she is sinking deeper & deeper into hell.

After he has committed the crime & become King all that is bad in his character bursts out. He is like a man who is mentally diseased, but the magnificence & courage of his nature remain till the end. He never becomes a brutish villain like Iago or Aaron.

Macbeth, Act III, Scene iv

(61)

Sit c stool

Act III Sc. iv

The secret'st man of blood. What is the night?
L.M. Almost at odds with morning, which is which.
Mac. How say'st thou, that Macduff denies his person †
At our great bidding?
L.M. Did you send to him, sir?
Mac. I hear it by the way: but I will send:
There's not a one of them but in his house
I keep a servant fee'd. I will to-morrow
(And betimes I will) to the weird sisters:
More shall they speak; for now I am bent to know,
By the worst means, the worst, for mine own good,
All causes shall give way: I am in blood
Stepp'd in so far, that should I wade no more,
Returning were as tedious as go o'er:
Strange things I have in head, that will to hand,
Which must be acted, ere they may be scann'd.
L.M. You lack the season of all natures, sleep.
Mac. Come, we'll to sleep. My strange and self-abuse
Is the initiate fear, that wants hard use:
We are yet but young in deed. *Exeunt.*

rises & look out of PS Ass

turns to him & moves slowly round PS end of table & up first two steps

rises & moves round OP end of table & goes OP of Lady M on to steps -

OP Lift followed by Lady M who sinks down on her knees leaning against Kings throne

Stops on throne steps & turns to her

SLOW CURTAIN

61

END OF PART II

Her loyalty to her husband is magnificent. The way she behaves in the banquet scene is beyond praise. In spite of her complete lack of compassion & goodness of heart one cannot but have the greatest admiration for her courage & loyalty.

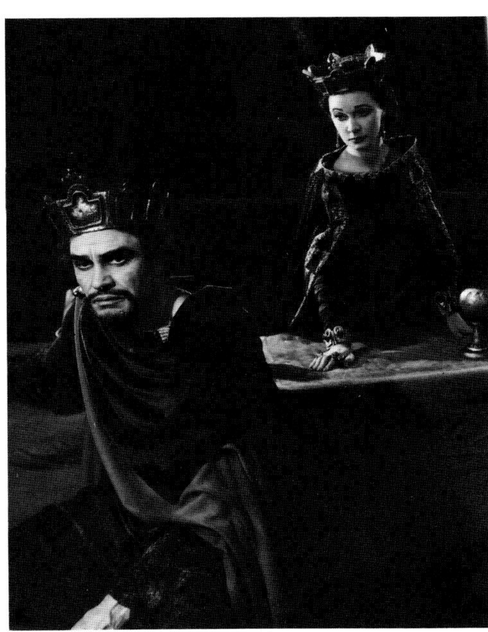

Act III, Scene iv.
"I am in blood stepp'd in so far."
Sir Laurence Olivier (Macbeth), Vivien Leigh (Lady Macbeth).

PART III (IV, i to V, ix). 49:00

Scene 1 (IV, i), Cauldron Scene. 8:10.

When the house lights go out there comes "a great crash of thunder echoing through a cavern out of which comes the hissing, bubbling sound of a boiling cauldron. . . . It must not be loud, but must come up in volume each time the Witches chant all together." Under blue and red lights we see the Witches circling their cauldron, into which they throw their charms and from which smoke rolls up. Overhead and behind them, rough stone walls rise up to a natural arch reminiscent of the arches in Macbeth's palace. The charm complete, the Witches stop circling and wait. As if conjured up by their charm, Macbeth's coming is signaled by a knocking sound and he steps forth from the darkness at the back of the cave. As he comes in the light grows redder, the Witches wait, crouched around the cauldron as they had crouched around the rock when Macbeth first met them.

The conjurations begin. From the fire there comes first "a great fierce hissing sound, as the flames shoot up," and then at the Witches' command, "Thy self and office deftly show!" there comes "a sharp crack of ear-splitting thunder," and the Armed Head, "which is Macbeth's own head cut from his body," rises from the cauldron. "Another crack of thunder," "a scream," and the Bloody Child appears, speaking in Macduff's voice. "Another crack of thunder, then sound of Malcolm's victorious trumpets and drums." From the cauldron rises the Child Crowned, with a tree in his hand, and it speaks in Malcolm's voice. The Witches draw together and, at Macbeth's demand to know more, a "strange, unearthly beautiful and serene music" fills the cavern. Across the forestage pass Banquo and his heirs dressed in dark gray robes with a darker gray drape and hood, "like shadows." As Banquo steps into the light to smile and claim them for his own, the "Witches disappear behind OP rock piece." The music stops, the light on Banquo fades out, and "he is left alone in their monstrous cave." The "noise of galloping horses" offstage brings him to himself, he summons Lennox, and the two men go out together at the back of the cave. As the lights go down, we hear a "short piece of music denoting Macbeth and followers galloping away." It fades to silence and the stage darkens to blackout.

Scene 2 (IV, ii), Lady Macduff Scene. 4:55.

During the blackout, the backcloth for the Lady Macduff Scene, painted to look like a frescoed wall, drops into place just in back of the runners, which are "swagged" or drawn up into a peaked opening. The lights come up and Lady Macduff, dressed in blue and carrying a baby, comes in with Ross. As they talk, her two young sons are laughing and play-fighting around them. They are a family at peace. The nobleman is close kin. "He kisses her," and as they speak of the children, he is touching the baby, "giving it his blessing." He leaves and Lady Macduff, sitting nursing the baby, banters with her oldest boy. Then a threat materializes in the form of an old Shepherd telling of dangers, "who is frightened himself and leaves as soon as he has given his warning." The tableau breaks, "Lady Mac rises," her sons draw near her. "Almost immediately the two terrible brutes who murdered Banquo appear." The younger son "sees Murderer & gives a frightened cry & turns to Lady Mac & holds on to her." "Her gallant eldest son defends his father's name. The first brute smashes his skull like an egg." Her baby in her arms, Lady Macduff flees shrieking.

Scene 3 (IV, iii), England Scene. 11:15.

During the blackout, a "Wall was rolled on from stage right," and the "Madcuff cloth" was flown out, revealing the England cut cloth (one with an opening in it) and the backcloth, which were already in place, so that when the lights came up the scene had changed to England, brightly lit (to look like noontime) and overhung with the arching boles of huge trees (the cut cloth). Malcolm and Macduff enter. "Malcolm is young & unsure of himself," boyish looking and small next to the tall, large-limbed Macduff. The two men are at first cautious with each other. The dissembling Malcolm sits, feigning indifference to test Macduff, who kneels as he pleads straightforwardly with Malcolm until, the testing nearly over, he rises and turns away in disgust before Malcolm reaches out and stops him. He succeeds, and they are friends. Ross then arrives, greetings are exchanged, the news of Macduff's slain family told, and, following Shakespeare literally, "Mac pulls his cap over his eyes," and Malcolm "gently pulls Mac's right arm away from his face. Malcolm and Macduff now trust each other completely." The three men leave together, the lights fade, and there is the sound of "music to link England Scene with Sc. 4."

Scene 4 (V, i), Sleepwalking Scene. 6:05.

During the blackout the England cloths are flown out, revealing the "Sleepwalking Cloths" already in place. The clock strikes two. "It is very early morning & the great long corridor leading to the Queen's apartments looks terrifyingly eerie and cold in the moonlight." The Doctor and the Waiting Gentlewoman watch anxiously from downstage. "Suddenly at the extreme end of the corridor they see a small light." Down the great corridor she comes, passing under one set of arches after another until she reaches the forestage. "She stands [the] light on floor, PS of her, then starts to rub her hands." She has a dazed, hypnotized look, her dark gray nightdress is disheveled, and her hair, now gray, hangs loose about her shoulders. "Serious and professional in his manner," the Doctor clutches his notebook, and watches. Her futile expiation performed, Lady Macbeth goes back into the darkness the way she came, to be seen no more. The Gentlewoman is worried, and fearful of the secrets she now possesses. As the Doctor gives his instructions to her, "we hear drums very softly in the distance." Bidding the Doctor good night, the Gentlewoman draws a curtain across the second arch, screening the corridor, and leaves.

Scene 5 (V, ii), Revolt Scene. 1:30.

Scots noblemen and soldiers rush in from stage right, and the stage brightens with the light from their lantern. Two other Scots soldiers, led by another nobleman, march in from stage left. Greetings are exchanged, and plans made, as all the while the drums beat softly and the morning light begins to brighten the gray arches of Dunsinane. Seyton enters behind the men, and stands listening to their marching orders. They stride off together stage right, Seyton watches them go, and then runs out to tell Macbeth as the drums fade away in the distance. The build toward the last scene has begun, and events occur ever swifter to the story's end.

Scene 6 (V, iii), Cream Fac'd Loon Scene. 4:00.

It is now dawn, and Dunsinane is bathed in light. Macbeth, who has not been seen since his meeting with the Witches, comes in with Seyton. The messenger comes, and he kneels to deliver his message to the King. We think momentarily of those who knelt before the kindly Duncan, as we watch Macbeth roar his anger at the messenger's bad tidings, then smash his fingers into the kneeling man's face and brutally shove him down the steps. Macbeth's mood swings from outbursts of violence to quiet despair. Alone, he sits on the forestage steps, and sadly speaks of his desolation. Then, when Seyton comes with the armor, Macbeth's active self returns. He rises and reaches for his spear. As he speaks, Seyton pulls off his cloak and straps on the brown leather armor. The Doctor (whom the Stratford promptbook brings on with Seyton, and whom Shaw's promptbook brings on later) stands silent until spoken to. When he does speak, his fawning, timid replies provoke scorn from Macbeth and from us. Armed once again, Macbeth marches out, with Seyton at his heels, and the Doctor scurries away. The runners close, as we hear "loud drums and trumpets for entrance of Malcolm, Old Siward, and the rest."

Scene 7 (V, iv), Birnam Wood Scene. 0:58.

Onto the brightly lit forestage march the soldiers: from stage right come Scotsmen in dark tartans led by Malcolm in white; from stage left, the English in blue tunics, led by Old Siward. The two leaders exchange greetings, dispatch Young Siward with orders for camouflage, and the two groups, now joined, march offstage together. The trumpets sound, the drums beat, and the pace of the action grows swifter, more intense.

Scene 8 (V, v to ix), Last Scene. 11:15.

The runners open, disclosing the battlements of Dunsinane. Macbeth marches in, flanked by his standard bearers, and strides up the steps to survey the field. There comes the cry of women. Macbeth is kneeling center stage when Seyton brings news of Lady Macbeth's death. The lights begin to fade as twilight comes; Macbeth rises, and steps forward to utter his despair—"Tomorrow, and tomorrow, and tomorrow"—"leaning against PS Pros," behind him, the soldiers and standard bearers complete the tableau. The sentry comes, and the tableau breaks as the soldiers stir to make room for him. Macbeth runs up, seizes him, and then, the message confirmed, throws him down. He shouts his orders. As the soldiers rush to their posts, the alarum bell crashes out, ringing again as it had for the discovery of Duncan's murder.

In the lull that follows we hear the sound of Malcolm's "drums and trumpets coming nearer and nearer." The soldiers enter, some of them with branches, and stand behind Old Siward, Malcolm, Macduff, and the Scots noblemen. As Malcolm raises his hand, the trumpets and drums stop. He gives his order, "Make all the trumpets speak; give them all breath / Those clamorous harbingers of blood and death." "Trumpets [sound] as loud as possible, out of which battle music starts: exciting, fierce, but it must not be too loud." The avengers storm out, shouting. Macbeth enters. His troops fight, and are routed by the English. Macbeth is everywhere, his longsword flashing in the dim light. He fells "an English sentry." With a few strokes, he cuts down Young Siward. He is alone with the two corpses, and he turns to mount the battlements when Macduff, a giant in armor, enters and snaps Macbeth round with his challenge: "Turn, hell-hound, turn!"

"Music stops suddenly." This is the moment toward which the action has been building for so long: the avenger at last has the tyrant within his sword's length, and Macbeth, again the warrior, can at last seek his fate as a fighting man. In the thrust and parry, Macbeth at first takes the offensive. Then, when he hears of Macduff's untimely birth, "Macbeth fights desperately, Macduff coldly." A drum begins to beat, throbbing like a pulse. The two men grapple high on the battlements stage left. Macduff knocks away Macbeth's sword. Each draws his dagger. Their furious struggle carries them up to the highest part of the battlements, where they fall to their knees, each locked in the other's grip. "Macduff pushes Macbeth's dagger with his own, grabs his wrist with L hand and pushes his R forearm under Macbeth's throat," then, exerting all his strength, he pushes him off the battlements to his death. The battle music, now "very loud," swells to retreat and flourish. Malcolm enters with Old Siward, Ross, and the soldiers. Macduff comes down to them from the battlements, hailing Malcolm as the new King of Scotland. A general shout "Hail, King of Scotland," and "a great flourish of victorious trumpets and drums" greet Malcolm, his young face shining like his bright garments, who makes his proclamations from the battlements. A flourish of trumpets, and the curtain falls.

This last part of the play, in which Macbeth's fate is foreshadowed in the Cauldron Scene, and then played out in the course of two acts, presents special problems. It is long, in that Macbeth's inevitable execution is delayed by seeming digressions—Lady Macduff's murder, Malcolm and Macduff's long parley in England, the Sleepwalking Scene. Because of these digressions from the main narrative, and the shifts of scene and interest they entail, the pace is especially tricky. Too much time and the wrong sort of attention on the Witches, on the Sleepwalking, or (unlikely) on Macduff's concerns, and the main thrust is blunted. The system of runners, drops, and cloths allows Shaw to minimize time lost through set changes. It thus keeps the pace rapid between scenes (the "running plot" allows only five seconds between some scenes), even if the pace could be slowed within a scene. The Cauldron Scene and the Lady Macduff Scene each end in a burst of action, but once passed, the scene following begins in a low key, reaching its lowest in the England Scene. Rather than hurrying through this scene (which is often said to be unplayable and therefore drastically shortened), Shaw gives it about a quarter of this part's running time, with the good effect that its slow pace, which continues through the Sleepwalking Scene, builds up a feeling of action, violent action, constrained, ready to blaze forth at any moment. After this slow stillness comes the blare of trumpets, the beat of drums, and the soldiers making ready for battle. Across the stage they march, gathering forces, preparing defenses, until the fighting starts. The movement from slow beginnings to violent endings recurs so regularly in each part that it can only be design, Shakespeare's design, which Shaw follows. Like the Macbeth-Macduff fight at the end of the third part, the discovery of Duncan's murder and the coming of Banquo's Ghost bring each of the first two parts to a violent climax.

The Witches' Cave.

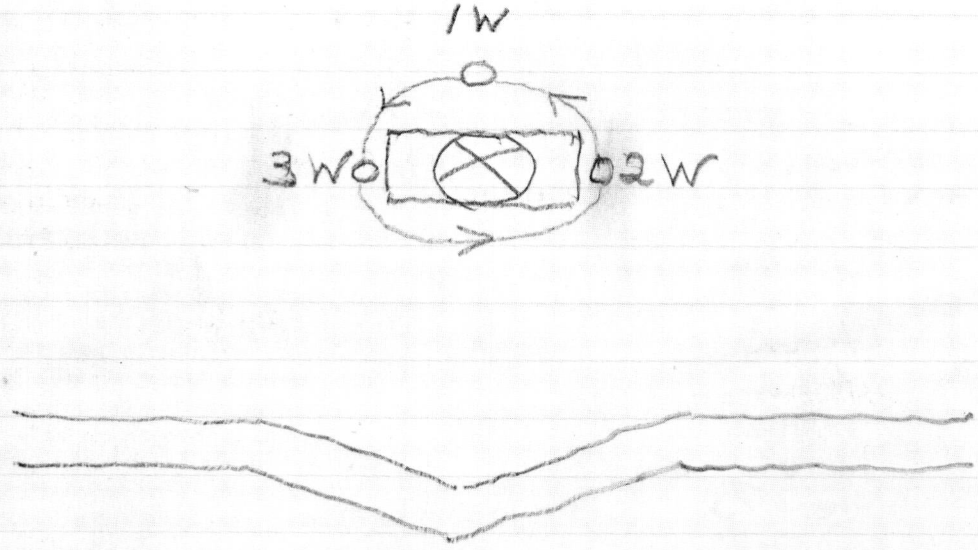

1W

3W 2W

Cauldron Scene. 4 am.

The first time we see the Witches they are "hovering in the fog & filthy air." The second time we see them they are on the earth & now we see them below the earth or as though they were in hell. They are preparing their black magic.

MACBETH

~~His message ere he come, that a swift blessing~~
~~May soon return to this our suffering country~~
~~Under a hand accurs'd!~~

~~*Lord.*~~ ~~I'll send my prayers with him.~~ ~~*Exeunt*~~

PART III

~~Act Fourth~~

SCENE I Cauldron 4AM

A cavern. In the middle, a boiling cauldron

Thunder. ~~*Enter*~~ *the three Witches*

HOUSE LIGHTS FADE OUT
THUNDER
CURTAIN UP
Cauldron Bubbling

1. *W.* Thrice the brinded cat hath mew'd.
2. *W.* Thrice, and once the hedge-pig whin'd.
3. *W.* Harpier cries ''Tis time, 'tis time.'
1. *W.* Round about the cauldron go: — moving round the Cauldron
In the poison'd entrails throw; — They stop with 1W US of Cauldron, 2W PS ", 3W OP "
Toad, that under cold stone
Days and nights has thirty one
Swelter'd venom sleeping got,
Boil thou first i' the charmed pot. — throws Toad into Cauldron
All. Double, double, toil and trouble; — They move round the cauldron again
Fire burn, and cauldron bubble.
2. *W.* Fillet of a fenny snake, — They stop 2W US of Cauldron, 1W OP " ", 3W PS " "

66

In the cauldron boil and bake;
Eye of newt, and toe of frog,
Wool of bat, and tongue of dog;
Adder's fork, and blind-worm's sting,
Lizard's leg, and howlet's wing;
For a charm of powerful trouble,
Like a hell-broth, boil and bubble. — Throws them all into cauldron

All. Double, double, toil and trouble,
Fire burn, and cauldron bubble.

move round the cauldron again

3. *W.* Scale of dragon, tooth of wolf,
Witches' mummy, maw, and gulf
Of the ravin'd salt-sea shark;
Root of hemlock, digg'd i' the dark;
Liver of blaspheming Jew,
Gall of goat, and slips of yew,
Sliver'd in the moon's eclipse;
Nose of Turk, and Tartar's lips;
Finger of birth-strangled babe,
Ditch-deliver'd by a drab,
Make the gruel thick and slab:
Add thereto a tiger's chaudron,
For the ingredients of our cauldron. — Throws them all into cauldron

They stop
3 W. US of Cauldron
1 W PS ..
2 W OP ..

All. Double, double, toil and trouble,
Fire burn, and cauldron bubble. — Stop suddenly 1 W US of Cauldron

move round the cauldron again

~~2. *W.* Cool it with a baboon's blood,~~

Macbeth, Act IV, Scene i

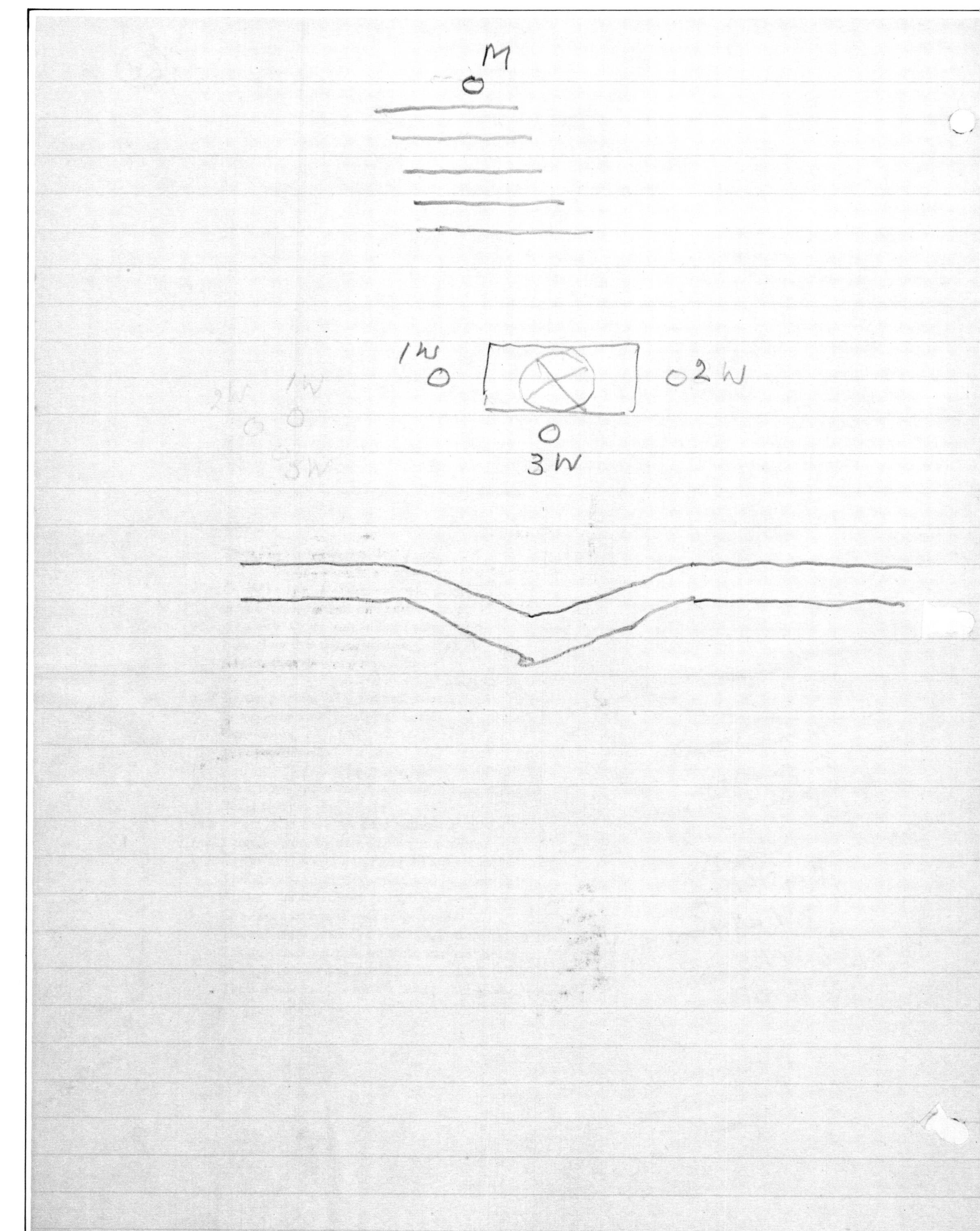
M
1W
O
O 2W
O
3W

MACBETH

~~Then the charm is firm and good.~~

~~*Enter Hecate to the other three Witches*~~

~~*Hec.* O, well done! I commend your pains,~~
~~And every one shall share i' the gains:~~
~~And now about the cauldron sing,~~
~~Like elves and fairies in a ring,~~
~~Enchanting all that you put in.~~

~~*Music and a song: 'Black spirits,' &c.*~~

1 *W.* By the pricking of my thumbs,
Something wicked this way comes: — KNOCKING
Open locks,
Whoever knocks! — LIGHT on BACK Steps

Enter Macbeth

Mac. How now, you secret, black, and midnight hags?
What is't you do?
All. A deed without a name.
Mac. I conjure you, by that which you profess,
(Howe'er you come to know it) answer me:
Though you untie the winds, and let them fight
Against the churches; though the yesty waves
Confound and swallow navigation up;
Though bladed corn be lodg'd, and trees blown down,
Though castles topple on their warders' heads;
Though palaces and pyramids do slope
Their heads to their foundations; though the treasure

68

1W moves to OP of Cauldron
2W moves to DS of DS Cauldron

coming half way done the steps

down back steps PS & moves to top of C Stage steps

They show no surprise when they sense the approach of Macbeth, for they probably know that he is coming to visit them as soon as he says so to his wife. Macbeth descends into their cavern & demands to know the answers to his questions. Now he has given himself up to evil completely & he is led into a feeling of false security by what he is told by the apparitions.

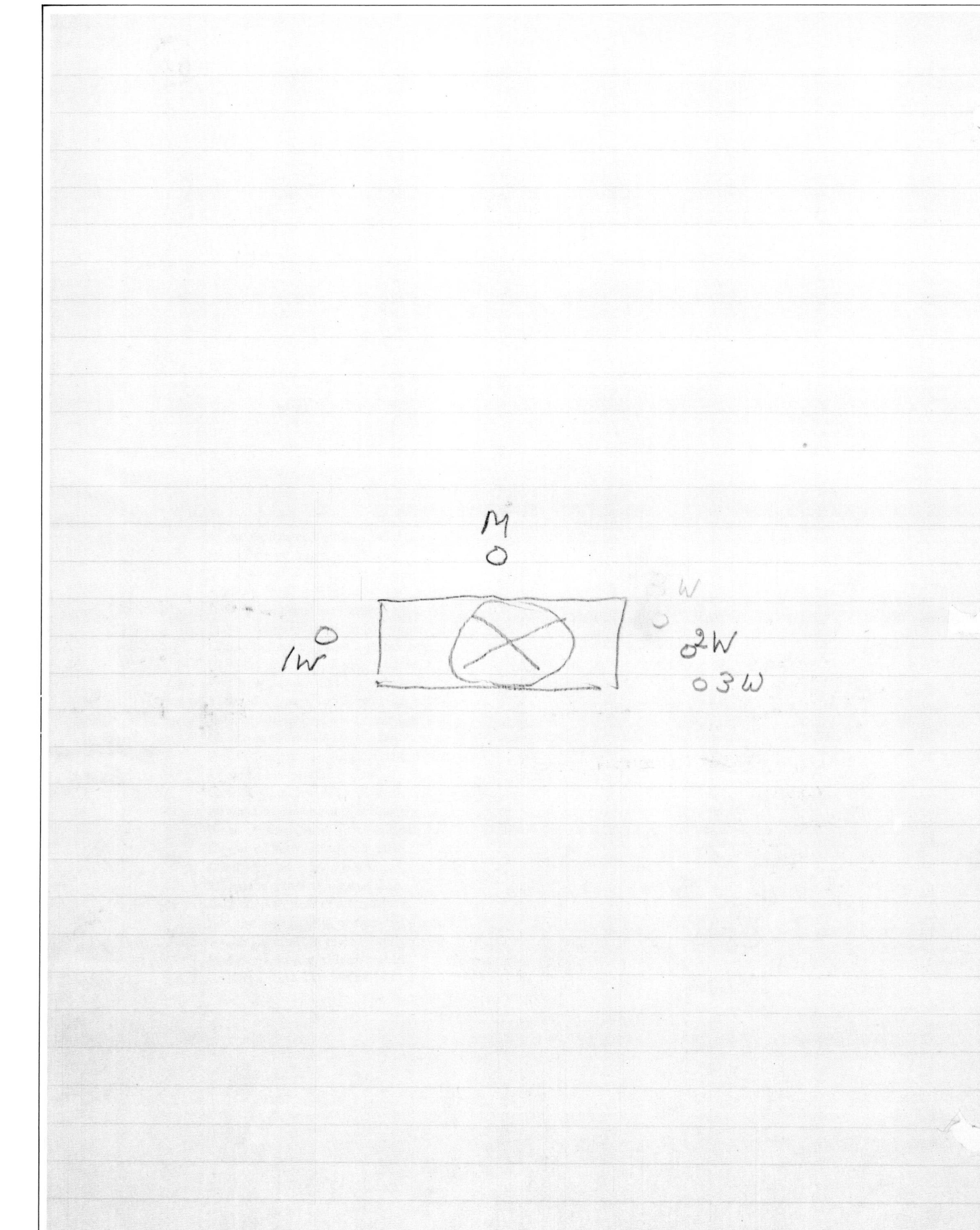
M
1W
2W
3W
3W

Act IV Sc. i

Of nature's germins tumble all together,
Even till destruction sicken; answer me
To what I ask you.

1. W. Speak.
2. W. Demand.
3. W. We 'll answer.
1. W. Say, if thou 'dst rather hear it from our mouths,
Or from our masters.
Mac. Call 'em: let me see 'em.

Coming down steps to US of Cauldron

1. W. Pour in sow's blood, that hath eaten
Her nine farrow; grease that 's sweaten
From the murderer's gibbet throw
Into the flame.

Hissing noise

2W & 3W pour blood & grease on to the fire from two vessels standing beside cauldron 2 W moves to DS PS of 3W

All. Come high or low:
Thyself and office deftly show!

Thunder. First Apparition: an armed Head

appears out of the cauldron

Mac. Tell me, thou unknown power,—
1. W. He knows thy thought:
Hear his speech, but say thou nought.
1. A. Macbeth! Macbeth! Macbeth! beware Macduff,
Beware the thane of Fife. Dismiss me: enough.

Descends

into the Cauldron

Mac. Whate'er thou art, for thy good caution, thanks;
Thou hast harp'd my fear aright: but one word more,—
1. W. He will not be commanded: here 's another,

69

The first apparition, which is his own head cut from his body, tells him to beware of Macduff.

(66)

MACBETH

More potent than the first.
Thunder. Second Apparition : a bloody Child

A Scream

appears out of the Cauldron

2. *A.* Macbeth ! Macbeth ! Macbeth !
~~*Mac.* Had I three ears, I'ld hear thee.~~
2. *A.* Be bloody, bold, and resolute ; laugh to scorn
The power of man : for none of woman born
Shall harm Macbeth. *Descends*

into the Cauldron

Mac. Then live Macduff : what need I fear of thee ?
But yet I 'll make assurance double sure,
And take a bond of fate : thou shalt not live,
That I may tell pale-hearted fear, it lies ;
And sleep in spite of thunder.
Thunder. Third Apparition : a Child crowned, with a tree in his hand

appears out of Cauldron

What is this,
That rises like the issue of a king,
And wears upon his baby-brow the round
And top of sovereignty ?
All. Listen, but speak not to 't.
3. *A.* Be lion-mettled, proud, and take no care
Who chafes, who frets, or where conspirers are :
Macbeth shall never vanquish'd be, until
Great Birnam wood to high Dunsinane hill
Shall come against him. *Descends*

into the Cauldron

Mac. That will never be :

70

The second apparition, which is the baby Macduff just after it has been ripped from its mother's womb, tells him that he need have no fear for he cannot be harmed by anyone who is born of woman.

The third apparition, which is Malcolm with a heavy bough from Birnam Wood, tells him that he will never be vanquished till Birnam Wood moves to the hill on which his Castle at Dunsinane is built.

Act IV, Scene i. The Cauldron Scene, The Armed Head. Mary Law (Witch), Sir Laurence Olivier (Macbeth), Dilys Hamlett, Nancye Stewart (Witches) (see opposite page).

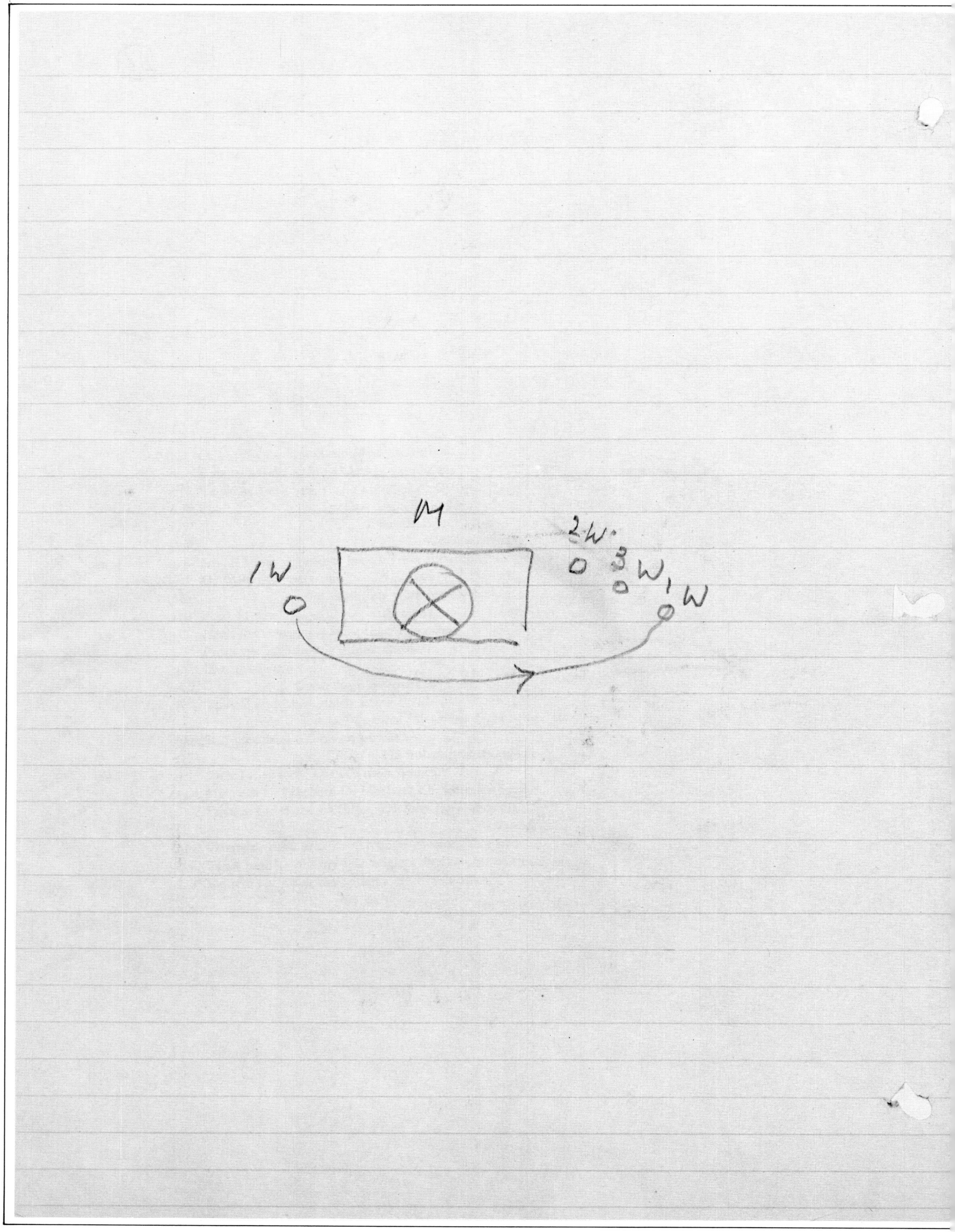

The Eight Kings.
The Witches say

> "Show his eyes, & grieve his heart
> Come like shadows, so depart!"

And that is exactly how the Kings should appear. Like Shadows.

Finally when he forces the Witches to tell him whether Banquo's heirs will reign in Scotland, he is tortured & driven into a state of fury by what he is shown.

Macbeth, Act IV, Scene i

1st King	Ian Holm
2nd "	Richard Coe
3rd "	Geoffrey Sassé
4th "	Rex Robinson
5th "	Leon Eagles
6th "	Emrys James
7th "	George Little
8th "	Paul Vieyra

Who can impress the forest, bid the tree
Unfix his earth-bound root? Sweet bodements! good!
Rebellious ~~dead~~ (head), rise never, till the wood †
Of Birnam rise, and our high-plac'd Macbeth
Shall live the lease of nature, pay his breath
To time, and mortal custom. Yet my heart
Throbs to know one thing: tell me, if your art
Can tell so much: shall Banquo's issue ever
Reign in this kingdom?

All. Seek to know no more.

(1 W moves round DS of cauldron to PS)

Mac. I will be satisfied: deny me this,
And an eternal curse fall on you! Let me know:
Why sinks that cauldron? and what noise is this?

(moves round OP of cauldron as it sinks)

Hautboys

2 ~~1~~. *W.* Show!
3 ~~2~~. *W.* Show!
1 ~~3~~. *W.* Show!
(pointing to OP Ass)

All. Show his eyes, and grieve his heart,
Come like shadows, so depart!

A show of eight Kings, the last with a glass in his hand;
Banquo's Ghost following

Mac. Thou art too like the spirit of Banquo: down!
Thy crown does sear mine eye-balls. And thy hair,
Thou other gold-bound brow, is like the first.
A third, is like the former. Filthy hags!

71

enter OP Ass
& move across forestage & exit PS Ass
Witches exit (unseen) PS Mid

The shadows disappear & also the Witches & he is left alone in their monstrous cave.

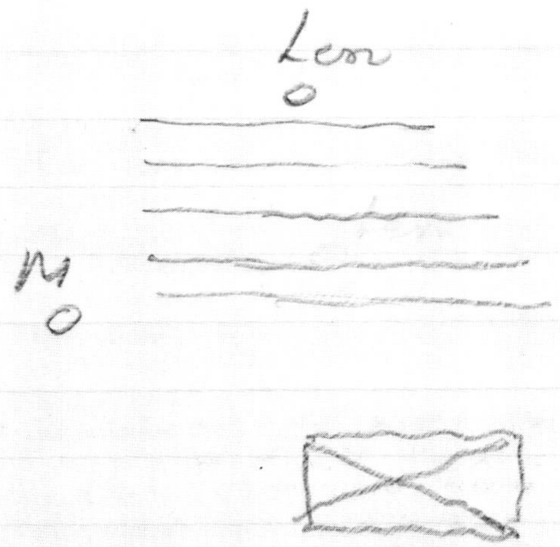

Macbeth, Act IV, Scene i

170

MACBETH

Why do you show me this ? A fourth ? Start, eyes !
What, will the line stretch out to the crack of doom ?
Another yet ? A seventh ? I 'll see no more :
And yet the eighth appears, who bears a glass
Which shows me many more ; and some I see
That two-fold balls and treble sceptres carry :
Horrible sight ! Now I see 'tis true,
For the blood-bolter'd Banquo smiles upon me,
And points at them for his. What, is this so ?

1. W. Ay, sir, all this is so : but why
Stands Macbeth thus amazedly ?
Come, sisters, cheer we up his sprites,
And show the best of our delights :
I'll charm the air to give a sound,
While you perform your antic round :
That this great king may kindly say,
Our duties did his welcome pay.

Music. The Witches dance, and then vanish, with Hecate

Mac. Where are they ? Gone ? Let this pernicious hour
Stand aye accursed in the calendar !
Come in, without there !

Enter Lennox

Len. What 's your grace's will ?

Mac. Saw you the weird sisters ?

72

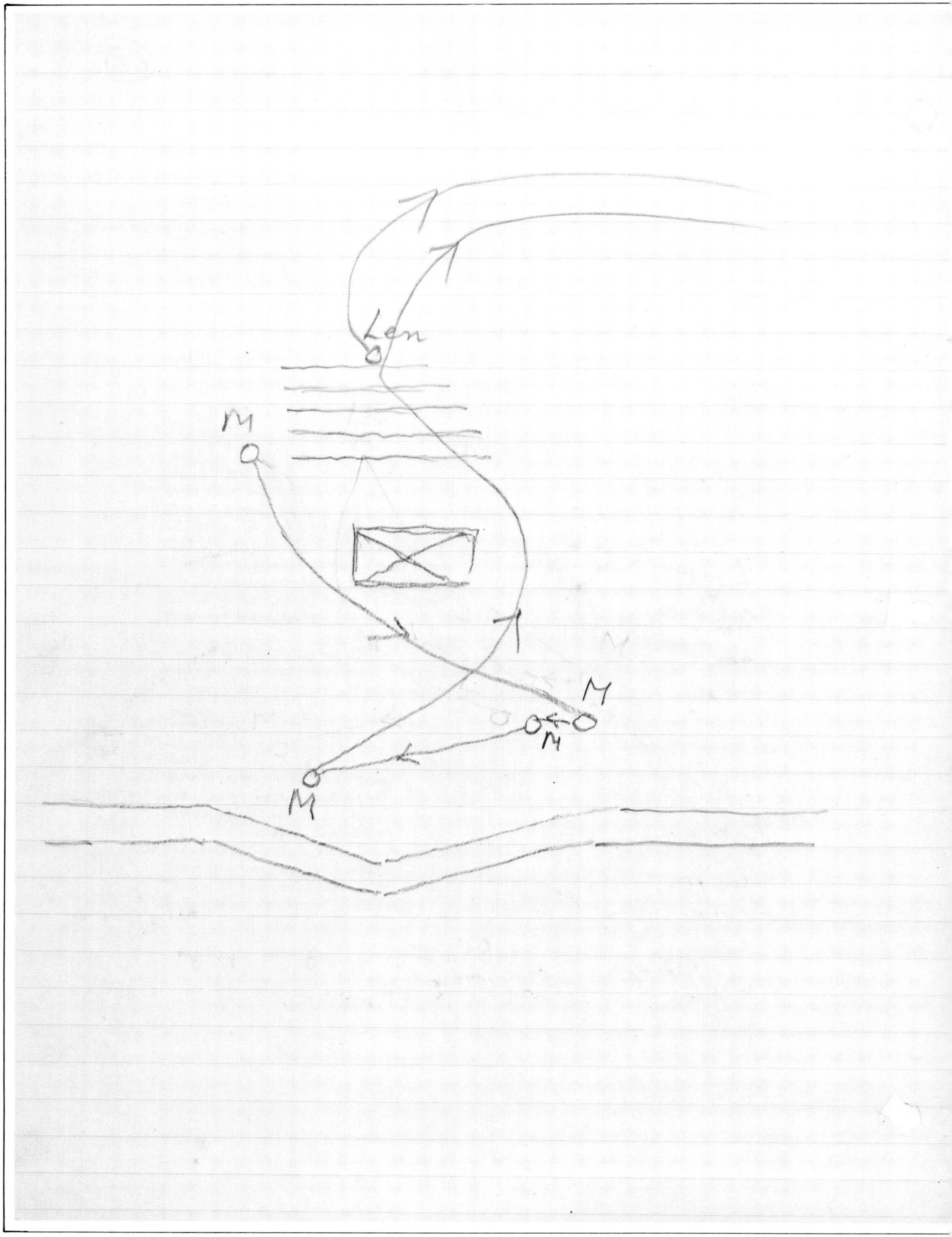

He calls Lennox in & is told that Macduff has fled to England & escaped him.

He immediately decides to carry out the most revolting revenge.

Len. No, my lord.
Mac. Came they not by you?
Len. No indeed, my lord.
Mac. Infected be the air whereon they ride,
And damn'd all those that trust them! I did hear
The galloping of horse: who was 't came by?
Len. 'Tis two or three, my lord, that bring you word
Macduff is fled to England.
Mac. Fled to England?
Len. Ay, my good lord.
Mac. (*aside*) Time, thou anticipat'st my dread exploits:
The flighty purpose never is o'ertook
Unless the deed go with it: from this moment
The very firstlings of my heart shall be
The firstlings of my hand. And even now,
To crown my thoughts with acts, be it thought and done:
The castle of Macduff I will surprise,
Seize upon Fife; give to the edge o' the sword
His wife, his babes, and all unfortunate souls
That trace him in his line. No boasting like a fool,
This deed I'll do, before this purpose cool,
But no more sights!—Where are these gentlemen?
Come, bring me where they are. *Exeunt*

21 g 73

moving DS to OP of M

X-ing in front of Len to DS PS

X-ing in front of Len to DS OP

turning & moving PS of cauldron to C steps

turning to Len

slight move to Len

MUSIC

Len & M up C steps & PS US steps

FADE to BLACK OUT CLOTH FLIED IN

Lady Macduff Scene. 5 pm.

For the first time in this play we hear children laughing. The two eldest sons of Macduff are playing together. Their mother comes in with their baby brother & their dear cousin Ross.

Lady Macduff is a simple sweet woman, she cannot understand how her husband could possibly leave her & his children without even saying "Good-bye" & go to a foreign country. Ross tries to calm her & explain, but it is no good. Her instinct as a mother tells her that her family is in great danger.

Lady Macduff. 28 [years old]. Maxine Audley.

She is a tender & loving mother & a devoted wife. She has her children round her. Two small sons & a baby in arms. She is very worried when we see her, but we should feel that, usually, she & Macduff & their children are very happy & love each other dearly. They are simple people, but Lady Macduff has the quiet dignity of a great lady.

Enter OP Pros — 1st & 2nd Sons. 1st Son is carrying a chair & defending himself with it. 2nd Son is attacking him with a wooden sword. They are laughing.
1st Son puts chair down in front of main stage PS of C. 2nd Son prods him with the sword & 1st Son falls back into chair pretending to die

MACBETH

FADE IN

SCENE II Lady Macduff

Fife. Macduff's castle 5PM.

carrying baby OP Pros → *Enter Lady Macduff, ~~her Son,~~ and Ross*

L.M. What had he done, to make him fly the land?
Ross. You must have patience, madam.
L.M. He had none:
His flight was madness: when our actions do not,
Our fears do make us traitors. — 1st Son looks at her
Ross. You know not
Whether it was his wisdom, or his fear. — Lady Mac moves to PS of C followed by Ross
L.M. Wisdom? to leave his wife, to leave his babes,
His mansion, and his titles, in a place
From whence himself does fly? He loves us not,
He wants the natural touch. For the poor wren
(The most diminutive of birds) will fight,
Her young ones in her nest, against the owl.
All is the fear, and nothing is the love;
As little is the wisdom, where the flight
So runs against all reason.
Ross. My dearest coz,
I pray you school yourself: but, for your husband,
He is noble, wise, judicious, and best knows
The fits o' the season. I dare not speak much further,

74

2nd Son starts to mend his sword with a piece of cord
1st Son joins him

She stops & turns to him

They sit on the floor OP of chair

Lady Macduff's Castle.

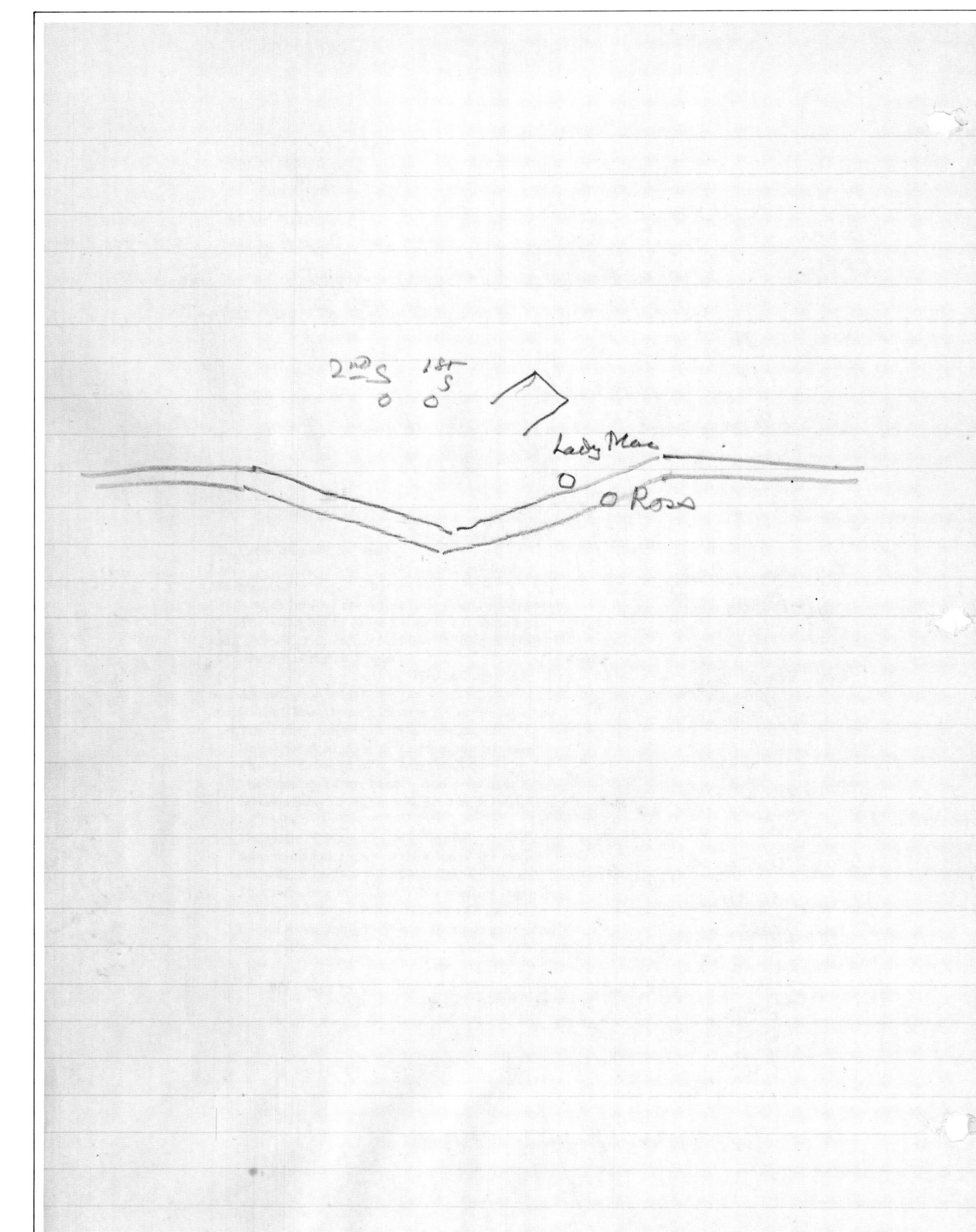
2nd S
1st S
Lady Mac
Ross

Act IV Sc. ii

But cruel are the times, when we are traitors
And do not know ourselves ; when we hold rumour
From what we fear, yet know not what we fear,
But float upon a wild and violent sea
Each way, and move. I take my leave of you : †
Shall not be long but I 'll be here again :
Things at the worst will cease, or else climb upward,
To what they were before. My pretty cousin,
Blessing upon you !

L.M. Father'd he is, and yet he 's fatherless.

Ross. I am so much a fool, should I stay longer,
It would be my disgrace and your discomfort :
I take my leave at once. *Exit*

L.M. Sirrah, your father 's dead,
And what will you do now ? How will you live ?

1st *Son.* As birds do, mother.

L.M. What, with worms and flies ?

1st *Son.* With what I get, I mean, and so do they.

L.M. Poor bird, thou 'ldst never fear the net nor lime,
The pitfall, nor the gin.

1st *Son.* Why should I, mother ? Poor birds they are not set for.
My father is not dead, for all your saying.

L.M. Yes, he is dead : ~~how wilt thou do for a father~~ ?

~~*Son.* Nay, how will you do for a husband ?~~

75

Xing in front of her to PS

turns to her

moves to chair & sits. 1st Son comes & looks at the baby & stands beside her L OPS.

Kisses her forehead

touching the baby

PS Ass

1st Son. John Rogers.
2nd Son. Philip Thomas.

They are two small boys. Happy, gay & perfectly ordinary by nature. Naturally the situation in which we see them is not at all ordinary, & they must, during the scene, re-act accordingly.

Ross leaves. Her eldest son talks to her as she nurses the baby.

MACBETH

~~L.M. Why, I can buy me twenty at any market.~~
~~Son. Then you'll buy 'em to sell again.~~
~~L.M. Thou speak'st with all thy wit, and yet, i' faith,~~
~~With wit enough for thee.~~

1st *Son.* Was my father a traitor, mother?

L.M. Ay, that he was.

1st *Son.* What is a traitor?

L.M. Why, one that swears, and lies.

1st *Son.* And be all traitors that do so?

L.M. Every one that does so is a traitor, and must be hang'd. — 2nd Son looks up

1st *Son.* And must they all be hang'd that swear and lie?

L.M. Every one.

1st *Son.* Who must hang them?

L.M. Why, the honest men.

1st *Son.* Then the liars and swearers are fools; for there are liars and swearers enow to beat the honest men, and hang up them. — 2nd Son laughs & Lady Mac hushes him

L.M. Now, God help thee, poor monkey!
But how wilt thou do for a father?

1st *Son.* If he were dead, you 'ld weep for him: if you would not, it were a good sign that I should quickly have a new father.

She laughs quickly — *L.M.* Poor prattler, how thou talk'st!

Enter a ~~Messenger~~ Shepherd — PS Ass

Shep ~~Mes~~. Bless you fair dame! I am not to you known,

76

Act IV, Scene ii. "Now, God help thee, poor monkey!" Philip Thomas (2d Son), John Rogers (1st Son), Maxine Audley (Lady Macduff) (see opposite page).

Suddenly an old Shepherd appears, begs her not to be alarmed, but warns her that she & her children are in great danger. He is frightened himself and leaves as soon as he has given his warning.

Almost immediately the two terrible brutes who murdered Banquo appear. In spite of her terror Lady Macduff retains her dignity as a great Lady & her gallant eldest son defends his father's name. The first brute smashes his skull like an egg. His mother has her baby in her arms & her other son clinging round her knees in terror.

Macbeth, Act IV, Scene ii

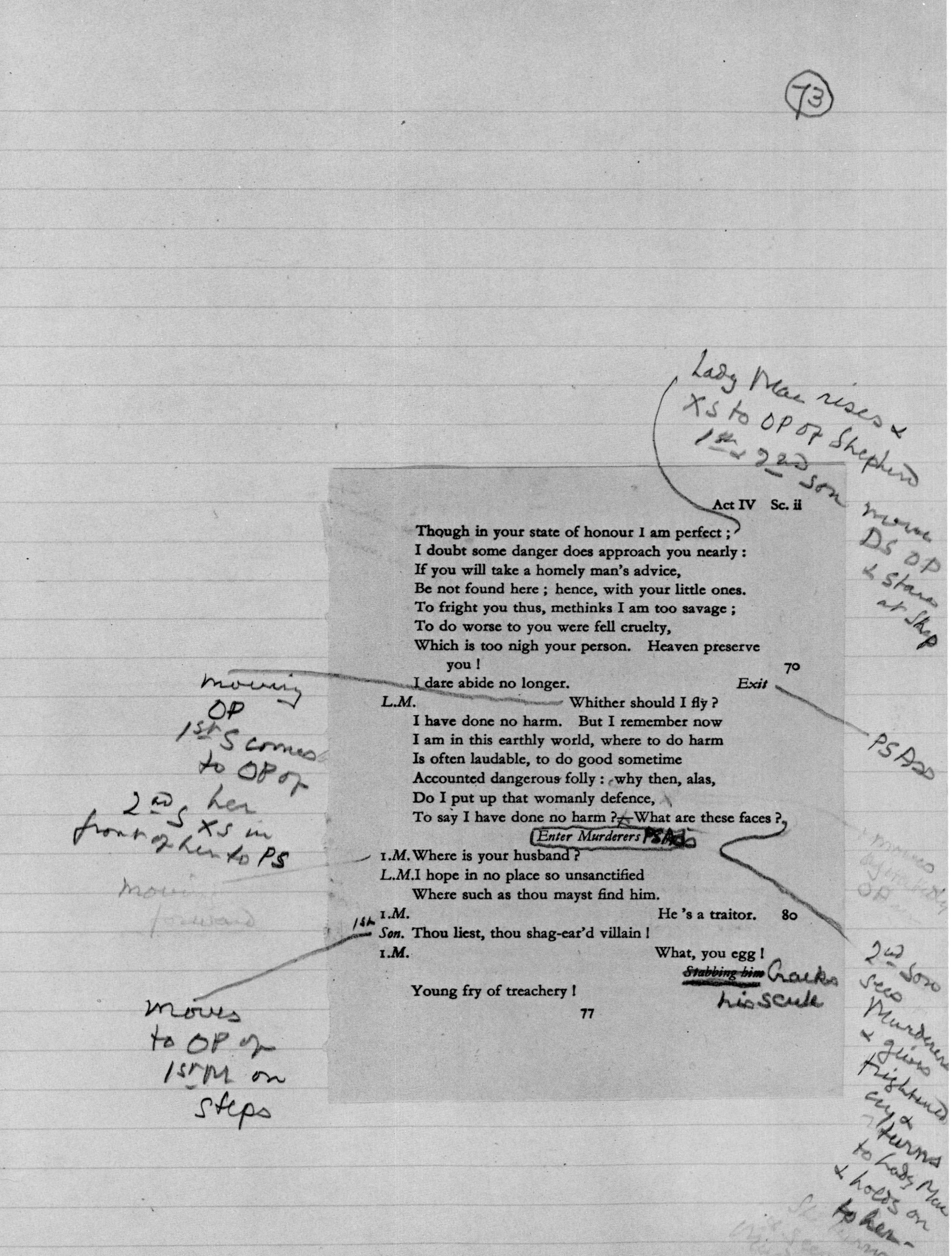

Act IV Sc. ii

Though in your state of honour I am perfect ;
I doubt some danger does approach you nearly :
If you will take a homely man's advice,
Be not found here ; hence, with your little ones.
To fright you thus, methinks I am too savage ;
To do worse to you were fell cruelty,
Which is too nigh your person. Heaven preserve
you !
I dare abide no longer. *Exit*

L.M. Whither should I fly ?
I have done no harm. But I remember now
I am in this earthly world, where to do harm
Is often laudable, to do good sometime
Accounted dangerous folly : why then, alas,
Do I put up that womanly defence,
To say I have done no harm ? What are these faces ?

Enter Murderers

1.*M.* Where is your husband ?

L.M. I hope in no place so unsanctified
Where such as thou mayst find him.

1.*M.* He 's a traitor.

Son. Thou liest, thou shag-ear'd villain !

1.*M.* What, you egg !
~~*Stabbing him*~~
Young fry of treachery !

77

Act IV, Scene ii. The Murderers Come. Philip Thomas (2d Son), Maxine Audley (Lady Macduff), John Rogers (1st Son), Ron Haddrick, Hugh Cross (Murderers) (see following pages).

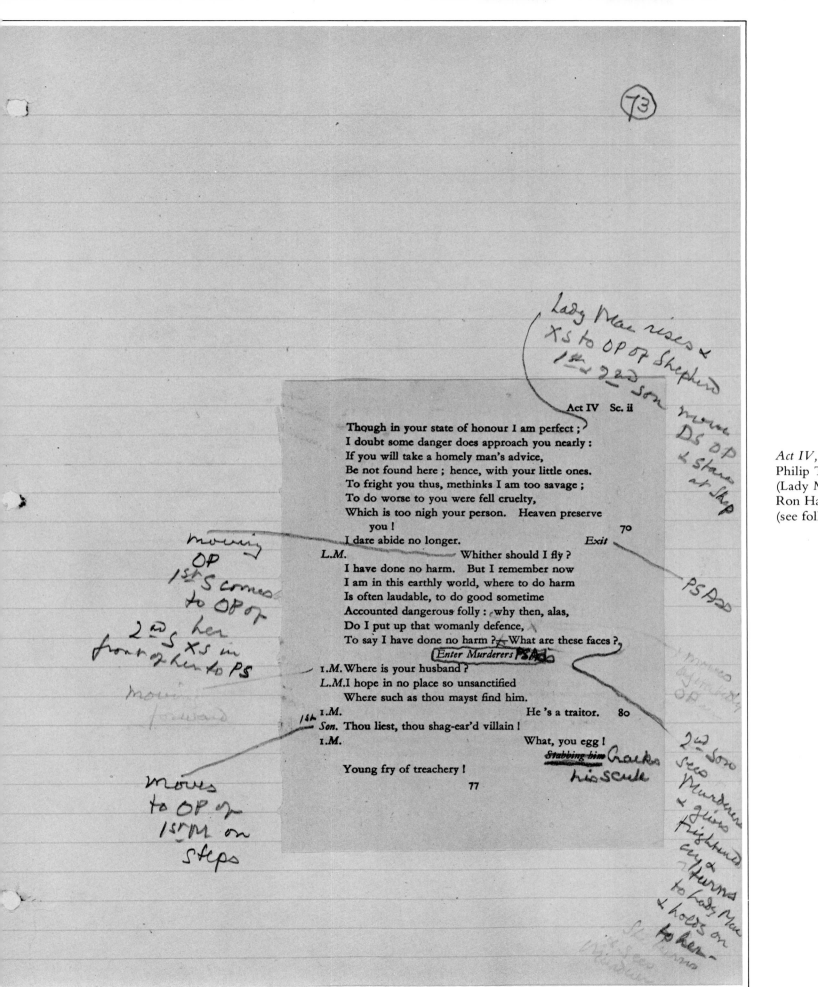

She starts to scream & both the Murderers set upon them.

Set for the England Scene.

2nd Son

Lady Mac

1st Son

1st Murd

2nd Murd

Mal

Mac

England Scene. 12 noon.

We are in England. It is peaceful, quiet & sunny. Malcolm is restless & unhappy in exile, but Macduff has come to England with the hope of getting him to lead an army of revolt against Macbeth.

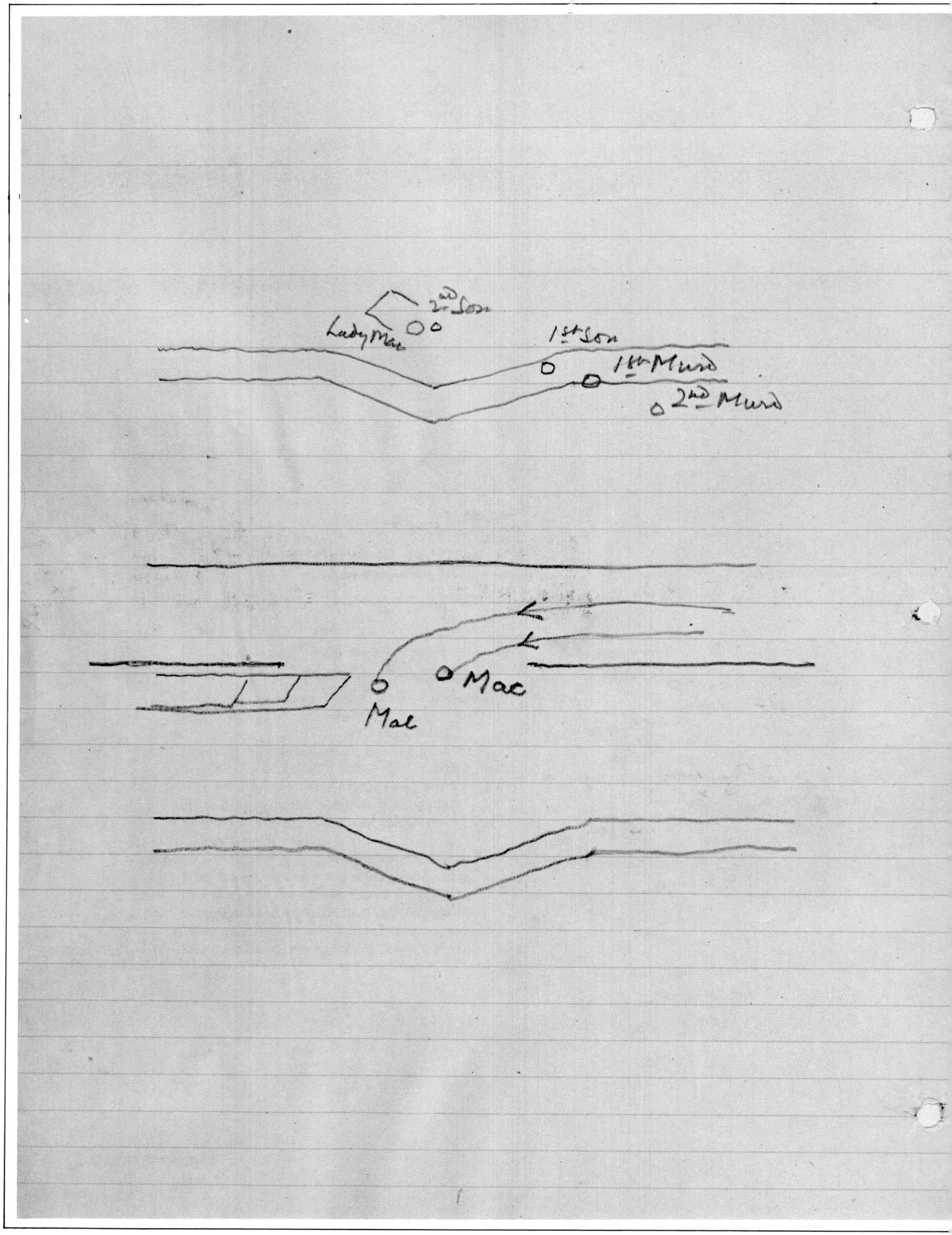

falls on his knees & turns to Lady Mac

MACBETH

Son. He has kill'd me, mother:
Run away, I pray you! *Dies*
~~*Exit*~~ *Lady Macduff*, ~~*crying 'Murder!'*~~ †Starts to Scream
~~*Exeunt murderers, following her*~~ (Exit OP Pros off (1st M takes chair (2nd M takes 1st, 3rd OP Pros

FADE to BLACK OUT DRAPE FLIED

MACDUFF FADE IN

SCENE III England 12noon

England. Before the King's palace

Enter Malcolm and Macduff — PS mid

Mal. Let us seek out some desolate shade, and there
Weep our sad bosoms empty.
Macd. Let us rather
Hold fast the mortal sword, and like good men
Bestride our down-fall'n birthdom: each new morn
New widows howl, new orphans cry, new sorrows
Strike heaven on the face, that it resounds — slight move DS
As if it felt with Scotland, and yell'd out
Like syllable of dolour.
Mal. What I believe, I'll wail; — Sits on end of Wall OP
What know, believe; and what I can redress,
As I shall find the time to friend, I will.
What you have spoke, it may be so perchance.
This tyrant, whose sole name blisters our tongues,
Was once thought honest: you have lov'd him well;

78

Act IV, Scene iii.
The England Scene.
Trader Faulkner (Malcolm),
Keith Michell (Macduff).

Malcolm is young & unsure of himself. He feels that he daren't trust anyone. Already Macbeth has been trying to inveigle him back to Scotland with promises of luxury & riches. The boy is on his guard.

One could accuse [Macduff] of stupidity for leaving his wife and children unprotected, but it would never enter such a man's head that anyone, not even Macbeth, could instigate such a dastardly crime as the murdering of his family. He is a man who has a simple & true belief in God.

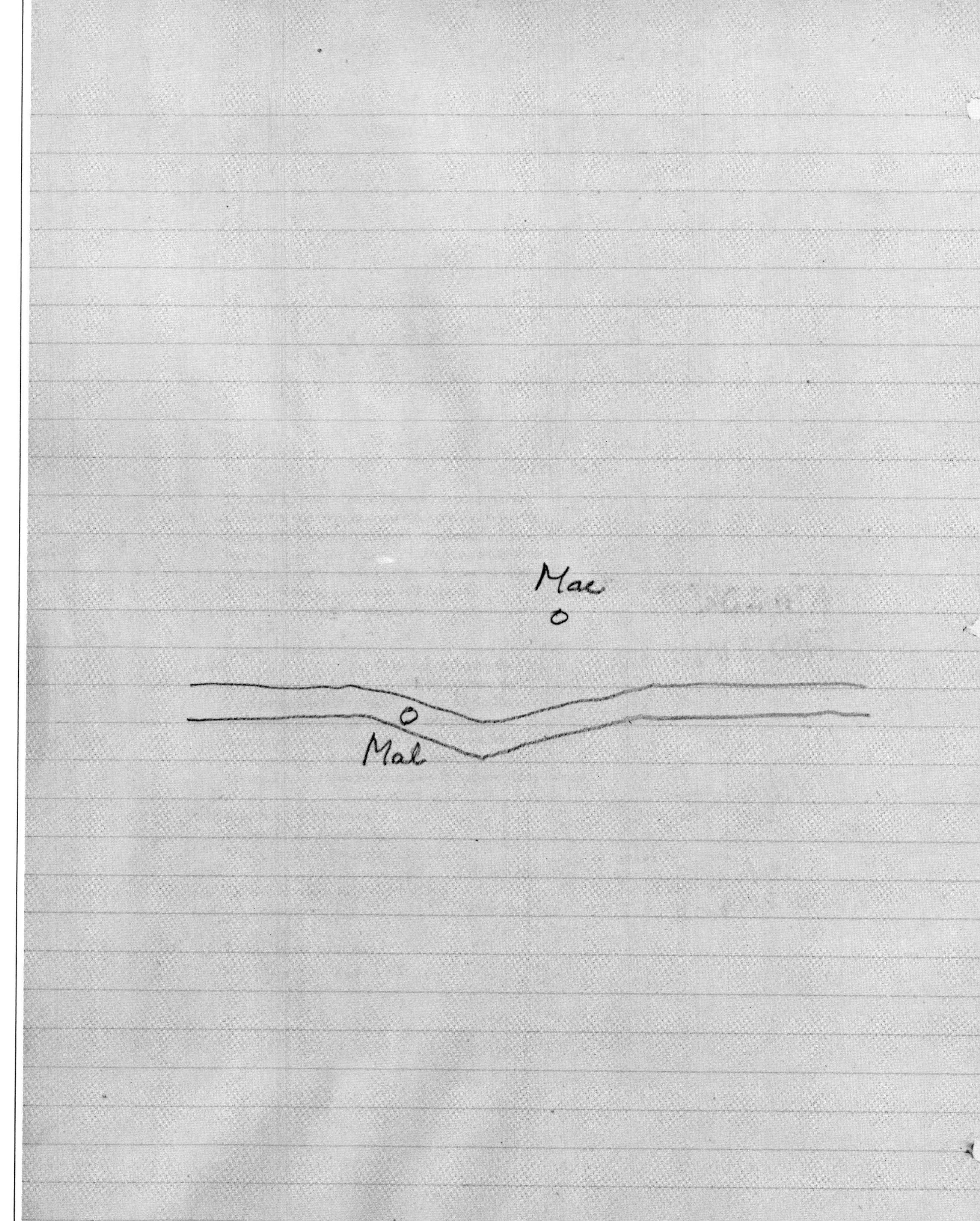

Macbeth, Act IV, Scene iii

(75)

Act IV Sc. iii

He hath not touch'd you yet. I am young; but something
You may ~~discern~~ *deserve* of him through me, and wisdom †
To offer up a weak, poor, innocent lamb
To appease an angry god.

Macd. I am not treacherous.

Mal. But Macbeth is.
A good and virtuous nature may recoil
In an imperial charge. But I shall crave your pardon:
That which you are, my thoughts cannot transpose;
Angels are bright still, though the brightest fell:
Though all things foul would wear the brows of grace,
Yet grace must still look so.

Macd. I have lost my hopes.

Mal. Perchance even there where I did find my doubts.
Why in that rawness left you wife and child,
~~Those precious motives, those strong knots of love,~~
Without leave-taking? I pray you,
Let not my jealousies be your dishonours,
But mine own safeties. You may be rightly just,
Whatever I shall think.

Macd. Bleed, bleed, poor country:
Great tyranny, lay thou thy basis sure,
For goodness dare not check thee: wear thou thy wrongs;

79

rises & comes to OP of Mac

Mac turns to Mal

turning DS

moving DS OP & sitting on front steps OP

He can't understand how Macduff could have left his family in the enemy's territory & come to England unless he was in league with Macbeth, so he tries him out to see what his re-action will be.

Macduff has no cunning or craftiness in his nature. He is supremely simple, direct, & honest & takes everything that the boy says about himself for the truth & is, naturally, appalled by it.

76

The title is affeer'd. Fare thee well, lord:
I would not be the villain that thou think'st
For the whole space that 's in the tyrant's grasp,
And the rich East to boot.

Mal. Be not offended:
I speak not as in absolute fear of you:
I think our country sinks beneath the yoke,
It weeps, it bleeds, and each new day a gash
Is added to her wounds: I think withal
There would be hands uplifted in my right;
And here from gracious England have I offer
Of goodly thousands: but for all this,
When I shall tread upon the tyrant's head,
Or wear it on my sword, yet my poor country
Shall have more vices than it had before,
More suffer, and more sundry ways than ever,
By him that shall succeed.

Macd. What should he be?

Mal. It is myself I mean: in whom I know
All the particulars of vice so grafted
That, when they shall be open'd, black Macbeth
Will seem as pure as snow, ~~and the poor state~~
~~Esteem him as a lamb, being compar'd~~
~~With my confineless harms~~.

Macd. Not in the legions

Macbeth, Act IV, Scene iii

77

Of horrid hell can come a devil more damn'd
In evils, to top Macbeth.
Mal. I grant him bloody,
Luxurious, avaricious, false, deceitful,
Sudden, malicious, smacking of every sin
That has a name: but there 's no bottom, none,
In my voluptuousness: your wives, your daughters,
Your matrons, and your maids, could not fill up
The cistern of my lust, ~~and my desire~~
~~All continent impediments would o'erbear,~~
~~That did oppose my will:~~ better Macbeth
Than such an one to reign.
Macd. Boundless intemperance
In nature is a tyranny; it hath been
The untimely emptying of the happy throne,
And fall of many kings. But fear not yet
To take upon you what is yours: ~~you may~~
~~Convey your pleasures in a spacious plenty,~~
~~And yet seem cold, the time you may so hoodwink:~~
We have willing dames enough; there cannot be
That vulture in you, to devour so many
As will to greatness dedicate themselves,
Finding it so inclined.
Mal. With this there grows,
In my most ill-compos'd affection, such

kneeling
beside
Mal PS
of him

MACBETH

A stanchless avarice, that, were I king,
I should cut off the nobles for their lands,
Desire his jewels, and this other's house:
And my more-having would be as a sauce
To make me hunger more~~, that I should forge~~
~~Quarrels unjust against the good and loyal,~~
~~Destroying them for wealth.~~

Macd. This avarice
Sticks deeper, grows with more pernicious root
Than summer-seeming lust, and it hath been
The sword of our slain kings: yet do not fear;
Scotland hath foisons to fill up your will
Of your mere own: all these are portable,
With other graces weigh'd.

Mal. But I have none: the king-becoming graces,
As justice, verity, temperance, stableness,
Bounty, perseverance, mercy, lowliness,
Devotion, patience, courage, fortitude,
I have no relish of them, but abound
In the division of each several crime,
Acting it many ways. Nay, had I power, I should
Pour the sweet milk of concord into hell,
Uproar the universal peace, confound
All unity on earth.

Macd. O Scotland, Scotland!

82

Macbeth, Act IV, Scene iii

79

Mal. If such a one be fit to govern, speak:
I am as I have spoken.
Macd. Fit to govern? — rising
No, not to live. O nation miserable!
With an untitled tyrant, bloody-scepter'd,
When shalt thou see thy wholesome days again,
Since that the truest issue of thy throne
By his own interdiction stands accurs'd,
And does blaspheme his breed? ~~Thy royal father~~
~~Was a most sainted king: the queen that bore thee,~~
~~Oftener upon her knees than on her feet,~~
~~Died every day she liv'd.~~ Fare thee well!
These evils thou repeat'st upon thyself
Have banish'd me from Scotland. O my breast,
Thy hope ends here! — US moves towards C opening
Mal. Macduff, this noble passion,
Child of integrity, hath from my soul
Wip'd the black scruples, reconcil'd my thoughts
To thy good truth and honour. Devilish Macbeth,
By many of these trains, hath sought to win me
Into his power; and modest wisdom plucks me
From over-credulous haste: but God above
Deal between thee and me! for even now
I put myself to thy direction, and
Unspeak mine own detraction; here abjure

83

rises & coming to OP of Mac & stopping him. Mac backs away from him DS PS. Mal follows him.

He turns from him in disgust & bitter disappointment. His re-action is so obviously genuine & true that Malcolm is convinced of his honesty & promises to join with him to destroy Macbeth.

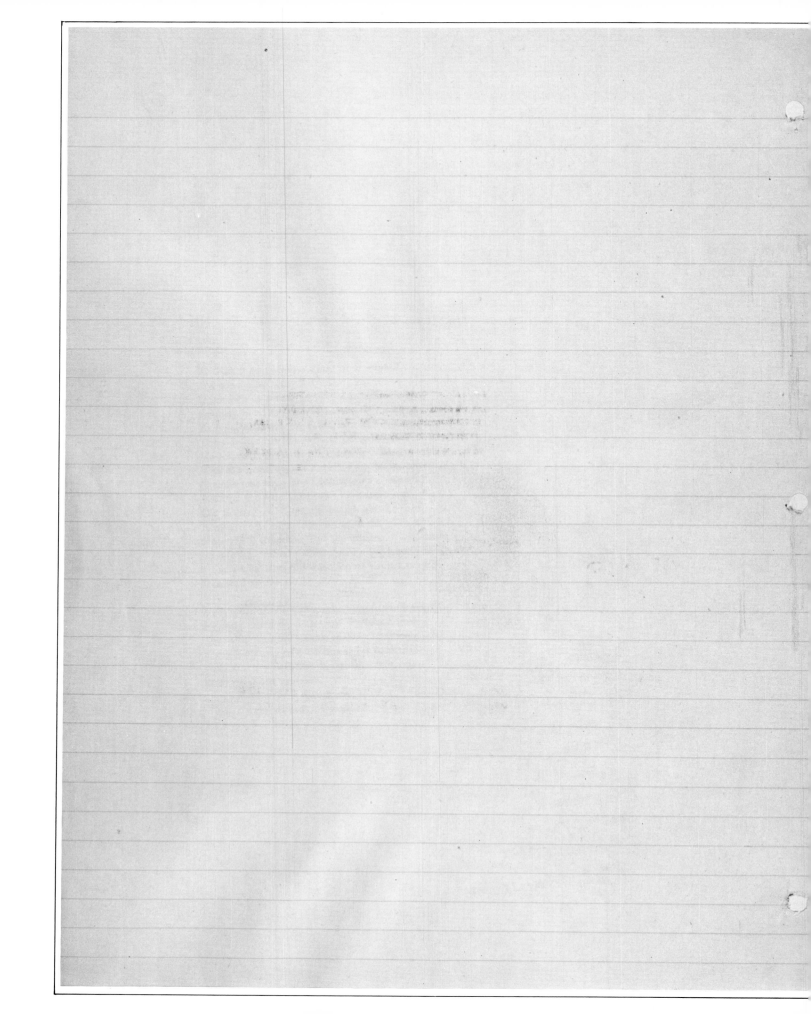

Macbeth, Act IV, Scene iii

MACBETH

The taints and blames I laid upon myself,
For strangers to my nature. ~~I am yet~~
~~Unknown to woman, never was forsworn,~~
~~Scarcely have coveted what was mine own,~~
~~At no time broke my faith, would not betray~~
~~The devil to his fellow, and delight~~
~~No less in truth than life: my first false speaking~~
~~Was this upon myself~~: what I am truly,
Is thine and my poor country's to command:
Whither indeed, before thy here-approach,
Old Siward, with ten thousand warlike men,
Already at a point, was setting forth.
Now we will together, ~~and the chance of goodness~~ †
~~Be like our warranted quarrel~~! Why are you silent?
Macd. Such welcome and unwelcome things at once
'Tis hard to reconcile.

~~*Enter a Doctor*~~

~~*Mal.* Well, more anon. Comes the king forth, I pray you?~~
~~*Doc.* Ay, sir; there are a crew of wretched souls~~
~~That stay his cure: their malady convinces~~
~~The great assay of art; but at his touch,~~
~~Such sanctity hath heaven given his hand,~~
~~They presently amend.~~
~~*Mal.* I thank you, doctor. *Exit Doctor*~~
~~*Macd.* What's the disease he means~~?

84

He tells him that he was on the point of invading Scotland with old Siward & an English army of ten thousand men.

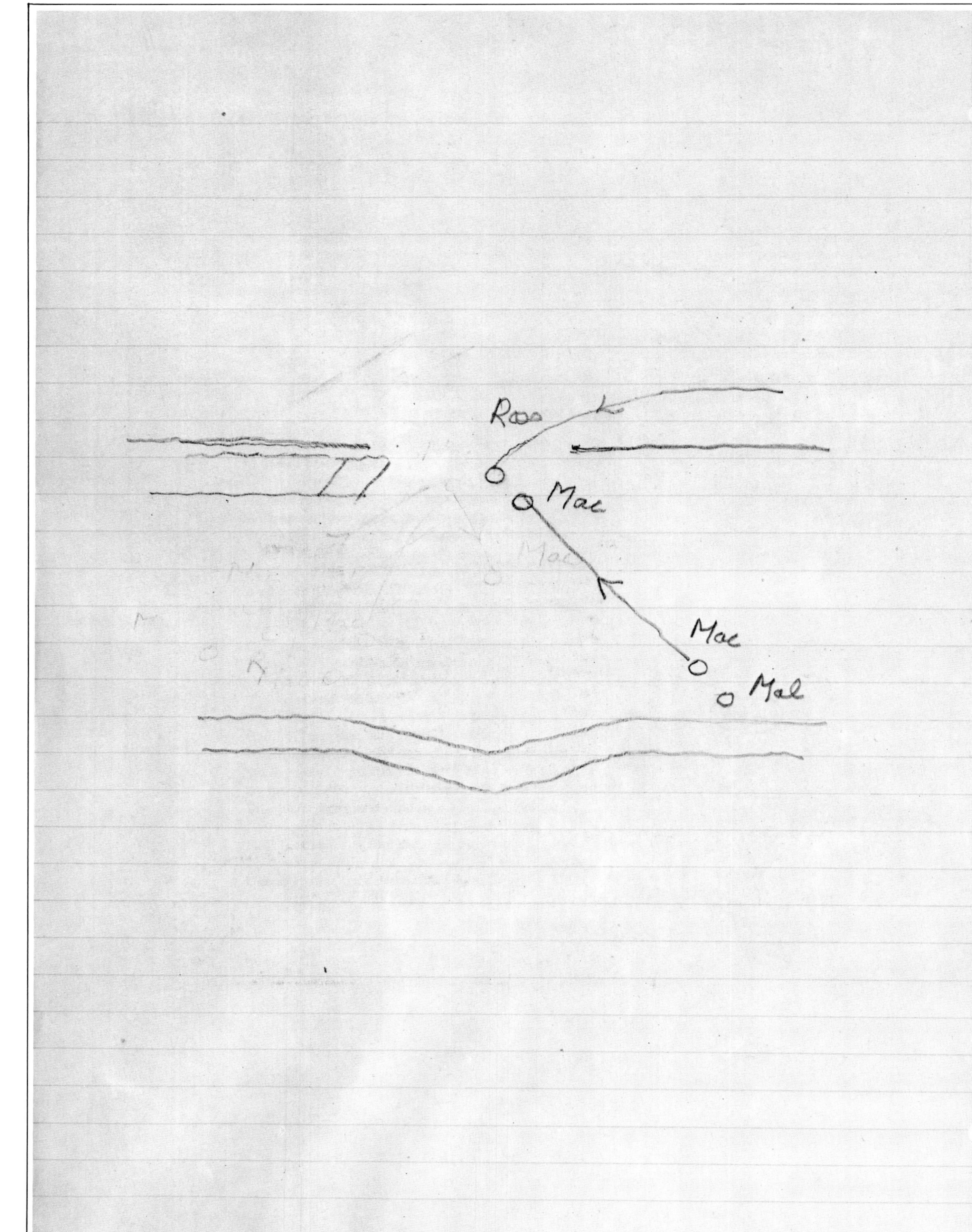
Ross
Mac
Mac
Mal

(81)

Act IV Sc. iii

~~*Mal.* 'Tis call'd the evil:~~
~~A most miraculous work in this good king,~~
~~Which often, since my here-remain in England,~~
~~I have seen him do. How he solicits heaven~~
~~Himself best knows: but strangely-visited people,~~
~~All swoln and ulcerous, pitiful to the eye,~~
~~The mere despair of surgery, he cures,~~
~~Hanging a golden stamp about their necks,~~
~~Put on with holy prayers, and 'tis spoken~~
~~To the succeeding royalty he leaves~~
~~The healing benediction. With this strange virtue~~
~~He hath a heavenly gift of prophecy,~~
~~And sundry blessings hang about his throne~~
~~That speak him full of grace.~~

Enter Ross PS mid

Macd. See, who comes here?
Mal. My countryman; but yet I know him not.
Macd. My ever gentle cousin, welcome hither.
Mal. I know him now; good God, betimes remove
The means that makes us strangers!
Ross. Sir, amen.
Macd. Stands Scotland where it did?
Ross. Alas, poor country!
Almost afraid to know itself! It cannot
Be call'd our mother, but our grave: ~~where nothing,~~

85

Mal turns DS OP of Mac

goes to PS of Ross

Slight move DS OP of Ross

Ross comes to Center of C opening

Ross Xs in front of Mac to OP of Mal

At this moment Ross arrives. He has terrible news & his gentle, kind nature makes it almost impossible for him to tell Macduff of the ghastly tragedy that has happened to his family.

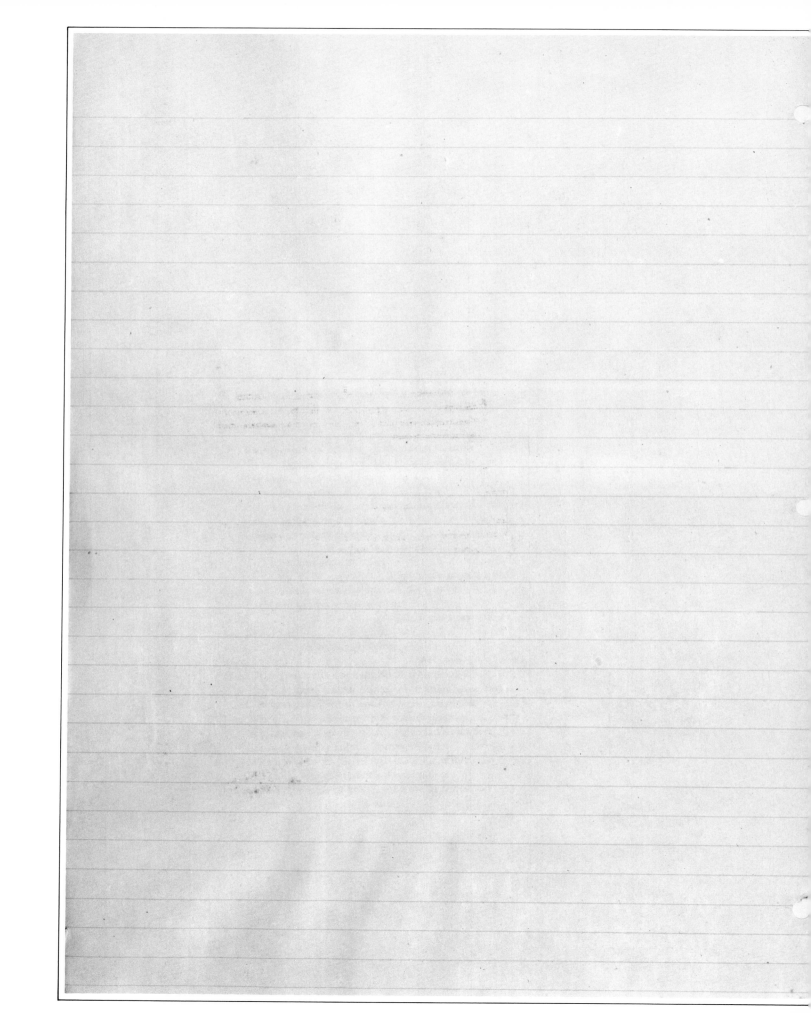

(82)

~~But who knows nothing, is once seen to smile;~~
~~Where sighs, and groans, and shrieks that rend the air,~~
~~Are made, not mark'd; where violent sorrow seems~~
~~A modern ecstasy~~: the dead man's knell †
Is there scarce ask'd for who, and good men's lives
Expire before the flowers in their caps,
Dying or ere they sicken.

~~*Macd.* O, relation~~
~~Too nice, and yet too true~~!

~~*Mal.* What 's the newest grief~~?

~~*Ross.* That of an hour's age doth hiss the speaker;~~
~~Each minute teems a new one~~.

Macd. How does my wife?

Ross. Why, well.

Macd. And all my children?

Ross. Well too.

Macd. The tyrant has not batter'd at their peace?

Ross. No, they were well at peace, when I did leave 'em.

Macd. Be not a niggard of your speech: how goes 't?

Ross. When I came hither to transport the tidings,
Which I have heavily borne, there ran a rumour
Of many worthy fellows that were out,
Which was to my belief witness'd the rather,
For that I saw the tyrant's power a-foot:
Now is the time of help; your eye in Scotland

turning to Mal

Mal. Would create soldiers, make our women fight,
To doff their dire distresses.
Mal. Be 't their comfort
We are coming thither: gracious England hath
Lent us good Siward, and ten thousand men;
~~An older and a better soldier none~~
~~That Christendom gives out.~~
Ross. Would I could answer
This comfort with the like! But I have words
That would be howl'd out in the desert air,
Where hearing should not latch them.
Macd. What concern they,
The general cause, or is it a fee-grief
Due to some single breast?
Ross. No mind that 's honest
But in it shares some woe, though the main part
Pertains to you alone.
Macd. If it be mine,
Keep it not from me, quickly let me have it.
Ross. Let not your ears despise my tongue for ever,
Which shall possess them with the heaviest sound
That ever yet they heard.
Macd. Hum! I guess at it.
Ross. Your castle is surpris'd; your wife, and babes,
Savagely slaughter'd: to relate the manner

half turning to Mac

At last he forces himself to tell him the truth.

MACBETH

Were on the quarry of these murder'd dear
To add the death of you.
Mal. Merciful heaven!
What, man, ne'er pull your hat upon your brows;
Give sorrow words; the grief that does not speak
Whispers the o'erfraught heart, and bids it break.
Macd. My children too?
Ross. Wife, children, servants, all
That could be found.
Macd. And I must be from thence?
My wife kill'd too?
Ross. I have said.
Mal. Be comforted.
Let 's make us medicines of our great revenge,
To cure this deadly grief.
Macd. He has no children. All my pretty ones?
Did you say all? O hell-kite! All?
What, all my pretty chickens, and their dam
At one fell swoop?
Mal. Dispute it like a man.
Macd. I shall do so;
But I must also feel it as a man:
I cannot but remember such things were,
That were most precious to me. Did heaven look on,
And would not take their part? Sinful Macduff,

88

Xing in front of R to PS of Mac & gently pulls Mac right arm away from his face

moves slightly DS

Mac pulls his cap over his eyes

moving to PS of Mac Ross moves DS PS of Mal

Macduff is overwhelmed with his grief, but he controls himself & swears to be revenged on Macbeth. Malcolm & Macduff now trust each other completely.

Act IV, Scene iii. "My wife kill'd too?" Keith Michell (Macduff), Trader Faulkner (Malcolm), William Devlin (Ross) (see opposite page).

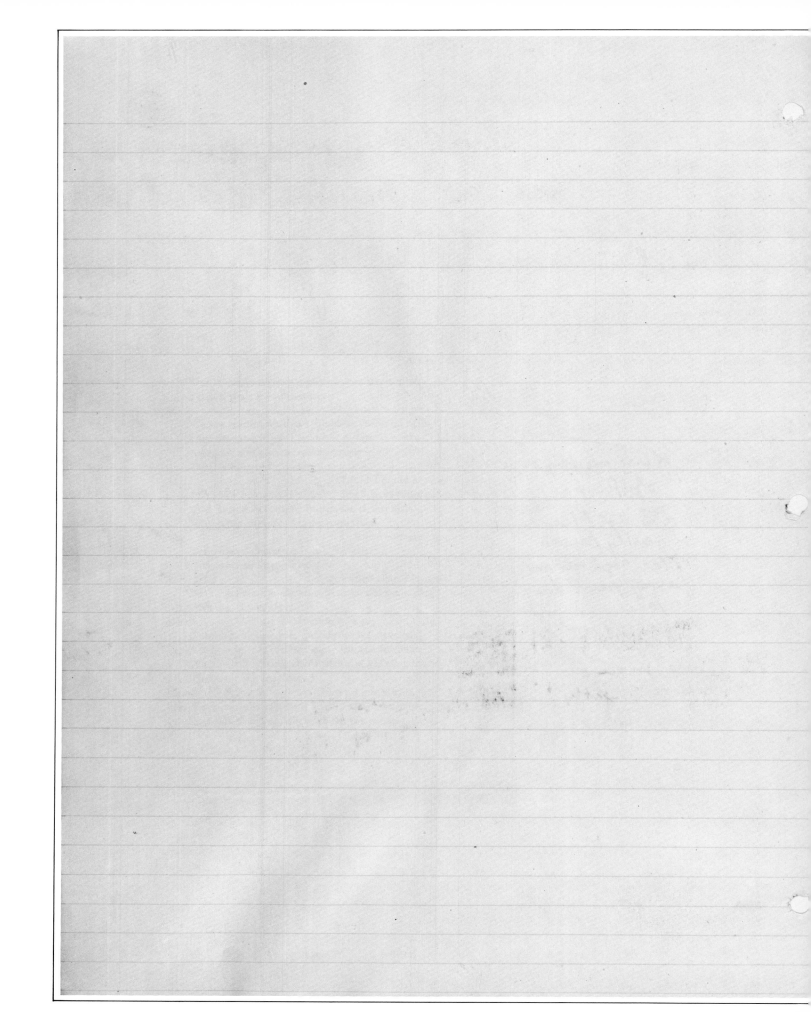

Ordr of Exit

Mal & Mac
Ross

They were all struck for thee! naught that I am,
Not for their own demerits, but for mine,
Fell slaughter on their souls: heaven rest them now!
Mal. Be this the whetstone of your sword, let grief
Convert to anger: blunt not the heart, enrage it.
Macd. O, I could play the woman with mine eyes,
And braggart with my tongue! But, gentle heavens,
Cut short all intermission; front to front
Bring thou this fiend of Scotland and myself,
Within my sword's length set him, if he 'scape,
Heaven forgive him too!
Mal. This tune goes manly.
Come, go we to the king; our power is ready,
Our lack is nothing but our leave. Macbeth
Is ripe for shaking, and the powers above
Put on their instruments. Receive what cheer you
may;
The night is long that never finds the day. *Exeunt*

PS mid

ENGLAND CLOTHES FLIED

FADE to BLACK OUT

MUSIC

TRUCK OFF

SLEEP WALKING CLOTHES FLIED IN

Doctor. 35 [years old]. Geoffrey Bayldon.

He is typically a Doctor. Serious & professional in his manner. A certain feeling of self-importance about him.

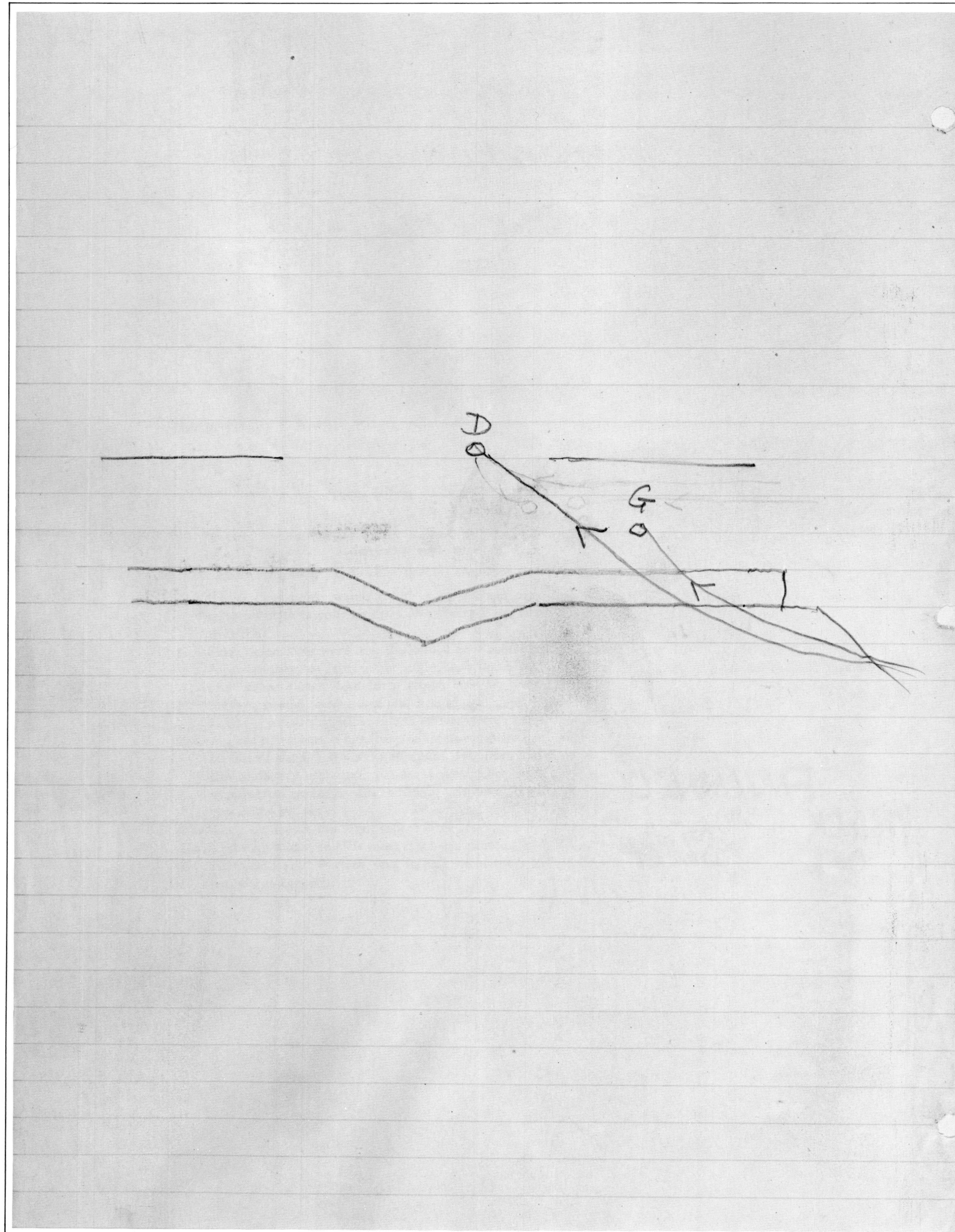

The Gentlewoman. 50 [years old]. Rosalind Atkinson.

The head Lady-in-waiting to the Queen & a trusted servant.

She is extremely worried by what she has heard & seen and has felt it her duty to inform the Doctor.

MACBETH

FADE IN

CLOCK STRIKES TWO

~~Act Fifth~~

SCENE 4 Sleep Walking

Dunsinane. Ante-room in the castle 2AM.

Enter a Doctor of Physic and a Waiting-Gentlewoman

PS Ass & moves to main stage PS / looks up corridor

Doc. I have two nights watch'd with you, but can perceive no truth in your report. When was it she last walk'd?

Gen. Since his majesty went into the field, I have seen her rise from her bed, throw her nightgown upon her, unlock her closet, take forth paper, fold it, write upon 't, read it, afterwards seal it, and again return to bed; yet all this while in a most fast sleep.

turns to G.W.

Doc. A great perturbation in nature, to receive at once the benefit of sleep, and do the effects of watching. In this slumbery agitation, besides her walking, and other actual performances, what (at any time) have you heard her say?

Gen. That, sir, which I will not report after her.

Doc. You may to me, and 'tis most meet you should.

Gen. Neither to you, nor any one, having no witness to confirm my speech.

90

Sleep Walking Scene. 2 am.

We are back in Scotland in Macbeth's Castle at Dunsinane. It is very early morning & the great long corridor leading to the Queen's apartment looks terrifyingly eerie & cold in the moonlight—One of her ladies-in-waiting is talking to the Doctor; she has told him that all is not well with her Majesty & that she walks & talks in her sleep, though she refuses to repeat anything that she has heard the Queen say. They have already watched for two nights & see nothing & the Doctor is beginning to doubt the truth of what the Gentlewoman has told him.

Dunsinane Castle, Sleepwalking Scene.

USC & coming DS OP of C line carrying standard light

Act V Sc. i

Enter Lady Macbeth, with a taper — change lighting

Lo you, here she comes! This is her very guise, and, upon my life, fast asleep. Observe her, stand close.

Doc. How came she by that light?

Gen. Why, it stood by her: she has light by her continually, 'tis her command.

Doc. You see her eyes are open.

Gen. Ay, but their sense is shut.

Doc. What is it she does now? Look how she rubs her hands.

Gen. It is an accustom'd action with her, to seem thus washing her hands: I have known her continue in this a quarter of an hour.

L.M. Yet here 's a spot.

Doc. Hark! she speaks, I will set down what comes from her, to satisfy my remembrance the more strongly.

L.M. Out damned spot! out I say! One: two: why then 'tis time to do 't: hell is murky. Fie, my lord, fie, a soldier, and afeard? What need we fear who knows it, when none can call our power to account? Yet who would have thought the old man to have had so much blood in him?

Doc. Do you mark that?

L.M. The thane of Fife, had a wife; where is she now?

91

Draws Doctor back into PS [illegible]

Lady M stands light on floor PS of her

Then starts to rub her hands

Suddenly stops rubbing her hands & listens

Sudden move slightly OP

Suddenly at the extreme end of the corridor they see a small light & the lady-in-waiting knows it is the Queen.

They take up a position so that they can see & hear all that she does & says.

Act V, Scene i. "Yet here's a spot." Vivien Leigh (Lady Macbeth) (see opposite page).

Act V, Scene i. "Lo you, here she comes!" Vivien Leigh (Lady Macbeth), Geoffrey Bayldon (Doctor), Rosalind Atkinson (Gentlewoman) (see following pages).

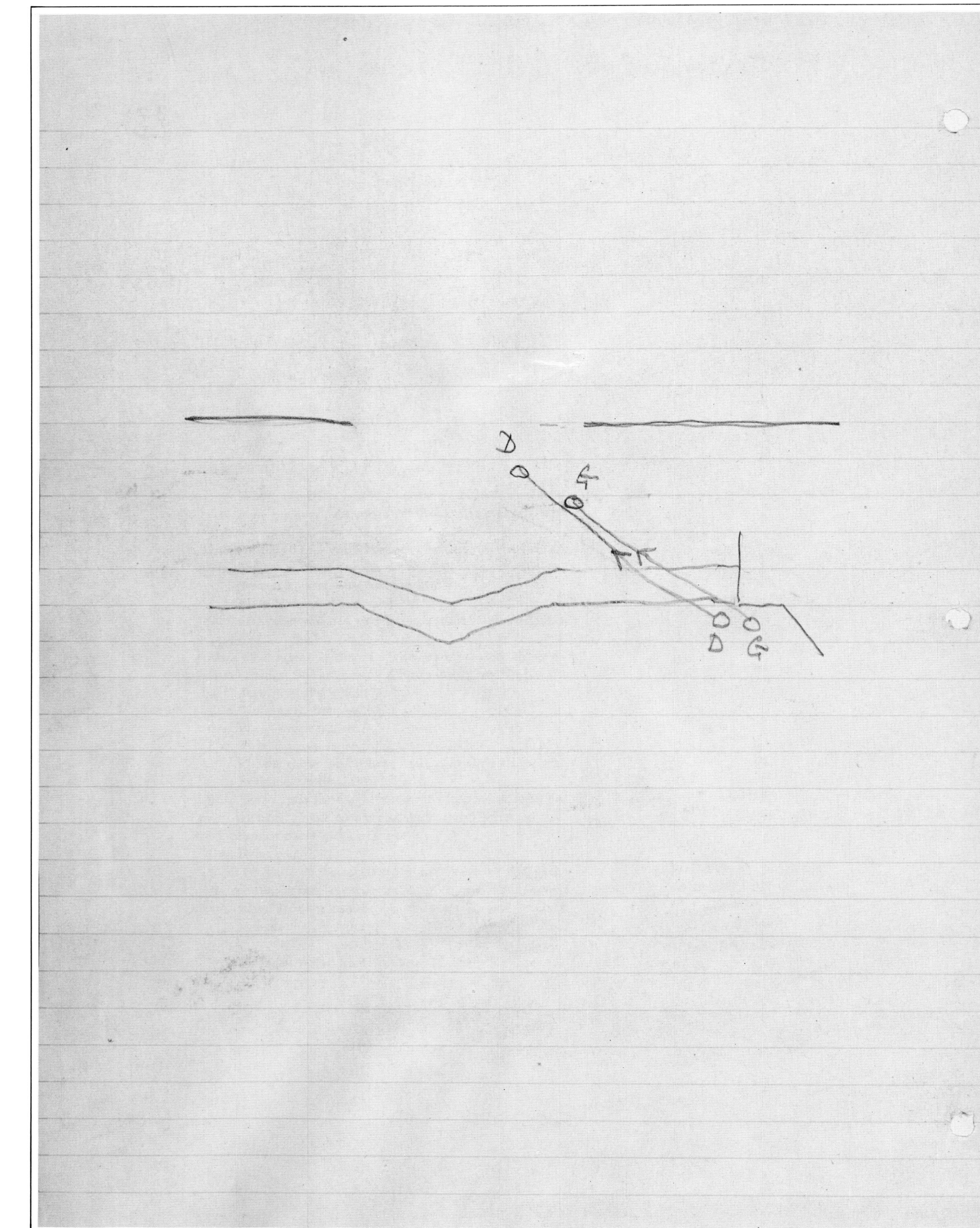
D
G
D
G

MACBETH

What, will these hands ne'er be clean? No more o' that, my lord, no more o' that; you mar all with this starting.

Doc. Go to, go to; you have known what you should not.

Gen. She has spoke what she should not, I am sure of that: heaven knows what she has known.

L.M. Here 's the smell of the blood still: all the perfumes of Arabia will not sweeten this little hand. Oh, oh, oh!

Doc. What a sigh is there! The heart is sorely charg'd.

Gen. I would not have such a heart in my bosom for the dignity of the whole body.

Doc. Well, well, well,—

Gen. Pray God it be, sir.

Doc. This disease is beyond my practice: yet I have known those which have walk'd in their sleep, who have died holily in their beds.

L.M. Wash your hands, put on your nightgown, look not so pale: I tell you yet again Banquo 's buried; he cannot come out on 's grave.

Doc. Even so?

L.M. To bed, to bed; there 's knocking at the gate: come, come, come, come, give me your hand: what 's done, cannot be undone: to bed, to bed, to bed. *Exit*

92

Starts rubbing her hands

Stops suddenly

Starts rubbing her hands again

Suddenly

Change lighting

Picks up lights Starts to go

US C Door Gentlewoman move forward to PSDC looking after her

Lady Macbeth is fast asleep, & unconsciously says things that betray her & her husband; things that no torture in the world would drag from her if she were conscious.

Her mind is diseased, but she is not mad.

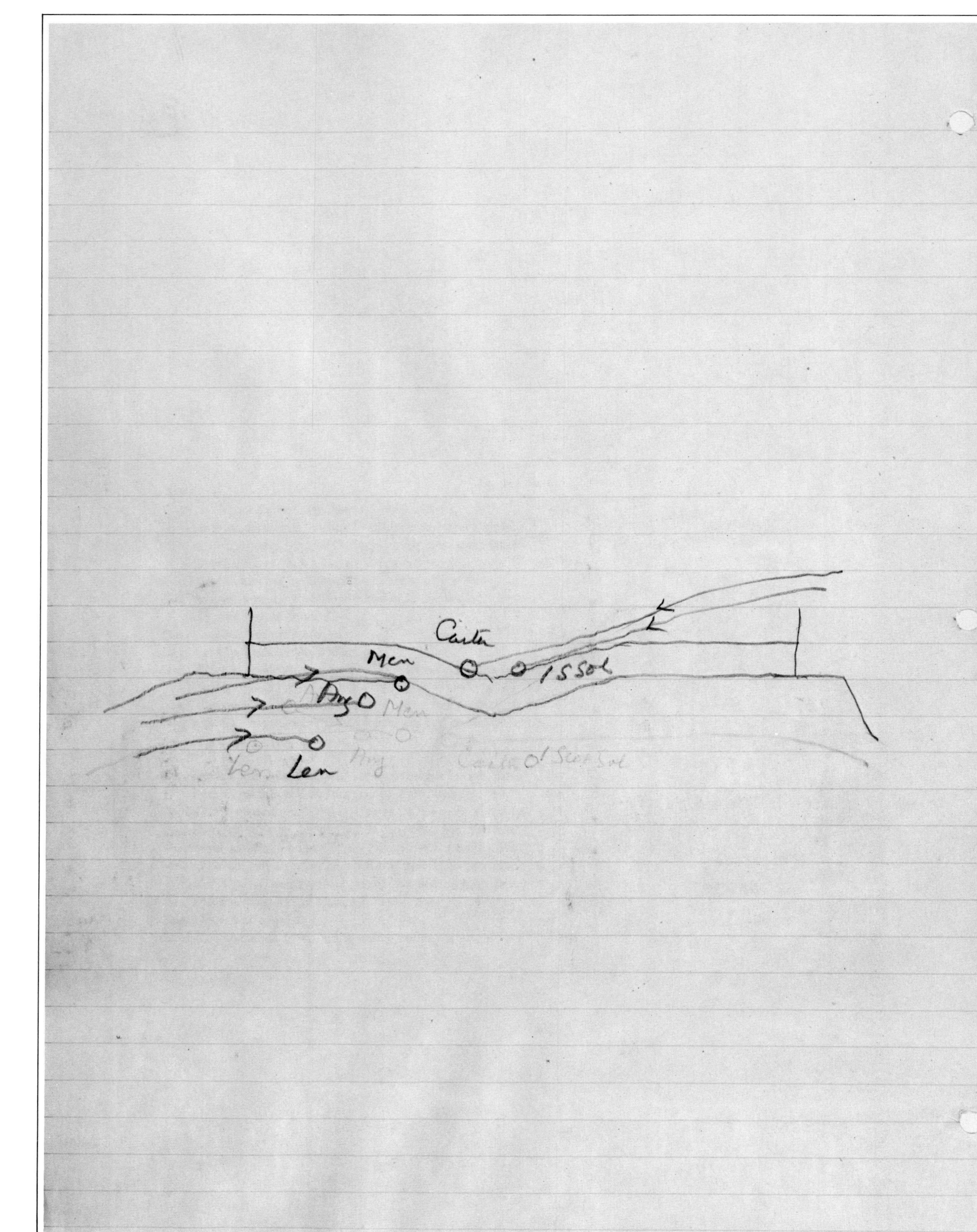

Revolt Scene. 4 am.

The nobles are leaving Macbeth to join the rebels' forces led by Malcolm & his Uncle Siward.

They meet together in the Castle & decide to go.

Macbeth, Act V, Scene ii

Act V Sc. ii

Doc. **Will she go now to bed?**
Gen. **Directly.**
Doc. **Foul whisperings are abroad: unnatural deeds**
Do breed unnatural troubles: infected minds
To their deaf pillows will discharge their secrets:
More needs she the divine than the physician.
God, God forgive us all! Look after her,
Remove from her the means of all annoyance,
And still keep eyes upon her. So good night:
My mind she has mated and amaz'd my sight:
I think, but dare not speak.
Gen. **Good night, good doctor.**
Exeunt

turning to G

turns to G

turns to Look up passage

draws Curtain over second area & exit behind it

G x s in front of D & moves up passage to second cloth

Doctor PS Ass

Change lighting SCENE 5 Revolt

Dunsinane 4AM

Drum. *Enter Menteith, Caithness, Angus, Lennox, and Soldiers*

With Lantern
Light change
in far distance

Menteith } enter 1st
Angus } OP
Lennox } Ass

Men. **The English power is near, led on by Malcolm,**
His uncle Siward, and the good Macduff:
Revenges burn in them; for their dear causes
Would to the bleeding and the grim alarm
Excite the mortified man.

93

Caithness } PS Pros
& 1 Scot Sol } quickly
with bundle & X to PS
(George Little) of Men

The doctor is deeply moved & up-set by what he hears. He fears that she will try to commit suicide & warns the Lady-in-Waiting to watch her most carefully.

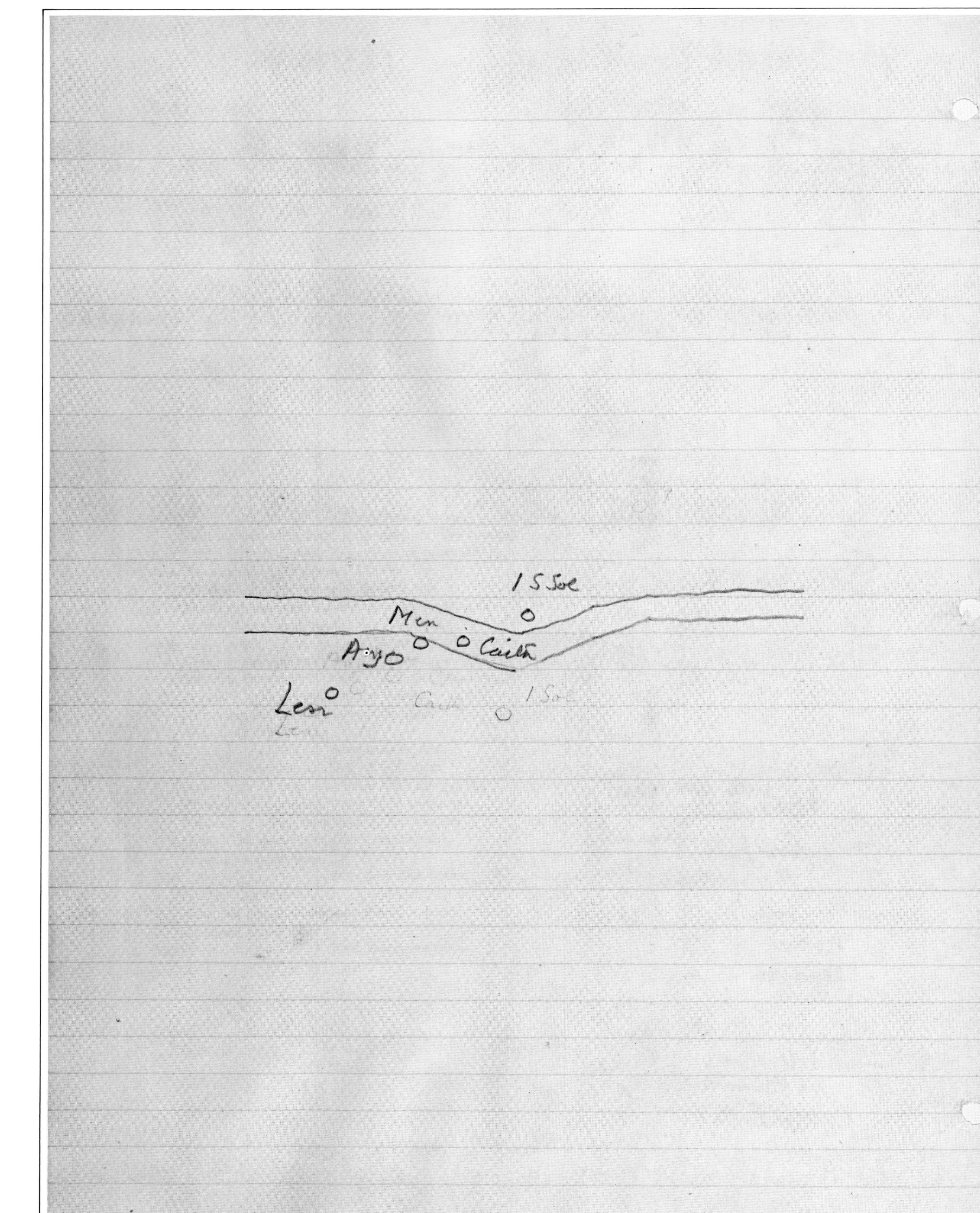

Macbeth, Act V, Scene ii

MACBETH

moves to OP of Men

Ang. Near Birnam wood
Shall we well meet them; that way are they coming.
Cai. Who knows if Donalbain be with his brother?
Len. For certain, sir, he is not: I have a file
Of all the gentry: there is Siward's son,
And many unrough youths, that even now
Protest their first of manhood.

moves down one step

Men. What does the tyrant?
Cai. Great Dunsinane he strongly fortifies:
Some say he 's mad; others, that lesser hate him,
Do call it valiant fury, but, for certain,
He cannot buckle his distemper'd cause
Within the belt of rule.

morning

Ang. Now does he feel
His secret murders sticking on his hands,
Now minutely revolts upbraid his faith-breach;
Those he commands move only in command,
Nothing in love: now does he feel his title
Hang loose about him, like a giant's robe
Upon a dwarfish thief.
Men. Who then shall blame
His pester'd senses to recoil, and start,
When all that is within him does condemn
Itself, for being there?
Cai. Well, march we on,

turns to Soe

94

Cream fac'd Loon Scene. 6 am.

As the nobles are leaving the Castle they are seen by Seyton who goes immediately to tell the King, but Macbeth realises that there is nothing he can do to stop them & pins his faith on the black magic of the Witches.

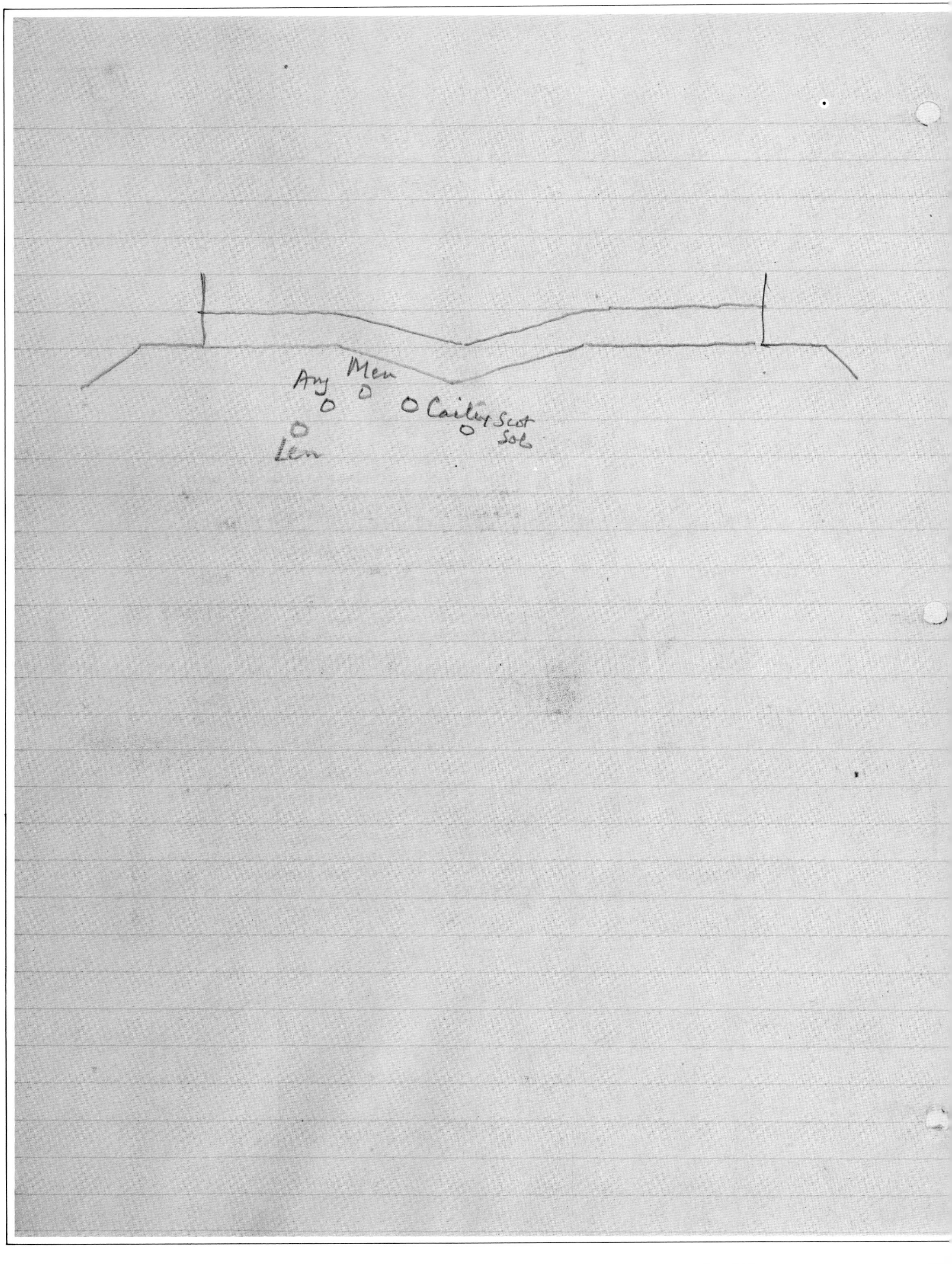

Macbeth, Act V, Scene iii

Order of exit — Len & Caith
Ang & Men
1 Sol

Enter Sey PS between 1st & 2nd Cloth

Act V Sc. iii

To give obedience, where 'tis truly owed:
~~Meet we the medicine of the sickly weal,~~
~~And with him pour we, in our country's purge,~~
~~Each drop of us.~~

Len. ~~Or so much as it needs,~~
~~To dew the sovereign flower, and drown the weeds:~~
Make we our march towards Birnam.

Exeunt, ~~*marching*~~ OP Ass

FADE AWAY

Light change

FADE IN

SCENE ~~III~~ 6 Cream fac'd Loon

* *Dunsinane.* ~~*A room in the castle*~~ 6AM

Enter Macbeth, ~~*Doctor, and Attendants*~~ followed by Seyton

Mac. Bring me no more reports, let them fly all:
Till Birnam wood remove to Dunsinane,
I cannot taint with fear. What's the boy Malcolm?
Was he not born of woman? The spirits that know
All mortal consequences have pronounc'd me thus:
'Fear not, Macbeth, no man that's born of woman
Shall e'er have power upon thee.' Then fly, false thanes,
And mingle with the English epicures:
The mind I sway by, and the heart I bear,
Shall never sag with doubt, nor shake with fear.

95

Moves slightly US

Ang moves slightly US
Men & Caith pass between them

PS Pros & move of OP of C stage looking at OP Ass

Seyton exit PS Ass X in front of M.

* Seyton moves quickly to OP after Lords exit then runs out PS Pros.

Dunsinane Castle, scene of the revolt.

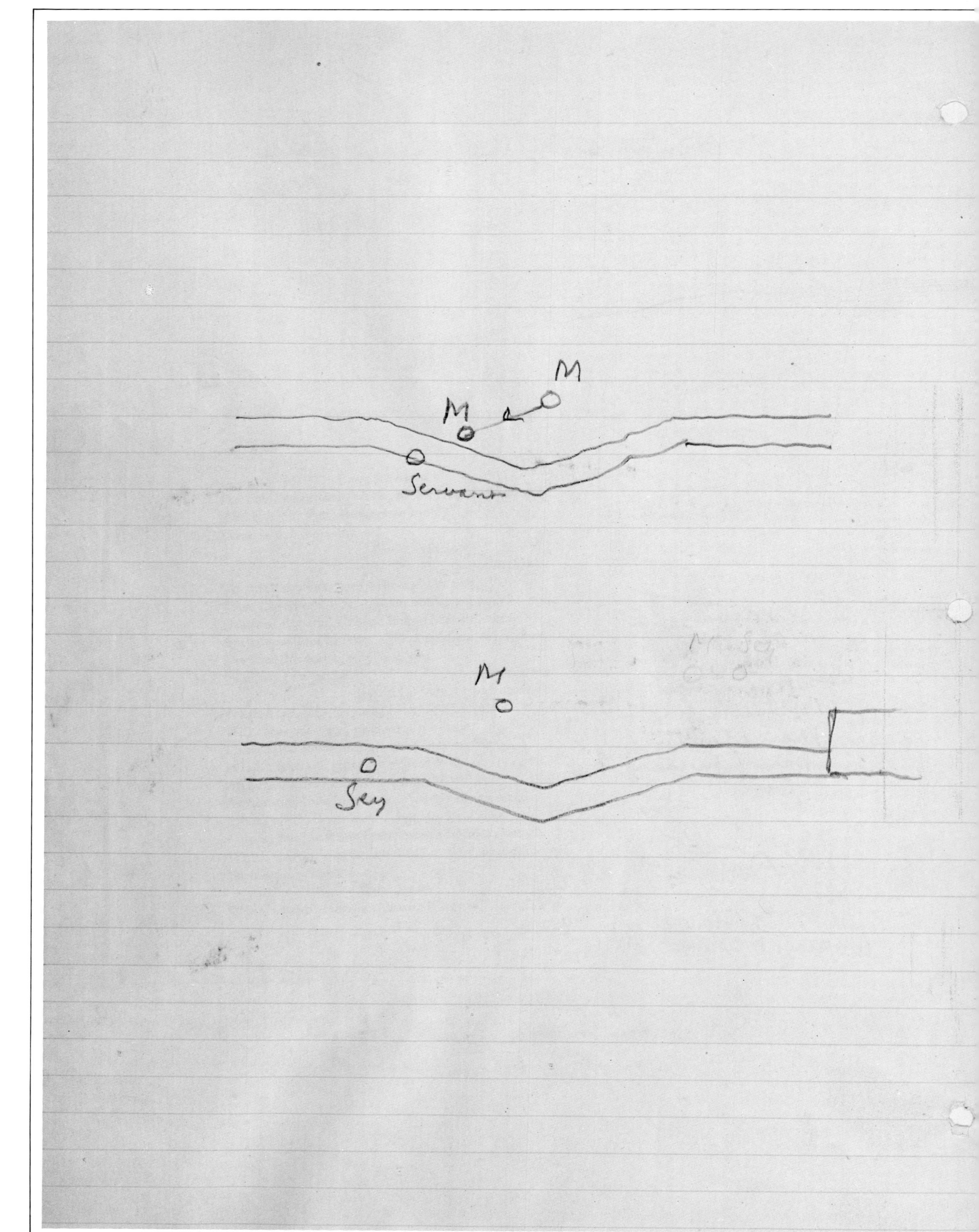

Macbeth, Act V, Scene iii

MACBETH

Enter a Servant OP Ass

The devil damn thee black, thou cream-fac'd loon!
Where got'st thou that goose look?

Ser. There is ten thousand—

Mac. Geese, villain?

Ser. Soldiers, sir.

Mac. Go prick thy face, and over-red thy fear,
Thou lily-liver'd boy. What soldiers, patch?
Death of thy soul! those linen cheeks of thine
Are counsellors to fear. What soldiers, whey-face?

Ser. The English force, so please you.

Mac. Take thy face hence. *Exit Servant*
Seyton!—I am sick at heart,
When I behold—Seyton, I say!—This push
Will ~~cheer~~ me ever, or disseat me now. †
I have liv'd long enough: my way of life
Is fall'n into the sear, the yellow leaf,
And that which should accompany old age,
As honour, love, obedience, troops of friends,
I must not look to have; but, in their stead,
Curses, not loud but deep, mouth-honour, breath,
Which the poor heart would fain deny, and dare not.
Seyton!

Enter Seyton

Sey. What's your gracious pleasure?

96

comes to OP of C steps

M moves to PS of him

Servant kneels

pushing him away towards PS & coming Down steps

OP Ass

Chair

moves to PS of forestage

Sits on front steps PS

rises & going up steps

OP Ass

He still has the courage of a lion & when one of his servants rushes in to tell him that an Army of ten thousand English soldiers is approaching he dismisses the boy with scorn & derision.

But he is, in another way, as sick at heart as his wife.

It is during the Sleep-Walking scene & this scene that we begin to admire their courage & endurance to the full. It is marvelous. Not for one second do either of them become self-pitying or disloyal to the other. They are already in hell but they are still human beings not monsters. Macbeth's attitude to the Doctor & medicine in general is magnificent. He dismisses it as rubbish & calls for his armour.

Macbeth, Act V, Scene iii

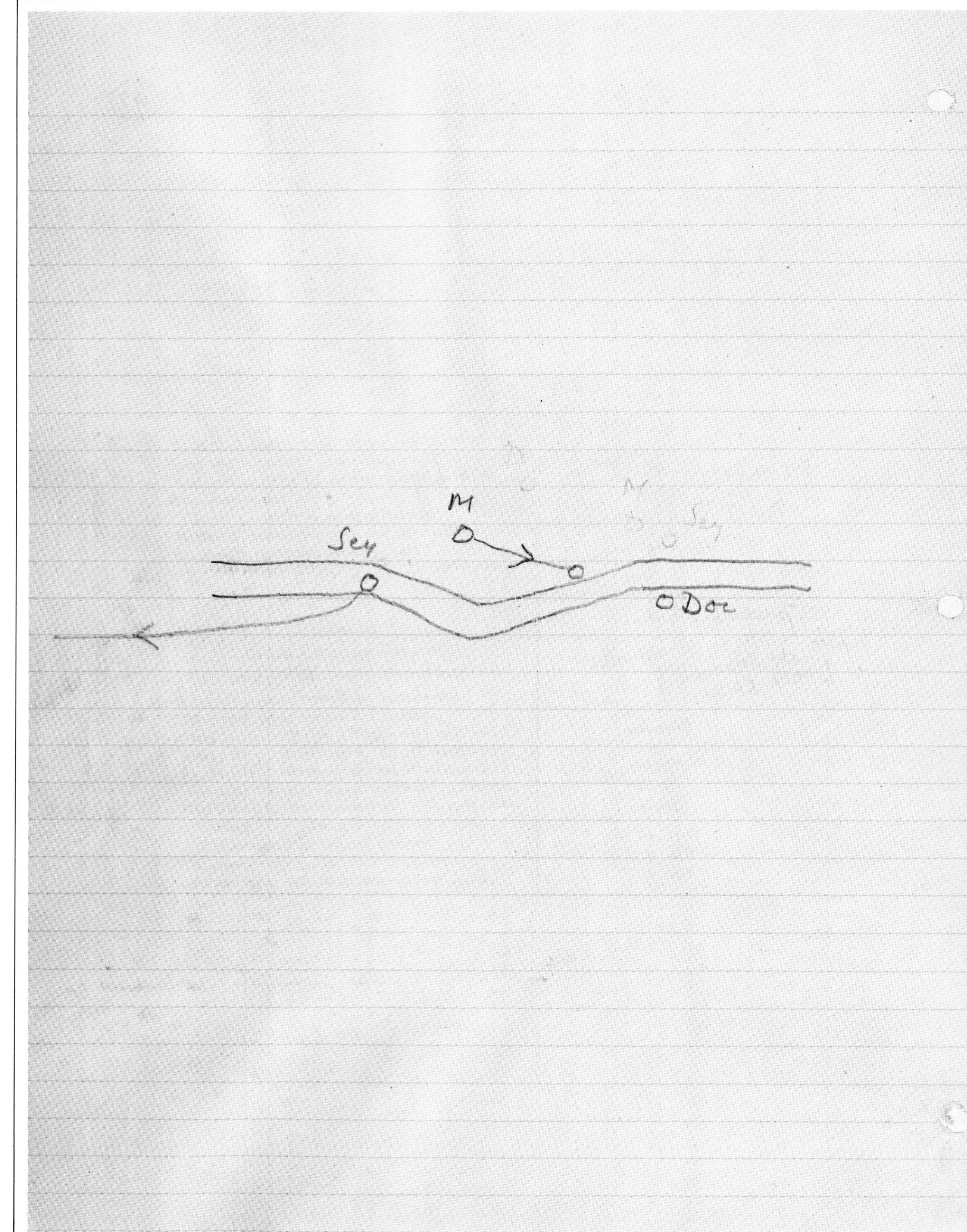

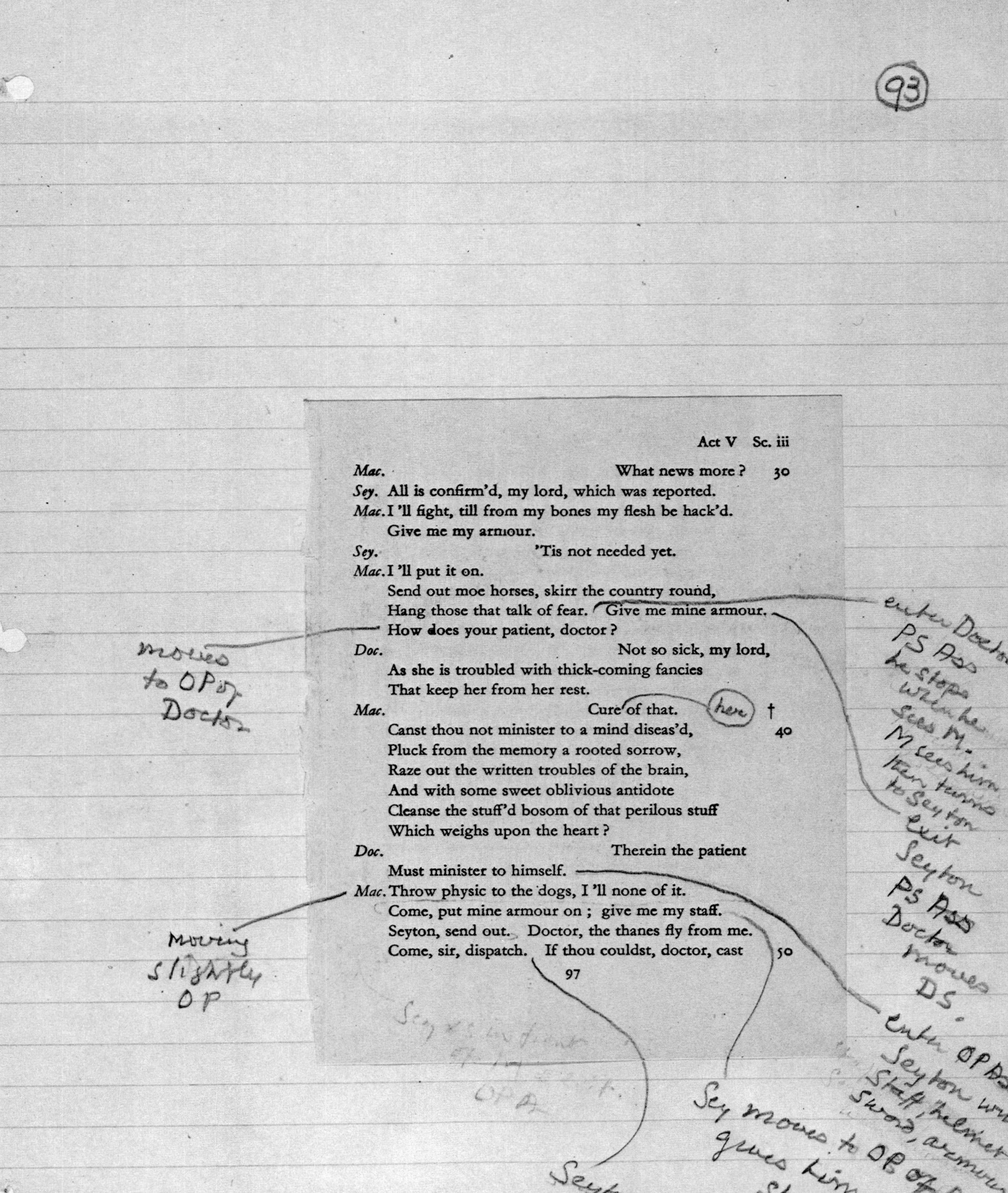

Act V Sc. iii

Mac. What news more?
Sey. All is confirm'd, my lord, which was reported.
Mac. I 'll fight, till from my bones my flesh be hack'd.
Give me my armour.
Sey. 'Tis not needed yet.
Mac. I 'll put it on.
Send out moe horses, skirr the country round,
Hang those that talk of fear. Give me mine armour.
How does your patient, doctor?
Doc. Not so sick, my lord,
As she is troubled with thick-coming fancies
That keep her from her rest.
Mac. Cure of that. †
Canst thou not minister to a mind diseas'd,
Pluck from the memory a rooted sorrow,
Raze out the written troubles of the brain,
And with some sweet oblivious antidote
Cleanse the stuff'd bosom of that perilous stuff
Which weighs upon the heart?
Doc. Therein the patient
Must minister to himself.
Mac. Throw physic to the dogs, I 'll none of it.
Come, put mine armour on; give me my staff.
Seyton, send out. Doctor, the thanes fly from me.
Come, sir, dispatch. If thou couldst, doctor, cast

97

93
here
moves to OP of Doctor
enter Doctor PS
he stops when he sees M. M sees him then turns to Seyton
Exit Seyton PS
Doctor moves DS.
Moving slightly OP
Enter OP Seyton with Staff, helmet, sword, armour
Sey moves to OP of M gives him his staff
Seyton starts to put armour on

Macbeth, Act V, Scene iii

Birnam Wood Scene. 5 pm.

The English Army led by Siward & Malcolm meet the rebel Scottish nobles & they join forces.

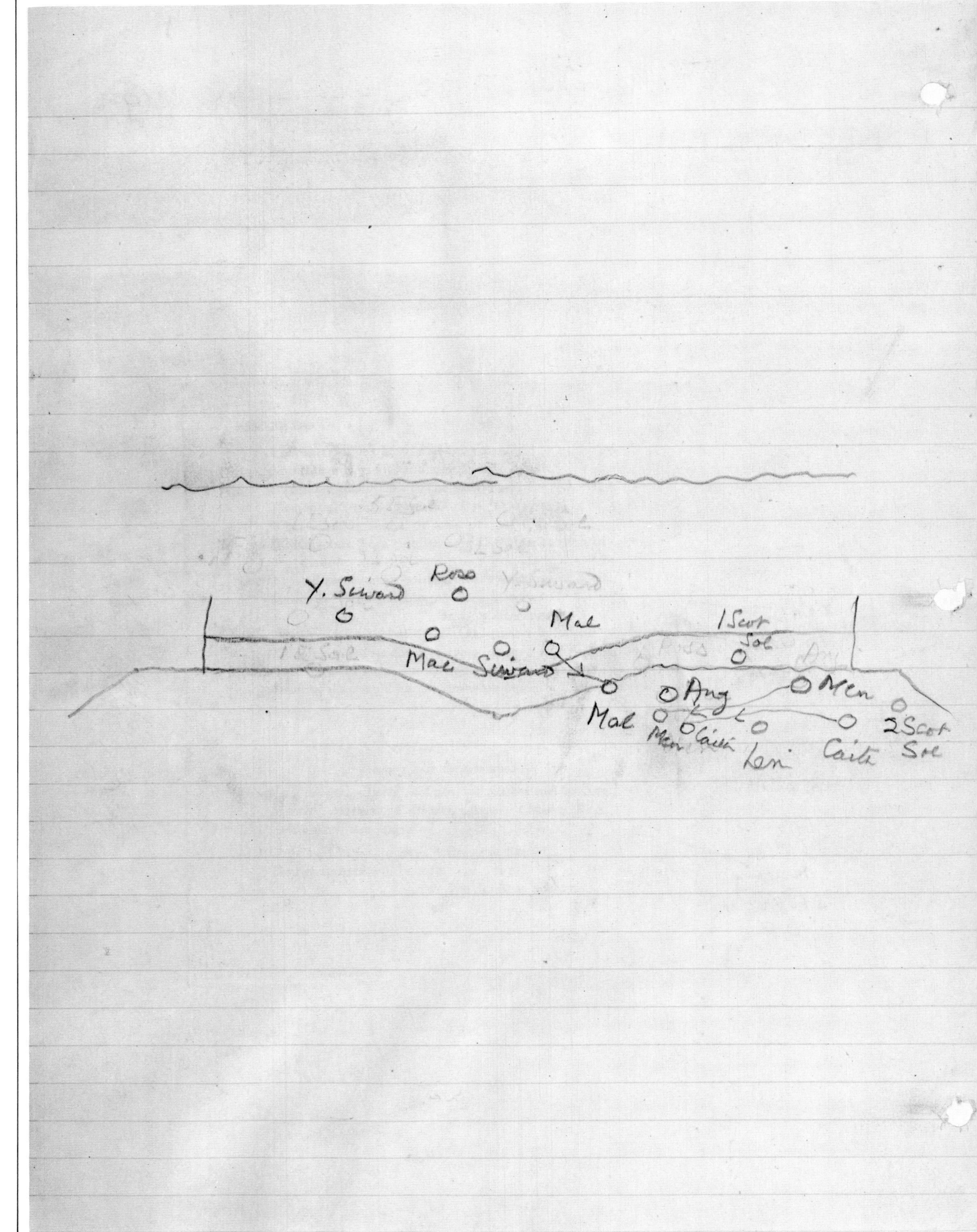

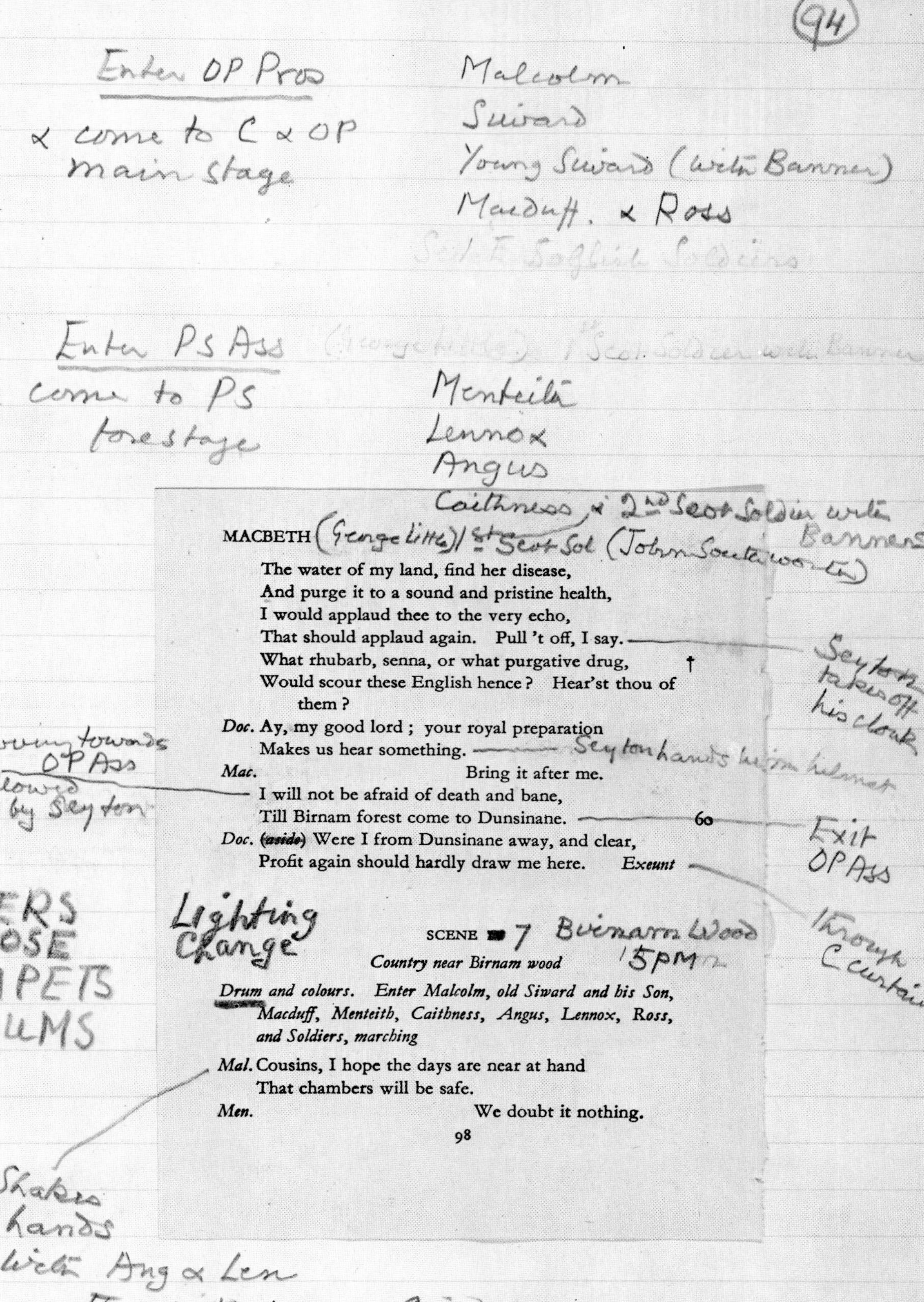

94

Enter OP Pros Malcolm
& come to C & OP Siward
main stage Young Siward (with Banner)
Macduff. & Ross

Enter PS Ass
& come to PS Menteith
forestage Lennox
Angus
Caithness & 2nd Scot Soldier with Banners

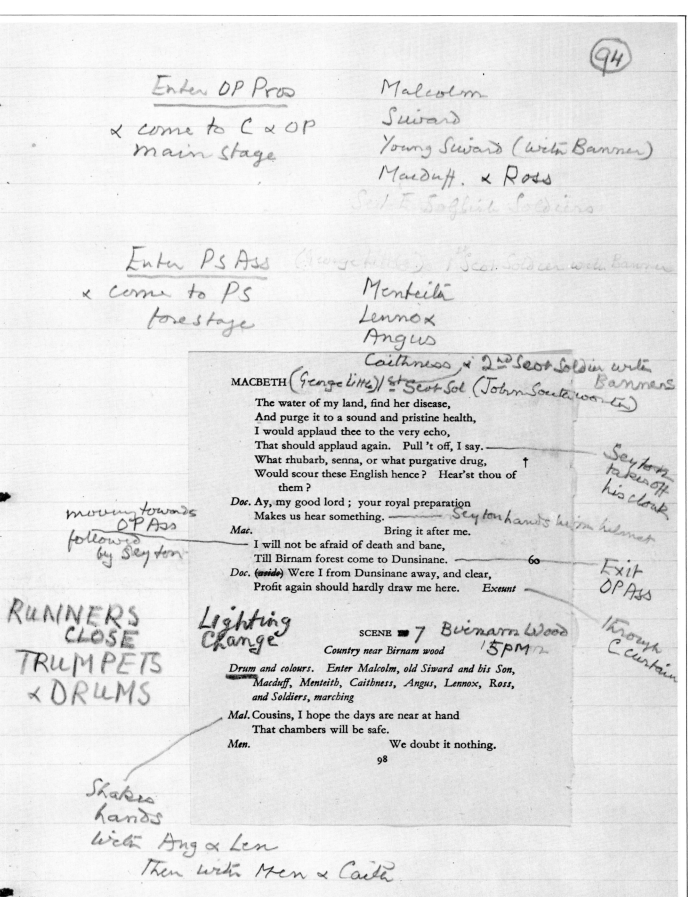

MACBETH (George Little) 1st Scot Sol (John Southworth)

The water of my land, find her disease,
And purge it to a sound and pristine health,
I would applaud thee to the very echo,
That should applaud again. Pull 't off, I say. — Seyton takes off his cloak
What rhubarb, senna, or what purgative drug, †
Would scour these English hence? Hear'st thou of
them?

Doc. Ay, my good lord; your royal preparation
Makes us hear something. — Seyton hands him helmet

Mac. Bring it after me.
I will not be afraid of death and bane, — moving towards OP Ass followed by Seyton
Till Birnam forest come to Dunsinane. — Exit OP Ass

Doc. ~~(aside)~~ Were I from Dunsinane away, and clear,
Profit again should hardly draw me here. *Exeunt* — through C curtain

RUNNERS CLOSE
TRUMPETS & DRUMS

Lighting Change

SCENE 7 Birnam Wood 5pm

Country near Birnam wood

Drum and colours. Enter Malcolm, old Siward and his Son, Macduff, Menteith, Caithness, Angus, Lennox, Ross, and Soldiers, marching

Mal. Cousins, I hope the days are near at hand
That chambers will be safe.

Men. We doubt it nothing.

98

Shakes hands with Ang & Len
Then with Men & Caith

We are left to despise the Doctor & his frightened, mercenary & almost laughably timid little remark at the end of the scene.

Malcolm orders the troops to use camouflage when they are approaching Dunsinane Castle.

Macbeth, Act V, Scene iv

Order of Exit — Siward & Malcolm
Macduff / Macduff
Ross & Menteith
1 Scot Sol
Angus & Caithness & Lenox
2 Scot Sol

Looking towards OP Ass

Xing to PS of Y Siward

Act V Sc. iv

Siw. What wood is this before us?
Men. The wood of Birnam.
Mal. Let every soldier hew him down a bough,
And bear 't before him, thereby shall we shadow
The numbers of our host, and make discovery
Err in report of us.
~~*Sol.*~~ Y. Siw It shall be done.

Exit Y Siw OP Ass

Siw. We learn no other but the confident tyrant
Keeps still in Dunsinane, and will endure
Our setting down before 't.
Mal. 'Tis his main hope:
For where there is advantage to be given,
Both more and less have given him the revolt,
And none serve with him but constrained things
Whose hearts are absent too.
~~*Macd.* Let our just censures~~
~~Attend the true event, and put we on~~
~~Industrious soldiership.~~
Siw. The time approaches,
That will with due decision make us know
What we shall say we have, and what we owe.
~~Thoughts speculative their unsure hopes relate,~~
~~But certain issue strokes must arbitrate:~~
Towards which, advance the war. *Exeunt, marching*

OP Ass

DRUMS & 99 TRUMPETS

The Battlements.

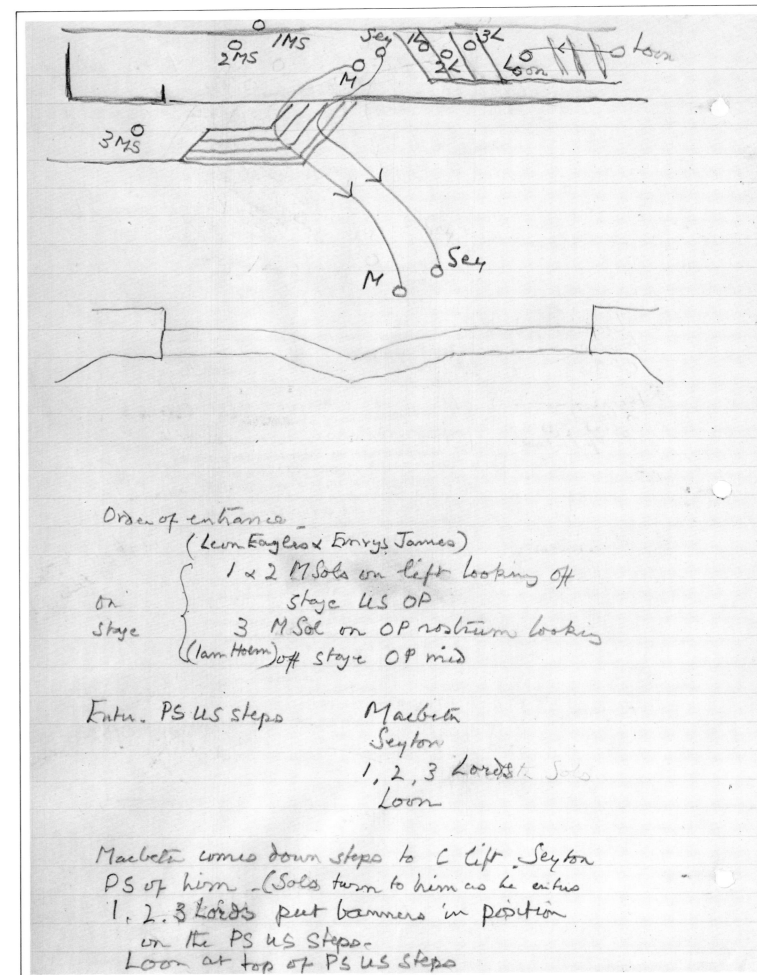

Order of entrance –

(Leon Eagles & Emrys James)

On stage { 1 & 2 M Sols on lift looking off stage US OP
3 M Sol on OP rostrum looking
(Ian Holm) off stage OP mid

Enter. PS US steps

Macbeth
Seyton
1, 2, 3 Lords
Loon

Macbeth comes down steps to C lift. Seyton
PS of him. (Sols turn to him as he enters
1. 2. 3 Lords put banners in position
on the PS US steps.
Loon at top of PS US steps

Lighting Pre-set behind runners

LIGHTING CHANGE

RUNNERS OPEN

MACBETH

SCENE ~~V~~ 8 Last

6PM to next morning

Dunsinane. ~~*Within the castle*~~

Enter Macbeth, Seyton, and Soldiers, with ~~*drum and*~~ *colours*

Mac. Hang out our banners on the outward walls ;
The cry is still ' They come : ' our castle's strength
Will laugh a siege to scorn : here let them lie
Till famine and the ague eat them up ;
Were they not forc'd with those that should be ours,
We might have met them dareful, beard to beard,
And beat them backward home.

A cry within of women

What is that noise ?

Sey. It is the cry of women, my good lord. *Exit*

Mac. I have almost forgot the taste of fears :
The time has been, my senses would have cool'd
To hear a night-shriek, and my fell of hair
Would at a dismal treatise rouse, and stir
As life were in 't : I have supp'd full with horrors,
Direness, familiar to my slaughterous thoughts,
Cannot once start me.

Re-enter Seyton

Wherefore was that cry ?

Sey. The queen, my lord, is dead.

100

UCP PS Steps

PSA00

moving towards PSA00

FADE

moves towards PS.

Coming to C main stage positions on opposite PSA00

PSA00

moving to PS P.co arch

Last Scene. 6 pm.

Macbeth prepares for the siege of his Castle. Suddenly a cry of women is heard. Seyton goes to find out the cause. He returns & tells Macbeth that the Queen is dead.

He has greatness of heart & soul even though he is damned.

A sentry arrives from his post & reports to Macbeth that he has seen Birnam Wood moving towards the Castle.

Macbeth, Act V, Scene v

Act V Sc. v

Mac. She should have died hereafter ;
There would have been a time for such a word.
To-morrow, and to-morrow, and to-morrow,
Creeps in this petty pace from day to day,
To the last syllable of recorded time ;
And all our yesterdays, have lighted fools
The way to dusty death. Out, out, brief candle,
Life 's but a walking shadow, a poor player
That struts and frets his hour upon the stage,
And then is heard no more. It is a tale
Told by an idiot, full of sound and fury,
Signifying nothing.

Leaning against PS Pros

Enter a ~~*Messenger*~~ Sentry

Thou com'st to use thy tongue ; thy story quickly.
Mes. Gracious my lord,
I should report that which I say I saw,
But know not how to do it.
Mac. Well, say, sir.
Mes. As I did stand my watch upon the hill,
I look'd toward Birnam, and anon methought
The wood began to move.
Mac. Liar, and slave !
Mes. Let me endure your wrath, if 't be not so :
Within this three mile may you see it coming ;
I say, a moving grove.

OP: mid

1, 2 & 3 Lords move off PS steps to main stage OP

Seize Sentry

101

Birnam Wood Sentry. 25 [years old]. Rex Robinson.

One of Macbeth's soldiers who has been posted on the hill overlooking the country below. He is amazed & alarmed by what he sees, but he doesn't, of course, know the terrible effect it will have on Macbeth.

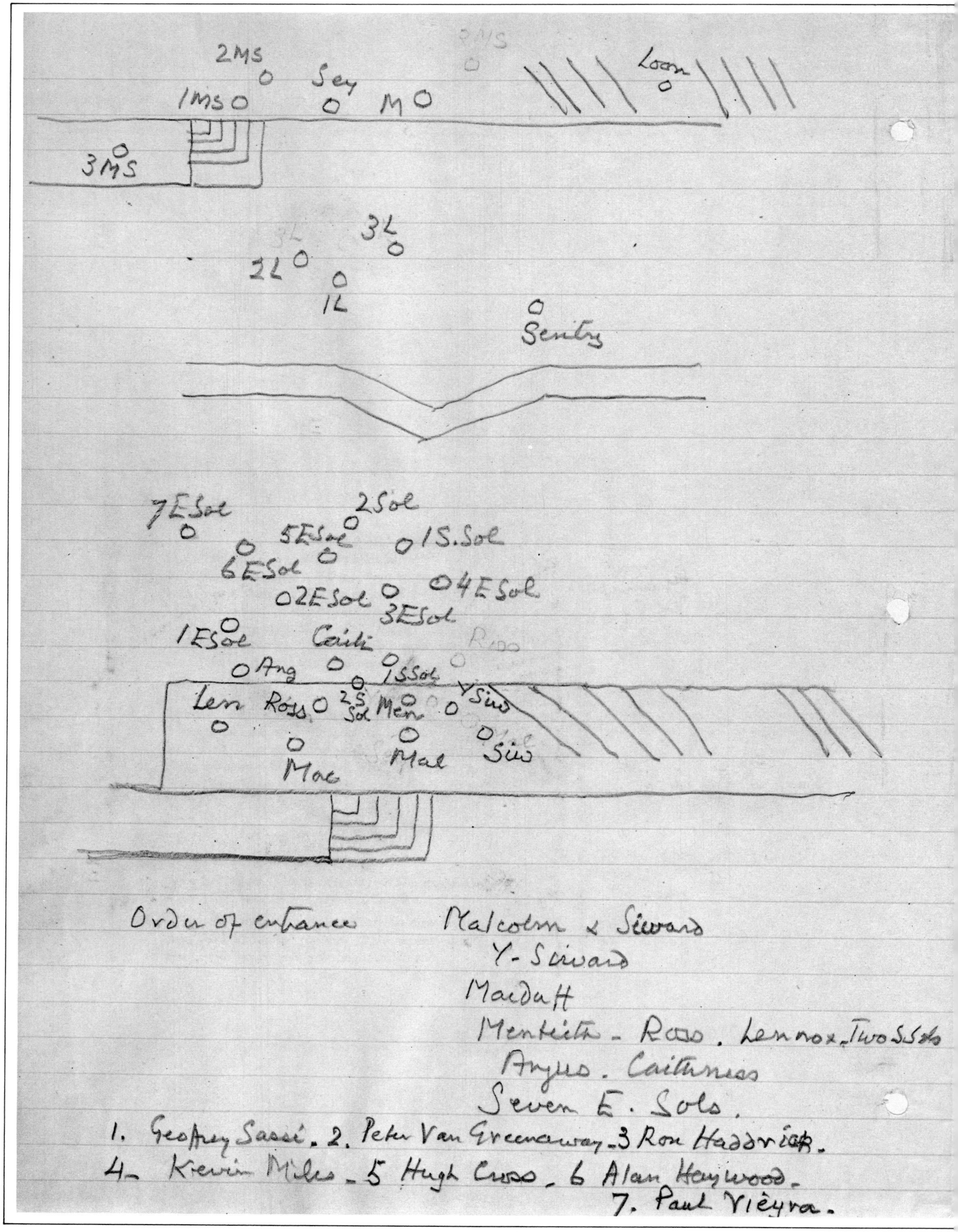

Malcolm, Siward, Macduff, & Young Siward with the Scottish Nobles & English soldiers arrive at the entrance to the Castle. Malcolm gives his orders for the assault & the trumpets sound the advance.

Macbeth, Act V, Scene vi

Order of entrance

Malcolm & Siward
Y - Siward
Macduff
Menteith - Ross. Lennox. Two S Sols
Angus. Caithness
Seven E. Sols.

1. Geoffrey Sassi. 2. Peter Van Greenaway. 3 Ron Haddrick.
4. Kevin Miles. 5 Hugh Cross. 6 Alan Haywood.
7. Paul Vieyra.

Order of Exit. Macbeth
Seyton
1, 2, 3 Mac Sols
1, 2 & 3 Lords.
Sentry

(pall pall)

Slight move DS.

turning US

turning DS

(followed by Seyton) moving US to OP steps & to C of left
Exit PS US steps
Loon

Slight move OP

TRUMPETS
DRUM

DRUM
LIGHT CHANGE

ALARUM BELL

throws Sentry downps

US PS steps

MACBETH

Mac. If thou speak'st false,
Upon the next tree shalt thou hang alive
Till famine cling thee: if thy speech be sooth,
I care not if thou dost for me as much.
I pull in resolution, and begin †
To doubt the equivocation of the fiend,
That lies like truth: 'Fear not, till Birnam wood
Do come to Dunsinane;' and now a wood
Comes toward Dunsinane. Arm, arm, and out!
If this which he avouches does appear,
There is nor flying hence nor tarrying here.
I 'gin to be a-weary of the sun,
And wish the estate o' the world were now undone.
Ring the alarum-bell! Blow, wind, come, wrack,
At least we'll die with harness on our back. *Exeunt*

~~SCENES VI, VII, AND VIII~~

Dunsinane. ~~*Before the castle*~~

Drum and colours. Enter Malcolm, old Siward, Macduff, ~~*and their Army,*~~ *with boughs* Menteith Angus - Lennox Caithness
7ESols 2S Sols

Mal. Now near enough; your leavy screens throw down,
And show like those you are. You, worthy uncle,
Shall, with my cousin, your right noble son,

102

→ George Little & John Southworth

The news is horrifying to Macbeth because he had believed that what the third apparition had said could never happen. He orders the Alarum bell to be sounded & he & his fellows retire into the Castle.

Act V, Scene vi. "Your leavy screens throw down." James Grout (Lennox), Keith Michell (Macduff), Trader Faulkner (Malcolm), Mervyn Blake (Siward, with shield), Robert Arnold (Young Siward, on steps), others unidentified (see following pages).

The English Soldiers
They should be different from the Scottish Soldiers in appearance, but they must look like fighting troops.

Order of Exit. Macbeth
Seyton
1, 2, 3 Mac Sols
1, 2 & 3 Lords
Sentry

(pall pall)

Slight move DS.

turning US

turning DS

(followed by Seyton) moving US to OP steps & to C of left Exit PS US steps

Slight move OP

TRUMPETS DRUM

→ George Little & John Southworth

MACBETH

Mac. If thou speak'st false,
Upon the next tree shalt thou hang alive
Till famine cling thee: if thy speech be sooth,
I care not if thou dost for me as much.
I pull in resolution, and begin
To doubt the equivocation of the fiend,
That lies like truth: 'Fear not, till Birnam wood
Do come to Dunsinane;' and now a wood
Comes toward Dunsinane. Arm, arm, and out!
If this which he avouches does appear,
There is nor flying hence nor tarrying here.
I 'gin to be a-weary of the sun,
And wish the estate o' the world were now undone.
Ring the alarum-bell! Blow, wind, come, wrack,
At least we'll die with harness on our back. *Exeunt*

DRUM
LIGHT CHANGE
ALARUM BELL

~~SCENES VI, VII, AND VIII~~

Dunsinane. ~~*Before the castle*~~

Drum and colours. Enter Malcolm, old Siward, Macduff, ~~*and their Army,*~~ *with boughs*
7 E Sols 2 S Sols Menteith Angus - Lennox Caithness

Mal. Now near enough; your leavy screens throw down,
And show like those you are. You, worthy uncle,
Shall, with my cousin, your right noble son,

102

throws Sentry down PS

US PS steps

The news is horrifying to Macbeth because he had believed that what the third apparition had said could never happen. He orders the Alarum bell to be sounded & he & his fellows retire into the Castle.

Act V, Scene vi. "Your leavy screens throw down." James Grout (Lennox), Keith Michell (Macduff), Trader Faulkner (Malcolm), Mervyn Blake (Siward, with shield), Robert Arnold (Young Siward, on steps), others unidentified (see following pages).

The English Soldiers

They should be different from the Scottish Soldiers in appearance, but they must look like fighting troops.

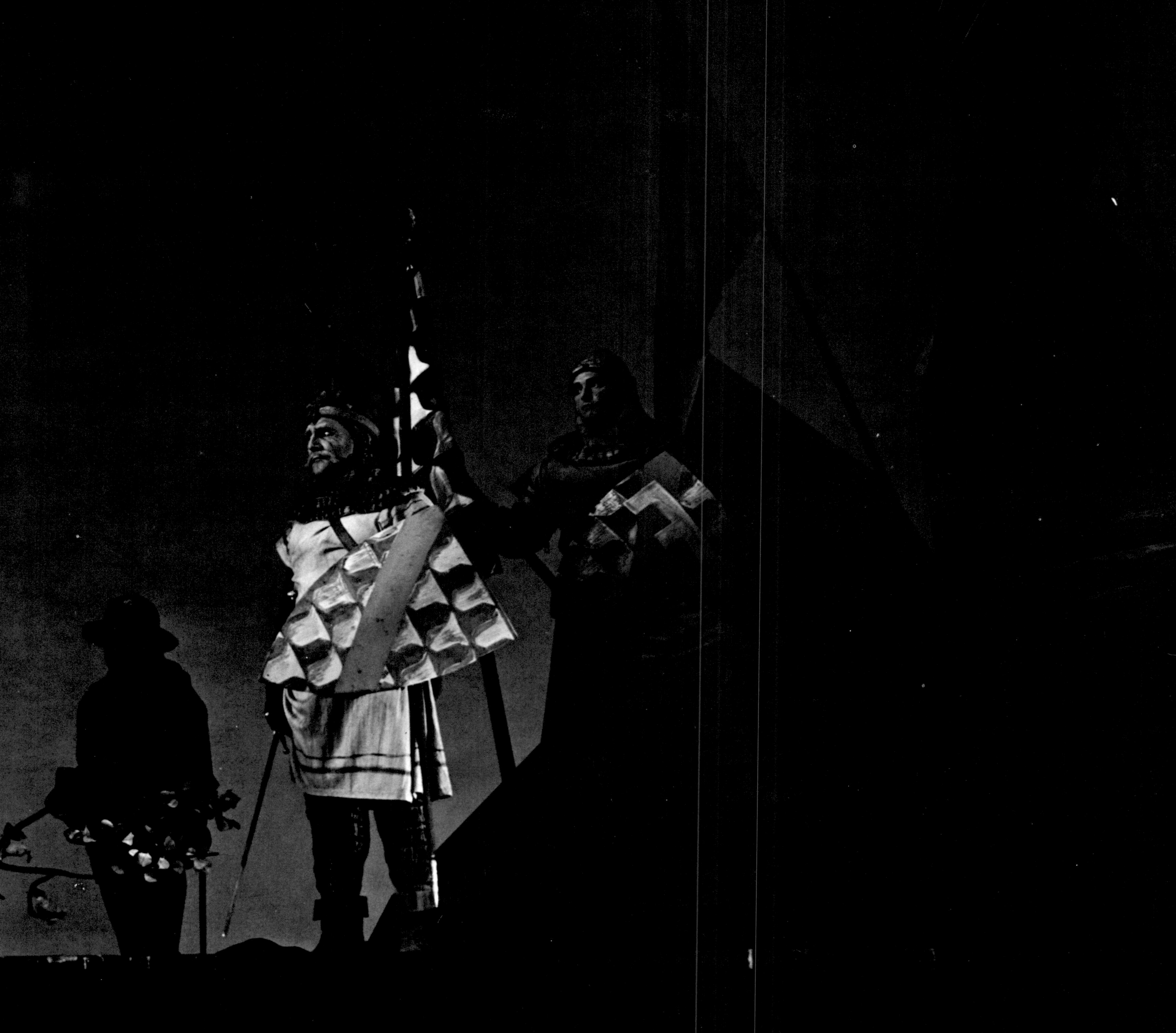

Old Siward. 50 [years old]. Mervyn Blake.

He is English & should look different from the Scottish Nobles. He is a real old War Horse. Rather like Erpingham in *Henry V*.

They hack their way into the castle.

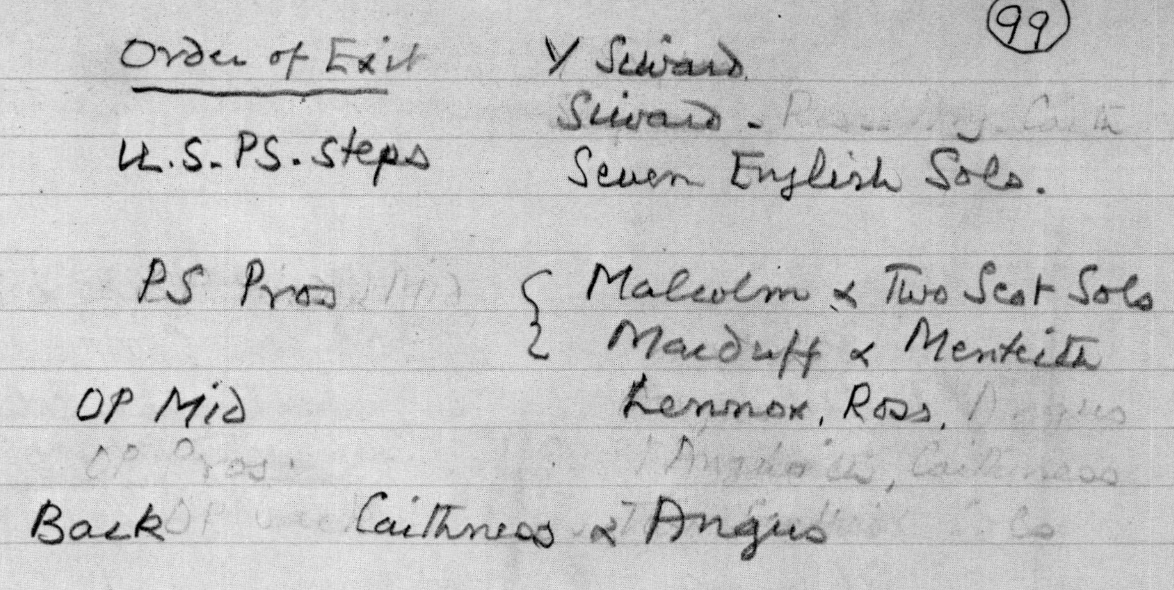

Order of Exit — Y Siward
Siward
U.S. PS. steps — Seven English Sols.

PS Pros — Malcolm & Two Scot Sols
Macduff & Menteith
OP Mid — Lennox, Ross,

OP Back — Caithness & Angus

Act V Sc. vii

Lead our first battle: worthy Macduff and we
Shall take upon 's what else remains to do,
According to our order.

Siw. Fare you well.
~~Do we but find the tyrant's power to-night,~~
~~Let us be beaten, if we cannot fight.~~

Macd. Make all our trumpets speak; give them all breath,
Those clamorous harbingers of blood and death.

Exeunt
Alarums continued

TRUMPETS Very Loud SHOUTING

Alarums. Enter Macbeth

PS Ass & comes to C main stage looking in all directions

Mac. They have tied me to a stake, I cannot fly,
But bear-like I must fight the course. What 's he
That was not born of woman? Such a one
Am I to fear, or none.

Enter young Siward

PS Pros & comes to PS 2 M

Young Si. What is thy name?
Mac. Thou 'lt be afraid to hear it.
Young Si. No; though thou call'st thyself a hotter name
Than any is in hell.
Mac. My name 's Macbeth.

103

Macbeth escapes from the first attack & comes into the Court yard.

He is met by young Siward who fights with him & is killed.

*

Enter down US PS steps fighting

1st & 2nd Lords & Sentry
Seyton, Caithness,
Three English soldiers (1, 2, 3) —

Enter OP back
Caithness & Angus &
attacks them from the back.
Angus drives Seyton off PS Pros

They exit OP Steps & OP mid

Enter PS mid fighting

Seyton & 3rd Lord & 1st, 2nd, 3rd M Sols
Three E Sols (4, 5, 6) ——

Enter OP mid
Angus & Lennox & attacks them from back – Angus drives Seyton off PS mid

They exit OP Ass

Macbeth joins in the fight
& kills 6 E. Sol on OP Steps

Sentry & 2 Lord killed one on back of lift OP
one on OP steps

M
O
Y. Siward

→ Geoffrey Sassé, Peter Van Greenaway, Ron Haddrick

DS PS
mainstage

→ Kevin Miles, Hugh Cross,
Alan Haywood

MACBETH

Young Si. The devil himself could not pronounce a title
More hateful to mine ear.
Mac. No, nor more fearful.
Young Si. Thou liest, abhorred tyrant; with my sword
I 'll prove the lie thou speak'st.
They fight, and young Siward is slain
Mac. Thou wast born of woman;
But swords I smile at, weapons laugh to scorn,
Brandish'd by man that 's of a woman born. *Exit*
Alarums. Enter Macduff
Macd. That way the noise is. Tyrant, show thy face!
If thou be'st slain and with no stroke of mine,
My wife and children's ghosts will haunt me still.
I cannot strike at wretched kerns, whose arms
Are hir'd to bear their staves: either thou, Macbeth,
Or else my sword with an unbatter'd edge
I sheathe again undeeded. There thou shouldst be;
By this great clatter, one of greatest note
Seems bruited: let me find him, fortune,
And more I beg not. *Exit. Alarums*
Enter Malcolm and old Siward
Siw. This way, my lord, the castle 's gently render'd:
The tyrant's people on both sides do fight,
The noble thanes do bravely in the war,
The day almost itself professes yours,

104

Young Siward. 18 [years old]. Robert Arnold.

He is a salty young chap. Full of enthusiasm & courage.

The Macbeth followers are driven out of the Castle & across the Court yard. Macbeth joins the fighting & kills one of the English soldiers.

Act V Sc. viii

~~And little is to do.~~

~~*Mal.*~~ ~~We have met with foes~~
~~That strike beside us.~~

~~*Siw.*~~ ~~Enter, sir, the castle.~~

~~*Exeunt.*~~ ~~*Alarum*~~

~~*Enter Macbeth*~~

Mac. Why should I play the Roman fool, and die
On mine own sword? whiles I see lives, the gashes
Do better upon them.

Enter Macduff

Macd. Turn, hell-hound, turn!

Mac. Of all men else I have avoided thee:
But get thee back, my soul is too much charg'd
With blood of thine already.

Macd. I have no words,
My voice is in my sword, thou bloodier villain
Than terms can give thee out! *They fight*

Mac. Thou losest labour;
As easy mayst thou the intrenchant air
With thy keen sword impress, as make me bleed:

11 105

Coming to OP of Macduff

DRUM

Macduff meets Macbeth. They are alone. They start to fight. Macbeth warns Macduff that he bears a charmed life & cannot be killed by anyone who was born of woman.

Act V, Scene viii. Macduff and Macbeth fighting. Keith Michell (Macduff), Sir Laurence Olivier (Macbeth) (see opposite page).

Macbeth, Act V, Scene viii

MACBETH

Let fall thy blade on vulnerable crests,
I bear a charmed life, which must not yield
To one of woman born.

Macd. Despair thy charm,
And let the angel whom thou still hast serv'd
Tell thee, Macduff was from his mother's womb
Untimely ripp'd.

Mac. Accursed be that tongue that tells me so;
For it hath cow'd my better part of man!
And be these juggling fiends no more believ'd,
That palter with us in a double sense,
That keep the word of promise to our ear,
And break it to our hope. I 'll not fight with thee.

They stop fighting

Macd. Then yield thee coward,
And live to be the show and gaze o' the time:
We 'll have thee, as our rarer monsters are, †
Painted upon a pole, and underwrit,
'Here may you see the tyrant.'

Mac. I will not yield
To kiss the ground before young Malcolm's feet,
And to be baited with the rabble's curse.
Though Birnam wood be come to Dunsinane,
And thou oppos'd, being of no woman born,
Yet I will try the last: before my body
I throw my warlike shield: lay on, Macduff;

106

Macduff tells him that he was prematurely ripped from his mother's womb. For a moment Macbeth despairs, but when Macduff orders him to yield & calls him a coward his courage comes back & he fights it out to the end.

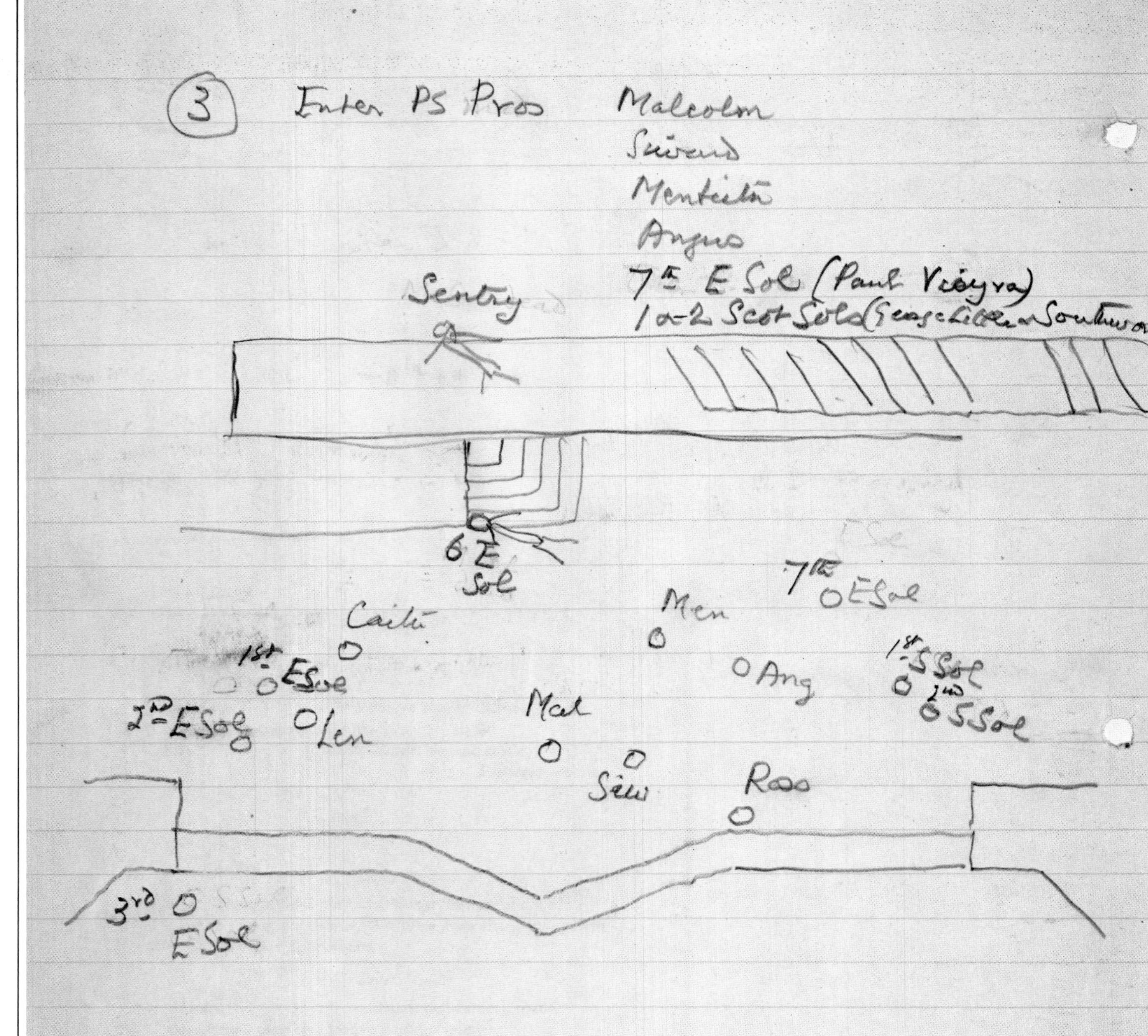

The battle is won & a retreat is sounded. Young Siward's body is carried off the field. His father and Malcolm with the Scottish nobles & English soldiers meet. Ross tells Siward that his son has been killed.

Macbeth, Act V, Scene viii

(103)

(1) Enter OP Ass Ross

3, 4, & 5 E Sols (Haddrick, Miles, Cross)

(2) Enter OP mid Lennox

Caithness

1 & 2 E Sols (Sassi, Van Greenaway)

Ross xs to body of Young Siward, recognises him – 3, 4 & 5 E Sols move forward lift up the body & carry it off PS Ass

Act V Sc. viii

And damn'd be him that first cries 'Hold, enough!'

Exeunt, fighting. *Alarums* → PS Steps

~~*Enter fighting, and Macbeth slain*~~

Retreat and flourish. Enter, with drum and colours, Malcolm, old Siward, Ross, the other Thanes, and Soldiers

Mal. I would the friends we miss were safe arriv'd.
Siw. Some must go off: and yet by these I see
So great a day as this is cheaply bought.
Mal. Macduff is missing, and your noble son.
Ross. Your son, my lord, has paid a soldier's debt:
He only liv'd but till he was a man,
The which no sooner had his prowess confirm'd
In the unshrinking station where he fought,
But like a man he died.
Siw. Then he is dead?
Ross. Ay, and brought off the field: your cause of sorrow
Must not be measur'd by his worth, for then
It hath no end.
Siw. Had he his hurts before?
Ross. Ay, on the front.
Siw. Why then, God's soldier be he!
Had I as many sons as I have hairs,
I would not wish them to a fairer death:
And so his knell is knoll'd.
~~*Mal.*~~ ~~He's worth more sorrow,~~

107

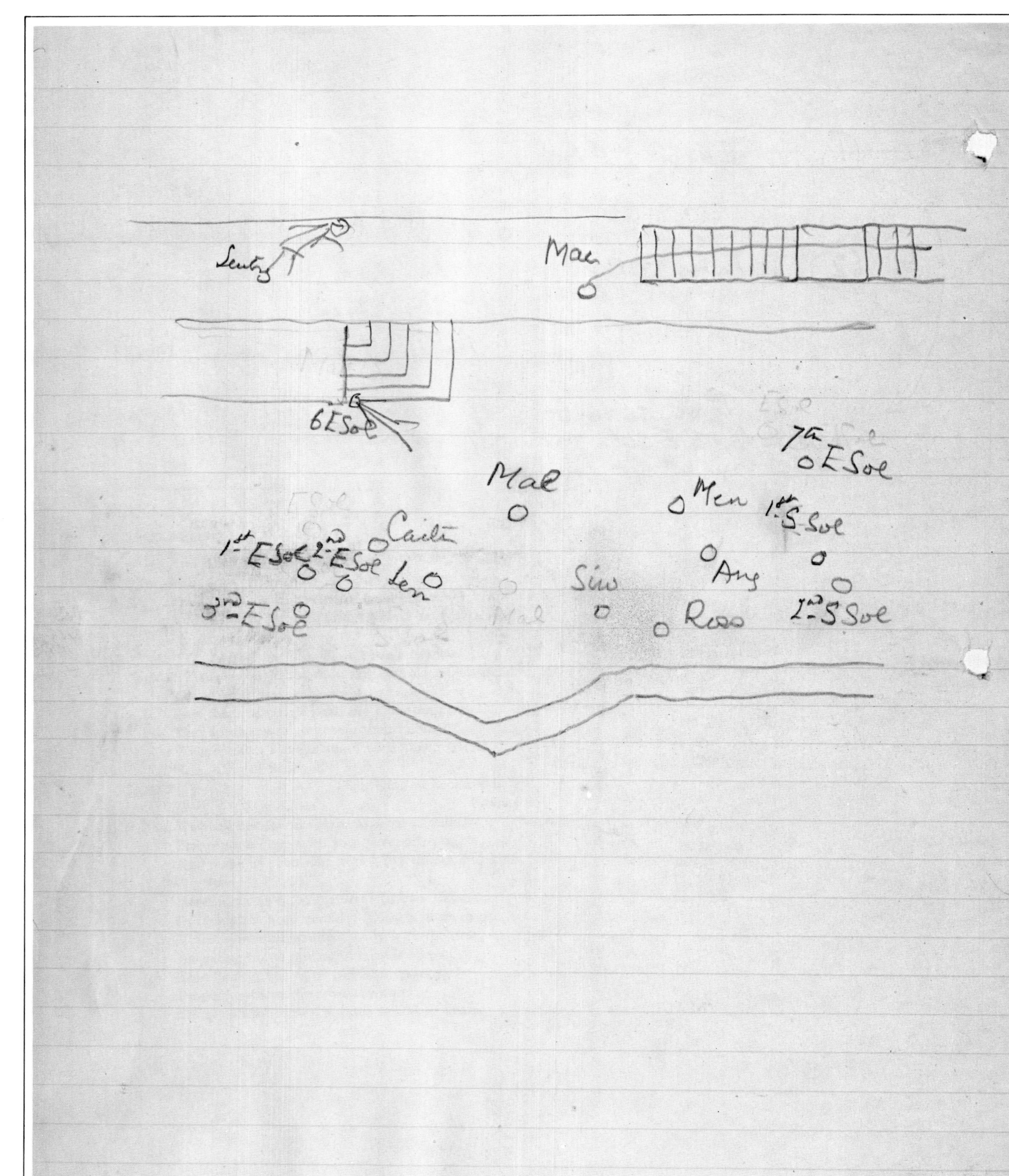

Macbeth, Act V, Scene viii

MACBETH

~~And that I'll spend for him.~~

~~*Siw.*~~ ~~He 's worth no more,~~
~~They say he parted well, and paid his score :~~
~~And so God be with him ! Here comes newer comfort.~~

Re-enter Macduff, ~~*with Macbeth's head*~~

Macd. Hail, king ! for so thou art : behold where stands
The usurper's cursed head : the time is free :
I see thee compass'd with thy kingdom's pearl,
That speak my salutation in their minds ;
Whose voices I desire aloud with mine :
Hail, King of Scotland !

All. Hail, King of Scotland !

Flourish

Mal. We shall not spend a large expense of time
Before we reckon with your several loves,
And make us even with you. My thanes and kinsmen,
Henceforth be earls, the first that ever Scotland
In such an honour nam'd. What 's more to do,
Which would be planted newly with the time,
As calling home our exil'd friends abroad,
That fled the snares of watchful tyranny,
Producing forth the cruel ministers
Of this dead butcher, and his fiend-like queen,

108

down PS Steps & Stands at bottom of them

Pointing off stage up PS steps

Mal goes up steps & stands C of lift Xing in front of Mac

Mal comes onto OP Steps

Macduff appears & hails Malcolm as King of Scotland & shows him Macbeth's head fixed on the battlement of his own Castle.

All the Nobles hail Malcolm as the new King. He tells them that it is rumoured that Lady Macbeth committed suicide.

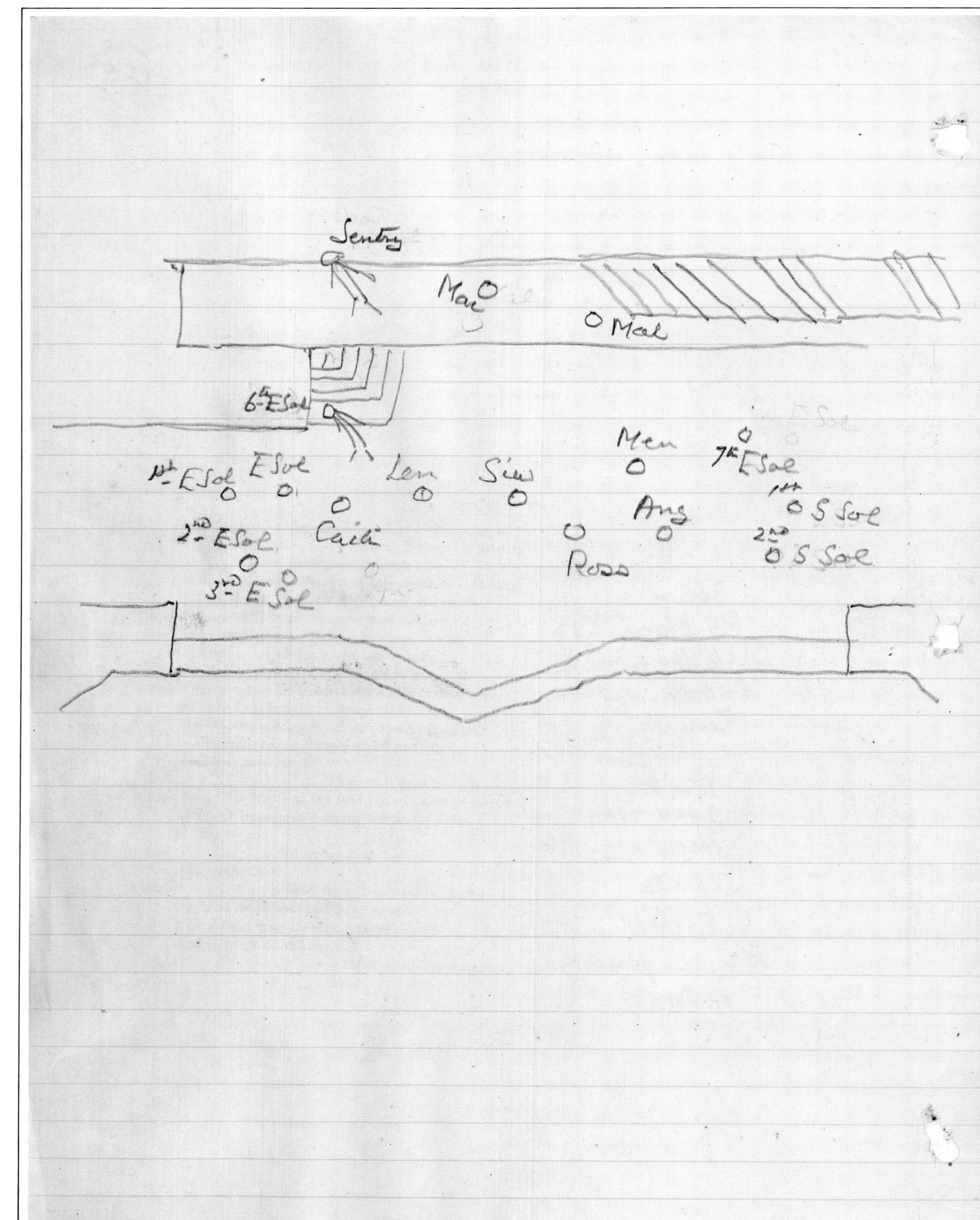

Macbeth, Act V, Scene viii

Act V Sc. viii

Who (as 'tis thought) by self and violent hands
Took off her life ; this, and what needful else
That calls upon us, by the grace of Grace
We will perform in measure, time and place :
So thanks to all at once, and to each one,
Whom we invite to see us crown'd at Scone.

Flourish.

CURTAIN

THE END.

109

He thanks them all for their help & invites them to his Coronation.

Act V, Scene viii. "Hail, King!" James Grout (Lennox, white tunic), Keith Michell (Macduff, hand raised, on platform), Trader Faulkner (Malcolm, in white), Mervyn Blake (Old Siward, helmeted), others unidentified (see following page).

CRITICS AND ACTORS

Olivier's interpretation of Macbeth met with the kind of consensus of approval among critics given in earlier years to players like Garrick and Mrs. Siddons.

—Richard David, *Shakespeare Survey*

Reactions of Reviewers

As the play is built around Macbeth, to the critics the production seemed to be built around Sir Laurence Olivier, and they were extravagant in their praise, judging his accomplishment equal to great performances of the past. "It is (let us be dogmatic) much the best performance of the part in our time; it may well be the best since William Charles Macready," wrote J. C. Trewin in the *Birmingham Post.* "This sinuous, tigerish Macbeth puts one continuously in mind of Edmund Kean; the deep, black-socketed, brooding eyes achieve a like, chilling effect to what we know of Edwin Booth," wrote Peter Foster in the *Financial Times.* Amidst some carping about underplaying in the early scenes, the critics agreed unanimously that Olivier's Macbeth was, to use one of their favorite words, "a triumph."

Olivier's special strengths as an actor shaped his approach to the role. What he *should* do and what he *could* do were in part a matter of practical choice. His athlete's ease of movement gave his Macbeth a sinewy, catlike grace, and in each of his "big" scenes he flew into a violent rage, leaping up on the banquet table in a swirl of red robes, or up on the battlements with his sword flashing. Ranging from ringing shouts of fear and defiance to drugged whispers, his voice twisted through the verse, rendering it utterly different both from nautral speech and from "Shakespearean" verse speaking. *Truth* reported:

> The ear must first accustom itself to Olivier's speech. . . . This initial difficulty is exaggerated by the unfamiliar stresses he gives to words to point his interpretation. But when this strangeness has worn off, a Macbeth is revealed whose obvious strength of personality is cabined, repressed, channelled into the single purpose of ambition. When his self-discipline snaps, it is a rare experience to witness, the more terrifying because of the restraint that preceded it.

The strange rhythms expressed great inner tension. "The storm is in Macbeth's mind. The actor does not try to reproduce it vocally," wrote James Courtenay in the *Stratford-upon-Avon Herald,* "He speaks the lines with extreme clarity and perception. The eyes are eloquent, the eyes of a man afflicted by terrible dreams." "When he whispers quietly," said the *Western Daily Press,* "it is almost as if one were trespassing within Macbeth's mind."

Olivier's talents for "big" acting allowed him to portray Macbeth as a man far from the normal run of men, a strong warrior who broke under the strain of very real threats—given special urgency by the literal powers of the Witches, by Malcolm's investiture, and by the visible presence of Banquo's Ghost. Olivier burned brightest where Shaw touched off great theatrical explosions—the discovery of Duncan's murder, the coming of Banquo's Ghost, the death fight atop the battlements—Macbeth's hidden goodness and strength blazing forth in displays of remorse and courage. While tension mounted in the quiet stretches, there grew the evidence of energy barely under the control of Macbeth's self-discipline in the flashing eyes, the rolling gait, the quick movements checked and slowed. Seeming to be a man with great things pent up inside him, Olivier made the soliloquies *necessary,* the revelations for which the audience yearned. Larger effects of staging and blocking transformed them into an intense communication between the actor downstage, cut off from others upstage, and the watching, listening audience. For all this, he was not a Macbeth who was *easy* to appreciate or understand. Not only was his speech mannered, his acting was restrained, especially during the first two acts. This quiet beginning puzzled and frustrated some in the audience who complained with Milton Shulman of the *Evening Standard* of "restraint run amok." The same restraint drew others into sympathy with Macbeth. "The opening, in a low key, is extraordinarily compelling; throughout we are in the mind of the doomed man, beset by fear and conscience," reported the *Sketch* (13 June). Listening hard, trying to infer meanings from the expressions that flickered over Macbeth's face, from his own movements and from the stage pictures that formed and re-formed around him, the audience became actively engaged in the interpretation of Macbeth's experience. "He is playing Macbeth from within," wrote Trewin in the *Illustrated London News,* which "means that the performance develops in our imaginations as it does in his. . . . Throughout we share his thought."

From the first moment, Olivier concentrated not upon Macbeth's fall from goodness, but upon his response to the evil that quickened within him. "His face is lean and sparsely bearded, the lines drawn down by sullen thoughts," said *Truth,* "the sisters do not incite ambition in him so much as they confirm and sustain it. There is nothing about the wild, impulsive warrior here. Each movement, each word he speaks, is the result of careful premeditation. . . . His speech is quiet, but heavy with evil intentions." The *Stratford-upon-Avon Herald* reported, "You watch this Macbeth's eyes. He is a haunted man from the moment the Witches speak, . . . their prophecy, we feel, has echoed his thought, . . . ambitions of which he is half-afraid."

As Duncan's murder drew nearer, Macbeth remained quiet. The dagger speech, famous as a "big" scene where actors pull out all the stops, Olivier played quietly, as Shaw had directed, because, wrote Kenneth Tynan in the *Observer,* he had "already killed Duncan time and again in his mind. Far from recoiling and popping his eyes, he greets the air-drawn dagger with sad familiarity; it is a fixture in the crooked furniture of his brain." Almost indifferent to the actual murder, it was only after the evil inside him blossomed forth into crime that the great shocks came. Harold Hobson of the *Sunday Times* commented:

> He accomplished the actual murder with the perfunctorily painted hands of an apparently bored actor, . . . then almost immediately began that superb upward leap. With "Methought I heard a voice cry, Sleep no more," Sir Laurence comes upon what he evidently considers the heart of Macbeth, namely not Macbeth's imagination of Duncan's murder, but his conscience after it. His "multitudinous seas incarnadine" is tremendous: it is greasy and slippery with immense revulsion. When, after the knocking on the door, he appears in a black monkish gown tied with a rope, he looks like . . . a Judas who, in his dark, brooding silence, has already begun to think of the potters' field and the gallows.

As the staging emphasized not thè murder, but the discovery of the murder, Olivier stressed not Macbeth's plunge into evil, but his horror-stricken discovery of the good he had lost.

From its quiet, puzzling beginnings, Olivier's Macbeth grew throughout the rest of the performance. Again and again, reviewers insisted on this: "Macbeth grew in stature throughout the evening" (*Birmingham Gazette*); he "grows steadily as he wades through his sea of blood towards doom" (*Birmingham Evening Despatch*); ". . . steadily gathers terrific momentum" (*Morning Advertiser*). As Trewin explained in the *Birmingham Post* (9 June):

> *Macbeth* came in at Stratford-upon-Avon in thunder, lightning and in rain. It thundered and flashed too, in our imaginations, though the storm did not begin at once. That is as it should be. The idea must grow . . . Macbeth, for many people, must strike twelve at once. For them he must be all sound and fury that, as we know on good authority, signify nothing. That has so often been the cause of disaster. A Macbeth has not been able to sustain his frenzy, and the play has sagged fatally to its end.

No simple villain, self-awareness infuses his words and looks with bitter irony and anguish. "Once on the throne . . . day cannot dawn for him again. He comes forward, despair in his eyes and voice, from one desperate expedient to another. Images of blood and darkness fill his mind" (*Stratford-upon-Avon Herald*). "Macbeth briefs the murderers of Banquo with a contempt for their trade which is exceeded by his contempt for himself, a contempt the more arresting because it is tinged with a bitter amusement," remembered Hobson (*Sunday Times*). When they leave, "the growing isolation of Macbeth is emphasized by [his] speeches being spoken as soliloquies downstage, with a puzzled and enthroned Queen upstage" (*Scotsman*). In the Banquet Scene, wrote Tynan (*Observer*), "he is seized with fits of desperate bewilderment as the prize is snatched out of his reach. There was true agony in 'I had else been perfect' . . . and the phrase about the dead rising 'to push us from our stools' was accomplished by a convulsive shoving gesture which few other actors would have risked." Then came the explosion of action. "His wonderfully histrionic jump on the table and his sudden challenge of Banquo's Ghost is not only a flourish of high theatre steeped in history, but it also lights up the courage of the man who can brave Russian bears and Hyrcan tigers," wrote Richard Findlater in the *Tribune*. That desperate bravery seized the audience's sympathies and imaginations. "The fury blended with panic on seeing Banquo's Ghost at his table, and his complaint at the unreasonableness of the apparition carried all before it. We see *his* point of view," said the reviewer for *Theatre World*.

> In the midst of all this remorse and terror, he never forgets that despair is the greatest of sins. . . . Yet despair he does not. In this refusal he discovers a terrible grandeur, so that when he reminds his wife that his enemies are still assailable, one's heart rises to him, both to the terrible pathos of a man who will not recognise an inevitable destruction, and to courage that may be evil, but is certainly unquenchable. (*Sunday Times*)

One after another, the reviewers remembered the terrible power at the scene's end as Macbeth looked toward the greater evils that lay ahead. "Sir Laurence opens a vista with the words 'We—and it sounds the royal *We*—are yet but young in deed.' Our plots and assassinations are only a modest beginning. The initiate fear past, we shall release lethal forces unknown to ordinary men" (*Theatre World*).

In Dunsinane Castle, despite consuming evil, Macbeth's courage became yet stronger. In appearance, he had become "a pale, tired figure, almost a ghost of his former self" (*Birmingham Post*, 9 June), but intellect and valor remained. "Even after events overtake him and he ceases to be master of his plans, he can still be seen balancing the moral score, withdrawn in the full consciousness of his own tragedy" (*Punch*). "When he says that his way of life is fallen into the sere and yellow leaf, you could swear that Macbeth, for all his wickedness, has a right to feel that the universe has monstrously betrayed him" (*Sunday Times*). And even at the last, as he strides across the stage in armor, there came a surge of pity for his suffering and admiration for his courage, a "sense of waste," the reviewer for *Truth* wrote: "As he approaches the final defeat . . . it is not a mad Macbeth that we are shown. . . . To watch him receive the news of his wife's suicide not with an explosion of insanity, but with resignation to a drooping tearless profundity is to be compelled to appalling fear, . . . deepest, empty dejection." After these quiet passages, the fight to the death came as a release. "On the battlements, Sir Laurence's throttled fury switches into top gear, and we see a lion, baffled, but still colossal" (*Observer*).

In many ways Vivien Leigh's performance was an extension of Olivier's: her delicate beauty, her brittle strength, and her pitiful nightmare made Macbeth's grim strength seem all the greater. Being married to Olivier, she was exceptionally convincing as Macbeth's wife: "Rarely does one feel in this play that Macbeth and his Lady were lovers before they were criminals. This time we know it," wrote Ivor Brown in *Drama*. In her sensual beauty there was ample explanation for Macbeth's fascination, and it implied a gain, not a loss, of manliness in his drive to fulfill her expectations. She eschewed Siddons's grandeur, and kept Lady Macbeth to a small scale, playing the vixen, not the man queller. During rehearsals she had extended the range of her voice, deepening it for the Murder Scene and the sleepwalking. "The dark red wig and serpent-green dress intensify her deadly pallor. Her frail, porcelain beauty takes on a new and stately strength, and her voice a new depth of authority," reported the *Daily Mail*. She did not shirk the great gestures that the role invites: she stretched her arms high above her head to invoke the unsexing spirits, and she held the daggers out in front of her, their blades thrust downwards, as if self-consciously striking a pose. Her real strength, however, lay not in these new skills, but in the modification of her established ability, sharpened in films, to play the Scarlett O'Hara heroine—a young beauty beset by dangers whose innocence conceals a steely strength of purpose. For Lady Macbeth she turned this formula around. As Olivier was restrained at the start, unleashing his full powers only later, Leigh was strongest at the start. Her charm as hostess was ominous: "With a ghoulish touch Lady Macbeth kissed Duncan before he went to his room" (*Leamington Spa Courier*). When Macbeth wavered, her strength grew until, as the full horror of the murder struck, she fainted. Lady Macbeth's attempts to play the Queen fell short: "Her crown gave her the top-heavy appearance of a child dressed up as a queen" (*Daily Mail*). Even before the banquet was disrupted, she had begun to fade, and as Macbeth burned brighter, "the evil, ruthless woman became a poor, broken wreck," said the *Birmingham Evening Despatch*. In the Sleepwalking Scene her self-destruction was complete. Down the long corridor she came, with hair now graying and disheveled, her finery changed into sackcloth. As if trying in nightmare to regain lost innocence, her voice became "childish," reported the *Evesham Journal*, then, as she relived the crime, guilt returned, and with it came "her own lovely diction," finally changing to the "gruffness" of the murder scene to give "awe-inspiring isolation to 'Hell is murky.'"

Star-system casting heightened the play's well-known imbalance between the Macbeths and the others, the spotlight on Olivier and Leigh throwing the rest of the cast into the shadows. Transferring from the characters to the actors their sense that a heroic Macbeth dwarfed those around him, reviewers often underpraised the cast for acting exactly as Shaw had insisted—portraying the group response to Macbeth's infamies, not developing strongly individualized characters. Scattered praise for Keith Michell as Macduff, Maxine Audley as Lady Macduff, Ralph Michael as Banquo, William Devlin as Ross, Patrick Wymark as the Porter, and Trader Faulkner as Malcolm was lost amidst the praise for and preoccupation with what Olivier and Leigh had conveyed in the title roles. Only the promptbook and Shaw's notes record what the supporting actors did, and why.

Interviews with Actors

What was it like to act in Shaw's *Macbeth*? Interviews with the actors who played Lady Macduff, Malcolm, and Seyton give us a different perspective on Shaw's work and on the play. Maxine Audley, who already had considerable experience when she came to play Lady Macduff, points out some of the problems the play holds for the actor. From Trader Faulkner, we get a sense of what it meant to be a young, relatively inexperienced actor working his way toward an understanding of Malcolm's character—and finding himself uncomfortably at odds with the director.

Lee Montague, who was Shaw's student at the Old Vic School, explains Shaw's methods, Olivier's approach to Macbeth, and his own approach to the part of Seyton.

Maxine Audley: Lady Macduff

Maxine Audley, who had been with the Shakespeare Memorial Theatre Company during the 1950 season, later played Lady Macbeth at the Edinburgh Festival. Besides extensive Shakespearean acting, she has often acted in contemporary plays and films. See Who's Who in the Theatre, *15th ed., London: 1972, pp. 482–83.*

In Rehearsal

Q. Tell me, what were the rehearsals like?
M. A. Well I do remember that the first reading was electrifying, you know.
Q. That's not the usual thing is it?
M. A. No. There were two electrifying runs through. One was the first reading of his [Olivier's] part—I don't think anyone else was quite up to it. It was electrifying, magical. I crept out. Big rehearsal room, a little bit echoey, and it was magical. The other outstanding rehearsal I personally wished could have been a performance was the last run-through in ordinary clothes, before the dress rehearsal, which was electrifying. And I thought, "Goddammit, now we're going to get into all those clothes and they're going to get in the way," which they did, so the first couple of dress rehearsals were terrible. But *that* was magical, so exciting.

Having played Lady Macbeth since then and got to know the play better, what I thought was so clever of Olivier was to realize that the part of Macbeth is one long build up to the end. Whoever's playing the part, it's a long, straight line upwards, ending with the great fight. The man is exhausted, but he's got to be on the top so they must start quietly and the whole of the first scene—all that must be in a low key. When he comes to his wife, she's up, she goes completely the other way. I always feel very strongly he's at his lowest ebb and she's absolutely at her peak and they completely change over.

I think they cross at the end of the Banquet Scene. She's geared herself and steeled herself to get through this terrific ordeal, and by the time they've all gone, she has already gone. She's finished. Absolutely marvelous part to do. And that's when he's getting into second or third gear of whatever. But this is what to me Olivier had above everybody else I've ever seen in the part. He had the gear changes really brilliantly cued, knew exactly when to change gear.

Danger Spots in Macbeth

M. A. *Macbeth* is full of danger spots. It's always on some school's curriculum, and during the season, whenever you do the play and wherever it's done, it's always on some examination syllabus. So after the first night, you always get school parties, usually matinees. "Is this a dagger that I see before me?" brings the house down. It *is* the funniest line in the play, and it gets a *roar* of laughter. Knowing this very well, [Olivier] used to say: "I've tried everything with this line. Tried taking it by surprise, turning my back and saying [very fast] 'IsthisadaggerthatIseebeforeme?'—to overcome this terrible thing, this gale of laughter which always bursts out." I do remember both Michael Redgrave and Donald Wolfit were guilty of what I thought was a terrible crime. I saw both at matinee performances unfortunately. On each occasion they came in front of the curtain before the show and said to the audience, mainly schools: "There is nothing funny in this play. Kindly do not laugh." Which of course incited them to laugh even more. Because not only that line, but all the cauldron bubble-bubble business gets gales of laughter from the kids.

There's an awful Spoonerism in [IV, iii]: All my shitty prickings and their dam at one swell foop. It's full of pitfalls.

Trader Faulkner: Malcolm

Trader Faulkner, who had joined the Shakespeare Memorial Theatre in 1955, later acted Seyton in the film of Macbeth *directed by George Schaefer for MGM. Besides his work in Shakespeare, Faulkner has acted in contemporary plays, arranged and performed flamenco recitals, and is currently preparing a BBC radio and stage presentation of the poems and music of Garcia Lorca.*

In Rehearsal

T. F. I can remember very, very well the first rehearsal in Stratford. Glen Byam Shaw said, "We have a very serious job in hand. We have exactly one hundred hours to do what is probably the most terrifying play ever written, a play about which there is a lot of evil in the ether." He gave a very interesting talk, I remember, about the intangible things which we can't rationalize. But then the sessions became closed sessions. He worked a lot with Laurence Olivier and Vivien Leigh alone and it was like men working far down in a submarine in different compartments and then the doors were opened and the compartments joined. I remember on the first night, there was a terrible thunderstorm in the afternoon. We went to the theatre, and the thing took off like a rocket.

The extraordinary thing was that Olivier played everything in the beginning in a very low key. He was like a man who was *dazed* by a lot of battle and by a lot of fighting. He played as an observer and everything was happening round him. He seemed at first almost passive. When he and Lady Macbeth met, you felt the tremendous control and discipline of two human beings who'd had no sexual intercourse. This was one of the key feelings of playing, her witholding because she wanted better things for him, and he, tired, very anxious to release himself physically with his wife, and of her holding back.

An Accident in Rehearsal

T. F. There was one night when he and Keith Michell were rehearsing the saber fight between Macbeth and Macduff, and the blade of Olivier's saber went in, I think, to the iris of Keith's eye, very near the pupil. And another night they were fighting backwards up the stairs—Macduff driving Macbeth upwards and out of sight before killing him— and the whole side of the stairs began to give way with the sheer weight of those gargantuan men battling it out. And I remember it started to crack and rock and we thought, "Oh well, this is it! They've had it!"—we were always expecting something dreadful to happen in this particular play. It's got that reputation and is surrounded by a great deal of theatrical superstition.

Olivier's Macbeth

T. F. The impression I got with him on stage was of a dangerous presence. He was not a man you went too near, with Olivier you felt the presence of what Lorca describes so well as the *Duende*.

Olivier grew and grew in strength in the play and she waned. This was I think deliberate policy of direction. In the end he became like a dangerous wounded bear and she became like a mad, spent butterfly. She went from this tremendous tensile strength she had at the beginning, and gradually the whole being disintegrated. She got the metaphysical, or if you prefer, the spiritual disintegration.

Faulkner's Malcolm

T. F. I remember at the first rehearsal I didn't discuss anything with Glen Byam Shaw because he was very busy. He had so much on his plate to make this production a key production with one of the leading actors of the world. And I felt rightly that I was a very minor potato and I would discuss what had to be discussed about Malcolm when they felt there was time to discuss it with me. So we went onstage and I started to play the role as a young, virile, resolute man of impeccable principles. I felt that he must be absolutely honest. He had seen what went on.

I began to play it in this way, but Glen Byam Shaw said that wasn't the way he'd seen it, or wanted me to do it. I was rather taken aback as I'd conceived it and we hadn't discussed it. He said he saw him as a rather effete young man without very much strength—rather decadent. I said I (Malcolm) don't feel I could supercede this Titan; I don't feel I can play it with conviction if I have to play it as a decadent—as a person too sheltered and without strength. I said I feel it's a young animal in its lair waiting and watching in the same way Macbeth has waited and watched while his strength grew. I said, "This boy to me is a very much younger bud, younger blossom, but with enormous potential, and you must feel that a greater strength will arise in time. He must give the suggestion of strength to come."

There was an unfortunate scene that I regret very much as it did me no good subsequently. Olivier came over in front of the cast and said, "This is the best Malcolm I've ever seen. You are the best one. I *know* it's a difficult part, and I know *how* difficult. What you're doing is dead right. Would you like me to coach you?" I said I'd be honored, but of course I didn't think what I was saying—very tactless—and naturally I meant no disrespect whatsoever to Glen Byam Shaw. It's just that I was young and I was very anxious to have any help, and there was the man who, I imagine, had probably done a near-definitive Malcolm as early as 1928 [in Barry Jackson's modern-dress *Macbeth*], so naturally I was anxious. And he was very helpful, and he was very critical, taking a personal interest in the way Malcolm developed throughout the run at Stratford-on-Avon.

This was the argument I had with Olivier and also with Keith Michell and with Byam Shaw. They said, "You're too convincing in the two contradictory aspects of the character. You're convincing when you say you're true and you're totally convincing when you say I didn't mean a word of it." I said, "Well, my answer to that is if you're sincere which I think Malcolm must be (otherwise he's boring, absolutely boring the audience) aren't there people who go right through their lives absolutely believing what they say at a given moment? Even though they may contradict themselves a day later, they may still totally believe it." I've seen this in human beings, this inconsistency in others and in myself very often. If the personality is attractive, it is what *makes* them attractive because one of the most important elements in the theatre is the unpredictable element. In other words, the element of not knowing, the element of surprise. So they agreed to let me go on and do what I believed.

In the first scene [I, ii] Malcolm is very much a witness when the Bloody Sergeant comes on, and he's watching, he's observing. He's very much an observer right through to the time he departs very quickly with his brother in their different directions. He's a witness, a mute observer, really.

I think Malcolm is in many ways immature. I think that the protected son of an old father (which I was) is very intuitive, but tends to be immature because it's the facing of life, the being flung out that tends to mature you quickly. I think Malcolm would be intuitively aware of a lot more than he would be rationally and analytically aware.

I think in [I, iv] he feels what a lot of immature people feel at sudden success—a glowing elation but really no idea what the future means or what the whole thing entails because I don't think that Malcolm has in any way really been submitted to reality—I'm sure he's always been surrounded by the nobility, by powerful Scots nobles and powerful men. But nothing would really hit him very hard until the death of his father, when he'd suddenly be flung and then all the processes that were going towards his maturity would suddenly be changed.

Malcolm represents light. What I did go for was spirituality. This is a quality I tried to stress more than anything. I think Malcolm at that stage would have been a man with his head very much in heaven and his feet well and truly on the rational earth. Obviously, this helps the play, and it helps the contrast of Malcolm as the son. This is why I disagreed with Glen Byam Shaw about the decadence, because I did not feel that decadence as a salient characteristic would allow for the element of spirituality in Malcolm needed to balance the dark forces of Olivier's Macbeth. I felt from Olivier's and Vivien Leigh's first reading that in the very difficult England Scene [IV, iii] I needed to provide the contrast and balance. Nor do I feel that utter decadence and true spirituality form a believable composite, especially in the character of Malcolm in that production.

He's the archetypal balance of spirituality that gets thrown into deep shadow in the blackness of the Macbeth theme and the Lady Macbeth theme, and the death of Macduff's children and the murder of Banquo. He's in a way the archetype of light, the archetype in society of the man with spiritual content, and I think Shakespeare shows through him the potential of what can come and the need for the restoration of the balance. This balance is driven out into England where it meets the spirituality of the people in England at that time where there was that mystical element, which culminated in Thomas á Becket. That ambience washed off on him and he came back to Scotland with that light. This is why the England Scene could, if handled by a director with an awareness of the spiritual implications, show this up in a white light of spirituality.

Costumes and Makeup

T. F. The colors were lovely. There were soft stone, buff-colored grays. The trimmings were russet, dried blood, browns. He had a uniformity of red, rust brown, those autumnal colors which offset the others. Vivien Leigh's costume was green, like something deep down under the ocean, a most marvelous costume, and it clung to her body and was like some Lorelei demon of the sea. She came up into this terrible dark, like some creature from the depth of the sea. His makeup was saturnine. Swarthy, dark, brooding, morose, obscure, are the adjectives I would use—oblique, very oblique.

In the Byam Shaw production, the lighting was very crepuscular and therefore that heavy painting. I don't know how it seemed from the front, but from a distance of ten or fifteen yards it was very impressive. So far as I remember, Roger Furse painted things on us. I know he painted women's navels and shadow lines under the breasts when the costumes were on. He achieved a marvelously evil and attractive sensuality.

Lee Montague: Seyton

Lee Montague studied under Glen Byam Shaw at the Old Vic School and joined the Shakespeare Memorial Theatre Company in 1955. Besides acting in Shakespearean and contemporary plays, he has often appeared in films and television. See Who's Who in the Theatre, *15th ed., London: 1972, p. 1199.*

In Rehearsal

L. M. I know that Glen from the school was very meticulous in his plotting [blocking] of the play. . . . He had such a strong framework (obviously there's room for maneuver within it), but he probably preempted that—even that—by suggestions of his own and because of the strong framework there were only certain channels you could go.
Q. He tells you where he wants you to go and to stand?
L. M. To within a few inches. He was pretty strict on it. And the thing is that in itself it would mean nothing to an actor, but I was brought up literally in his school so

he never just said "Go there" as lots of other directors do, and I've never in fact got over his way of teaching, which I think is admirable. It wasn't just a question of "Go there." He would provide a reason, a motivation, a very good motivation. And at the time you couldn't really in a way argue with it. He wouldn't give you the deepest motivation. He'd give you a motivation that was sufficient enough for you to go *there*.

Q. That would satisfy you.

L. M. That would satisfy you, which would satisfy you at the time. When in fact you started to drop the book and started to talk about it and really rehearse it, then he would provide you with even more, and deeper motivations.

Q. Can you remember much about the rehearsal itself?

L. M. The thing I do remember—there was a lot of work done with Vivien. I think they felt happier rehearsing it away from all the other actors. There's a rehearsal room at Stratford [where] she and Olivier and Glen would rehearse their main scenes, which they felt happier about. It was a very strict rehearsal schedule. But then with Glen it always was. . . .We'd always have a read-through.

Q. Just with book in hand?

L. M. Oh yes. Even though Olivier would know the lines he'd still read it, and he'd ask us to, say it quite quietly—no acting at all—just quite quietly go through it. And then he'd start to plot [block] it. I don't think I'm making this up. I mean, it would probably last, the actual plotting of the play—he wouldn't just give the moves. He obviously would talk at length about the play and about his feelings of what it should be finally. And when it came to plotting it again, it wouldn't just be a question of "You move there, and you move there," and right on to the next scene. A certain *time* would be taken over it.

Q. To know where you're going and what you're feeling?

L. M. Yes, in fact, to know basically why you're there, why you come onto the stage at that particular point. And probably that part would take nearly two days for each act—about ten days. So far as I remember, rehearsal was about five weeks.

It was very sort of stark—well *Macbeth* is always stark to rehearse. There's never much joy with *Macbeth*. It's just one of those plays that it's never much joy to rehearse. In fact, unless you're playing Macbeth, Lady Macbeth, the Porter (nice little part—contained), Macduff maybe, the rest of the parts I don't think for actors are awfully interesting. I mean, although honestly it was a marvelous production to be in, [Seyton] was very bitty to do. You came on and said one odd line and then you stood there for a long time. I suppose at the time one ought to have been, and in fact one was, very thankful to be in a production with Olivier who was then in fact at the height of his powers. What was actually very exciting—he'd been very quiet and not done a great deal, just walking through quite quietly, and then, we were going to do a run-through, one of the final run-throughs onstage—and he decided to give a performance. Then suddenly one realized what a tremendous performance it was going to be. It was very exciting. Suddenly on a Saturday morning or something like that, when we were trying to do yet another run-through, he suddenly decided to try all-out what he'd been thinking about, probably doing in his own room, mumbling over to himself.

He gives such tremendous realism to the character. When he came on at the beginning as Macbeth, he was a soldier, very real, his feet on the ground. And so the tragedy unfolded and you felt "Ah, if only it hadn't happened, if only he hadn't been married to that bauble!" . . . I think he disdained the Witches to begin with—couldn't quite believe them that it was all going to be like that. But his wife was such a strong character, their love for each other was so strong and so intertwined, their destinies were so intertwined, you felt that she did have this terrific hold on him. You could really understand the hold she had over him. After he had established himself as a soldier and a poet, he comes back and they meet. There's a terrific contact between them emotionally, intellectually.

Playing Seyton

L. M. I never took my eyes off him [Macbeth]. I remember that—never took my eyes off him. I think I was there even when I didn't have very much to say in any case. But I think I was there all the time, except for the soliloquies possibly. But even that one "Tomorrow and tomorrow and tomorrow"—while he was there obviously.

Q. What did you do then? I would think it would be uncomfortable.

L. M. I knelt. In that particular one, I knelt and just watched.

Q. And he was unconscious of your presence?

L. M. Yes, completely. He took it as read that I'd always be there.

Well, in fact before [V, iii] it wasn't really Seyton I was playing, it was all the messengers.

Q. Did you change costumes?

L. M. No. It was one character. He made it all Seyton, just the *one* character all the time.

Q. So in point of fact, here he's simply named Seyton, but he's been Seyton all the time.

L. M. It was rather a good idea because instead of it being anonymous messengers, in fact, it was the one character—armorer, secretary, if you like, right from start to finish. I think it's a good idea, gives continuity to the piece in the background of the castle.

One thing, as a character, Macbeth was never angry with Seyton. He was angry with some of the others—with the chap who comes in. And here, when the doctor came in, if I remember, he wouldn't allow the news of his wife's illness to weigh upon him.

Q. He tried to push it away?

L. M. It obviously did worry him a fair amount but he rose above it. He was demented. There was a sort of gleam in his eye. It has got hold of him—power, and the smell of blood, and that's why in a frightening way it was so intensely real.

Shaw's Methods

L. M. He was *so* meticulous. I can remember, not with this one, at the Vic, going into his room sometimes at the school and seeing all the little figures on the table. He was working out something we were doing at the school. And he would work all that out, and there'd be very little deviation from these moves. You would have had to provide pretty good reason for changing a move. Because it was so much part of the look of things. I always remember he said [in *Henry V*], talking about soldiers: "Soldiers, when they get up, have always been in most uncomfortable positions." So when he said, "Go, I want you to lie down and go to sleep," we all got into comfortable positions. He said, "No!" In fact, what finally happened, arms were askew, legs were up in the air, necks were lolling about so when in fact you got up, there were lots of "Oh! Aough!" It was absolutely splendid.

It was touches like that which made productions live. Instead of it becoming all walk-ons, although one played a small part and lots of other people played small parts, he was capable of making you feel you were an intrinsic and very important part of the production, which obviously helped the principals—either the atmosphere or the background. And indeed you cannot play *The Tragedy of Macbeth* with just Macbeth and Lady Macbeth and Banquo and Macduff—you've *got* to have all the other small parts which provide the atmosphere.

AFTERWORD

> The production as a whole is remarkable for its neutrality and integration. . . . Mr. Shaw has no time for directorial fantasy, . . . concentrating on guiding the play to speak for itself.—*The Stage*

Shaw is not a great experimentalist—like Meyerhold, Guthrie, or Brook, insisting on putting his personal stamp upon his production. Indeed, he appears to be a self-effacing artist, and his production seems an ideal one: solid, "straight" Shakespeare. Yet the great difference between Shaw's staging and Shakespeare's in an Elizabethan playhouse reminds us that this *Macbeth* is but one of many *Macbeths*, and that, like Shakespeare, Shaw is bound by conventions of the theatre. To put the production and the promptbook in proper perspective, we first need to recognize these conventions, which are difficult to discern clearly, because they belong to the modern theatre, and we take them for granted.

Shaw's staging is governed by the basic convention of the proscenium arch—that we are looking through a window on another world, which possesses a literal, objective reality. The words of the text imply objects, and they take on concrete reality onstage—the castle, for example, the table with meat and drink, or the cauldron. This realism extends to the supernatural, which is made visible, concrete, "really there": the Witches literally hover in the air, Banquo's Ghost is real, and his successors move "like shadows" but are real actors. Shaw follows the script literally, accepting as given the essentials of the play's theology: belief in God and the Devil, in the powers of witchcraft, and in spirits that can sometimes be seen and heard. If his audience wishes to rationalize the supernatural as Macbeth's hallucinations, they may, but Shaw does not make the choice for them. The action is located in "real" time. Without insisting upon historical accuracy, sets and costumes suggest the Middle Ages; the lighting or the striking of the clock sets the time of day. Reports of battles, the sound of music, a drum, or a clock—these give a sense of a world offstage, just out of sight.

Following the conventions of naturalistic acting, the characters too are "real," with an inner life, and an imagined past, which Shaw spells out in his notebooks. Olivier's Macbeth is not of course *ordinary*, yet Shaw treated his extraordinary personality as explicable by the norms of human behavior: he is a man of strength and imagination, whose peculiar susceptibility to the temptations of the Witches and his wife is caused by a secret sorrow (the loss of their child) gnawing at his heart. Shaw assigns more ordinary motives to the other characters, for they belong to the everyday "normal" world that reacts in horror to Macbeth's excesses. Shaw's Scots are a national type well known to his actors and audience. Malcolm is the inexperienced son of an old father; Duncan, the King whose good breeding makes it impossible to call Lady Macbeth "fair hostess" had she been a plain woman; Macduff, the blunt "man of God"; Lady Macduff, the loving wife and mother; the Doctor, "typically a Doctor"; and so on. Wherever possible, Shaw finds a line of motivation that suits the modern sensibilities of his actors and his audience. Even when he cannot, the Old Man as a holy hermit, for instance, or when differences between characters are negligible, as with Ross, Angus, Caithness, and Menteith, Shaw assumes that every character possesses a full personality the actor must try to convey.

These conventions of acting and staging are Shaw's strength, making the play accessible to his actors and his audience. Yet they are but one set of possibilities chosen from many. Other directors, for example, might prefer settings and characterizations much less specific and realistic than Shaw's, so that, as in Komisarjevsky's 1933 *Macbeth*, with its tall aluminum scrolls and robotlike actors, the action may seem to take place outside time, in a surreal, nightmare world. Whatever the limitations imposed by the conventions Shaw followed, there remains in his production a distinctive "non-verbal" dimension. Shaw's promptbook traces the rhythms that control both the movement of actors onstage and the audience's response. Each scene rises to its climax, each of the three great movements builds from still beginnings to violent endings followed by quiet reflections. The carefully orchestrated blocking that forms these rhythms goes far beyond the director's responsibility to move the actors on and off stage efficiently, and to keep the speakers in view. To see this, we need to step back and view the performance as a whole, a composite of recurring patterns of action. When we do, we see that the blocking consistently isolates Macbeth from others onstage—from Banquo, Ross, and Angus after he meets the Witches (I, iii), from Duncan, and his court after Malcolm is invested (I, iv), from the banquet (I, vii), from his own court (III, i and ii), from his guests (III, iv), from the Witches and their infernal masters (IV, i), and from his own men (V, iii and v). In each instance Shaw moves Macbeth downstage—often down onto the forestage—and has him speak directly to the audience with the setting and the other actors posed behind him, as in a *tableau vivant*. By this arrangement of the action, Shaw emphasizes the distance between Macbeth's quiet meditations and his frenzied ecstasies. When Macbeth comes downstage, the audience's attention focuses on him and on the workings of his mind. The others onstage become witnesses of his derangement, allies against him, not individuals speaking of private doubts and fears. Macbeth is at once at the center of the action and outside it, as if somehow, as in dreams, the events were projections from deep within his consciousness.

As the blocking consistently isolates Macbeth, it brings those who surround him together, creating images of unity, fellowship, and mutual trust. Shaw set this pattern early in the play. The Bloody Sergeant Scene (I, ii) is the first of three enactments of social unity. The King and his assembled entourage form a picture of an ordered society at stage left, balanced by the excited entry of the wounded Sergeant stage right. Where Macbeth will find himself thrust from that society, the Sergeant, another bloody man, is drawn into it and given succour. After Angus and Ross enter stage right, there is a greeting and "general movement in[ward]" of the assemblage, implying a common cause that is made explicit when they "cheer" at news of the victory and "exeunt cheering" at the end of the scene. The Forres Scene follows the same pattern, extending it to include the ceremonies of greeting (Macbeth and Banquo making their obeisance) and of investiture (Malcolm taking the coronet). So too, the blocking and stage business for Duncan's entry into Inverness reinforce the sense of community embodied in courtly language and ceremony, when "the King greets his hostess with great courtesy and charm" before he and his company go in through the center arch. The sounds of feasting in the next scene (I, vii) continue the sense of a thriving society.

Having been firmly established at the play's opening, this dramatic image of an ordered society becomes the model toward which group scenes move in the acts that follow Duncan's murder, culminating in Malcolm's restoration of order at the play's end. Immediately after the murder, only fear unites them—"those strained white faces peering" at Macbeth and Lady Macbeth; then, at the banquet, alarm and suspicion replace confusion, and only in the last act does purposeful reunion bring them together. Viewed in this context, Shaw's blocking and stage business take on added significance. The nobles who rush from the banquet through every available exit are a living representation of the community in disarray. Macbeth's attempts to play the humble host (which on Roger Furse's set require an actual physical descent from the royal dais) become improprieties when compared with Duncan's constancy in dignity and courtesy. The scene thus illustrates not only Macbeth's derangement, but also society's loss of the ceremonies of community and all they represent.

Even as group scenes depict society's disorder, there are other, smaller scenes, which depict remedy to come. These are remarkably similar in design, and the blocking reinforces that similarity. The first foreshadow a pattern of greeting and alliance that becomes dominant in Act V. In the meeting of the Old Man, Ross, and Macduff (II, iv), or later, of Lennox and Another Lord (III, vi, a scene Shaw omitted), men gather somewhere outside Macbeth's sphere of influence, and assess the state of the community. These choric scenes anticipate the long scene in England (IV, iii). As the third dramatic image depicting the re-forming of society, part of the scene's power is cumulative, and Shaw's blocking and stage business bring this out, repeating as they do the pattern of greeting, testing, and alliance. In the last act, the blocking for Malcolm and his allies elevates this procedure almost to the level of ritual. In V, ii, Menteith, Angus, and Lennox enter stage right; Caithness and a Scots soldier enter stage left. The two groups meet center stage, declare their common cause, and then leave together. So too, the Birnam Wood Scene (V, iv) enacts a meeting and an alliance between Malcolm's party and the Scots rebels from V, ii. As they did for Duncan, trumpets and drums sound; Malcolm and his English allies enter stage right, the Scots, stage left; and, meeting center stage, Malcolm "shakes hands with Ang & Len, then with Men & Caith." Their plans concluded, they leave together, marching to "Drums and trumpets." To the same music in V, vi, they enter as a group, now grown to twenty, with their leafy screens, and then disperse in several directions to hunt out Macbeth. Finally, in the last scene they reassemble around Malcolm, whose position at the center of the tableau marks him as Duncan's successor as surely as do his white robes, the trumpets, and the cheers of his subjects.

These dramatic rhythms and patterns of movement are an essential part of the play's structure, and Shaw's promptbook shows how they may be staged—not only in Shaw's theatre, but in any theatre that permits continuous action. To understand Shaw's work, readers must discover it for themselves. The faded erasures in the promptbook remind us of the bewildering possibilities *Macbeth* offers. By keeping other possibilities in mind, we may share the director's active decision in choosing what to stage and how to stage it. Shaw's promptbook takes us directly into the practical world of the theatre. Directors and actors will want to look closely at how Shaw solved the practical problems of script and blocking (especially at his skillful composition of scenes and groups of scenes), and also at how he decided the larger problems of interpretation. His straightforward remarks on the supernatural and his steady eye on the narrative purpose of each scene are especially helpful. Theatre historians, particularly experts in Shakespearean stage history, will want to compare Shaw's *Macbeth* with other great *Macbeths*: the stagings of Davenant, Garrick, Macready, Irving, Tree, and Komisarjevsky—to name only a few famous productions of the past. In the classroom, instructors might wish to re-enact or read through a scene, as Shaw maps it out, then look for other ways it could be done, sorting out the shifts in meaning that come with different stagings. For directors, actors, scholars, and teachers, and for those who first encounter the richness and ambiguity of the play in this promptbook, it is my hope that it will stimulate a fuller understanding of *Macbeth*, and, in the future, will inspire more *Macbeths* to stand with Shaw's as fully realized stagings of Shakespeare's play.